THE ARDEN SHAKESPEARE

GENERAL EDITOR: RICHARD PROUDFOOT

THE POEMS

THE ARDEN SHAKESPEARE

All's Well That Ends Well: edited by G. K. Hunter
Antony and Cleopatra: edited by M. R. Ridley
As You Like It: edited by Agnes Latham
The Comedy of Errors: edited by R. A. Foakes
Coriolanus: edited by Philip Brockbank
Cymbeline: edited by J. M. Nosworthy
Hamlet: edited by Harold Jenkins
Julius Caesar: edited by T. S. Dorsch
King Henry IV, Parts 1 & 2: edited by A. R. Humphreys
King Henry V: edited by J. H. Walter
King Henry VI, Parts 1, 2 & 3: edited by Andrew S. Cairncross
King Henry VIII: edited by R. A. Foakes
King John: edited by E. A. J. Honigmann
King Lear: edited by Kenneth Muir
King Richard II: edited by Peter Ure
King Richard III: edited by Antony Hammond
Love's Labour's Lost: edited by Richard David
Macbeth: edited by Kenneth Muir
Measure for Measure: edited by J. W. Lever
The Merchant of Venice: edited by John Russell Brown
The Merry Wives of Windsor: edited by H. J. Oliver
A Midsummer Night's Dream: edited by Harold F. Brooks
Much Ado About Nothing: edited by A. R. Humphreys
Othello: edited by M. R. Ridley
Pericles: edited by F. D. Hoeniger
The Poems: edited by F. T. Prince
Romeo and Juliet: edited by Brian Gibbons
The Taming of the Shrew: edited by Brian Morris
The Tempest: edited by Frank Kermode
Timon of Athens: edited by H. J. Oliver
Titus Andronicus: edited by J. C. Maxwell
Troilus and Cressida: edited by Kenneth Palmer
Twelfth Night: edited by J. M. Lothian and T. W. Craik
The Two Gentlemen of Verona: edited by Clifford Leech
The Winter's Tale: edited by J. H. P. Pafford

THE ARDEN EDITION OF THE
WORKS OF WILLIAM SHAKESPEARE

THE POEMS

Edited by
F. T. PRINCE

ROUTLEDGE

LONDON and NEW YORK

The general editors of the Arden Shakespeare have been
W. J. Craig (1899–1906), R. H. Case (1909–44),
Una Ellis-Fermor (1946–58), Harold F. Brooks (1952–82),
Harold Jenkins (1958–82) and Brian Morris (1975–82)

Present general editor: Richard Proudfoot

This edition of *The Poems*, by F. T Prince,
first published in 1960 by
Methuen & Co. Ltd
11 New Fetter Lane, London EC4P 4EE
Reprinted 1961

First published as a University Paperback 1969
Reprinted three times
Reprinted 1985
Reprinted 1988 by Routledge

Published in the USA by
Routledge
a division of Routledge, Chapman and Hall, Inc.
29 West 35th Street, New York, NY 10001

Editorial matter © 1960 Methuen & Co. Ltd

ISBN (hardbound) 0 416 47610 4
ISBN (paperback) 0 415 02752 7

Printed and bound in Great Britain by
Richard Clay Ltd, Bungay, Suffolk

CONTENTS

	PAGE
PREFACE	vii
ABBREVIATIONS	ix
INTRODUCTION	xi
I. The Texts	xi
II. The Poems	xxiv
VENUS AND ADONIS	1
LUCRECE	63
THE PASSIONATE PILGRIM	151
THE PHOENIX AND TURTLE	177

APPENDICES

I. The Stories of Venus and Adonis and of Hermaphroditus and Salmacis from *The XV Bookes of P. Ovidius Naso, entytuled Metamorphosis, translated oute of Latin into English meeter, by Arthur Golding Gentleman . . . 1567*   185

II. (a) Chaucer, *The Legende of Good Women*, ll. 1680–1885   189
   (b) Extract from Painter's *The Pallace of Pleasure* (1566)   199
   (c) Ovid, *Fasti*, II, 721–852   196
   (d) Translation of Ovid, *Fasti*, II. 721–852   193

PREFACE

I owe much to the advice of the late General Editor, who read and commented upon a first draft of this edition. I have also been helped, to an extent I can hardly stress too much, by Dr Harold F. Brooks. What virtues my treatment of the texts may have, derive from his criticism and guidance. I must thank him also for many suggestions embodied in the Commentary; this was also seen in proof by Mr J. C. Maxwell, to whom I am grateful for some valuable points of detail. I owe some important corrections and improvements to the vigilance of Professor Harold Jenkins. My thanks are also due to Miss B. Wotton and Miss D. Cross, of the Arts Faculty Secretariat in this University, for retyping much of the book in its later stages.

F. T. PRINCE

The University, Southampton
  February 1960

ABBREVIATIONS

The abbreviations used for Shakespeare's plays are from C. T. Onions, *A Shakespeare Glossary*. The most frequently used abbreviations for other works are:

Abbott   E. Abbott, *A Shakespearian Grammar.*

O.E.D.   *A New English Dictionary on Historical Principles* (Oxford, 1888–1933).

O.D.E.P.   *Oxford Dictionary of English Proverbs* (Oxford, 1935).

Rollins   New Variorum Edition of *The Poems* (*Venus and Adonis, Lucrece, The Passionate Pilgrim, The Phoenix and the Turtle, A Lover's Complaint*), edited by Hyder Edward Rollins (Philadelphia, 1938).

INTRODUCTION

I. THE TEXTS

(i)

The texts which are now given in editions of Shakespeare under the title of *The Poems* were not included in the First Folio.[1] *Venus and Adonis* and *Lucrece*, after many appearances in the first twenty years of their existence, were reprinted at intervals in the seventeenth century; but they were not brought together until 1707, in the collection oddly entitled *Poems on Affairs of State*. They soon appeared again, in Bernard Lintott's *Collection of Poems* of 1709, and were then joined for the first time by *The Passionate Pilgrim*. In the same year they were published also in an unauthorized 'seventh volume' of Rowe's edition of the plays. This supplementary volume may have been edited by Charles Gildon, who wrote the critical essays it contained; it gave also the 'miscellany poems' from John Benson's volume of 1640, *Poems Written by Wil. Shake-speare. Gent.*, and thus included *The Phoenix and Turtle*.

The collection of 1709 was reprinted several times as a supplement to various editions of the plays; but no editorial work of any value was done until 1780, when Malone began to revise the texts in the light of the early editions.[2] He carried this task further in 1790, in Volume x of his own edition of the *Plays and Poems*; and 'it is due to Malone's example that *Venus and Adonis* and the rest of Shakespeare's non-dramatic writings were finally admitted to the Shakespearean canon'.[3]

(ii)

Venus and Adonis was first published, in quarto, in 1593:[4]

Q1 [Ornament] / VENUS / AND ADONIS / *Vilia miretur vulgus: mihi flauus Apollo* / *Pocula Castalia plena ministret aqua.* / [Device,

---

1. In the Arden edition, *A Lover's Complaint* is printed with the Sonnets, with which it first appeared in 1609.
2. See Malone, *Supplement to the Edition of Shakespeare's Plays Published in 1778.*
3. Sidney Lee, *Poems and* Pericles, London, 1905, p. 75.
4. The only known copy of Q1 is in the Bodleian.

McKerrow 192] / LONDON / Imprinted by Richard Field, and are to be fold at / the fign of the white Greyhound in / Paules Churchyard. / 1593. /

    4°: [A²], B—G⁴, H¹.

The title-page is A1ʳ, the dedication (in which the author's name first appears) A2ʳ

The poem had been entered in the Register at Stationers' Hall by Richard Field on 18 April 1593:

[S.R. 1593.] xviii° Aprilis. Richard Feild Assigned ouer to master Harrison senior 25 Junii 1594. Entred for his copie under thandes of the Archbisshop of Canterbury and master warden Stirrop, a booke intituled, Venus and Adonis, vjᵈ S.[1]

At least eleven editions were printed before 1620, of which ten are extant. In addition to Q1, these are:

Q2 (1594), Q3 (1595?), Q4 (1596), Q5 (1599), Q6 (1599), Q7 (1602?), Q8 (1602), Q9 (1602), Q10 (1617).[2]

Five other editions appeared before 1640, one of them at Edinburgh in 1627.

Lucrece was first published, in quarto, in 1594:

Q1 [Ornament] / LUCRECE. / [Device, McKerrow 222] / LONDON. / Printed by Richard Field, for Iohn Harrifon, and are / to be fold at the figne of the white Greyhound / in Paules Churh-yard [*sic*]. 1594. /

    4°: A², B—M⁴, N¹.

The title-page is A1ʳ, the dedication is A2ʳ, the Argument A2ᵛ. The text begins on B1ʳ, and has the heading 'The Rape of Lucrece', which is also the running-title of every later page.[3]

The poem had been entered by Harrison at Stationers' Hall in May 1594:

1. Arber, *Transcript*, II, p. 630. In *Shakespeare's Sonnets Dated* (London, 1949) Leslie Hotson maintains that the book appeared a few days before 21 September 1593 (pp. 141–6). His evidence comes from letters written by William Renoldes, 'a sufferer from persecution mania and religious frenzy', and preserved among the Lansdowne MSS. in the British Museum.

2. The editions after Q2 were in octavo, but are usually referred to as Q3, Q4, etc. See E. K. Chambers, *William Shakespeare* (Oxford, 1930), vol. I, p. 544. Chambers cautiously accepts the suggestion by H. Farr (*The Library*, March 1923, p. 244), that some of the editions dated 1602 were really printed later (probably in 1607 and 1608). A fourth edition dated 1602 is known only from the title-page, which is in the British Museum.

3. Eleven copies (some imperfect) are known, distributed as follows: British Museum (2), Bodley (2), Sion College, Huntington, Folger (3), Yale, Rosenbach.

[S. R. 1594.] 9 Maij Master Harrison Senior Entred for his copie vnder thand of Master Cawood Warden, a booke intituled the Ravyshement of Lucrece vi^d C.[1]

Lucrece was almost as successful as *Venus and Adonis*. Five further editions were printed before 1616 (all are in octavo, but are usually referred to as Q2, Q3, etc.):

Q2 (1598), Q3 (1600), Q4 (1600), Q5 (1607), Q6 (1616).

Two other editions appeared before 1640.[2] In certain copies of Q1[3] there are variant readings which show that corrections were made in the type after a number of sheets had been printed; there is little to indicate whether these alterations were made by the author or by the printer, but C. J. Sisson believes they should be attributed to the latter.[4]

(iii)

The modernized texts of *Venus and Adonis* and *Lucrece* which are given in the present edition are based on the First Quartos, which have been generally accepted as well printed, probably from the poet's fair copies.[5] Some trouble would probably be taken, both by author and printer, in the production of pieces such as these: they were the poet's first publications, and were dedicated to a noble patron. That the First Quartos have greater authority than any other editions can hardly be disputed. It remains, however, to consider their relationship to the later Quartos, and to decide what, if any, degree of authority these may claim.

It may be said at once that the later Quartos have every appearance of belonging to a series of reprints, each based upon one or more of its predecessors; none of the new readings they contain are such as to suggest the author's intervention, or any recourse to fresh MS. material. But it will be well to give the grounds for this impression, by examining details of the texts.

Bibliographers have not yet challenged, indeed they have endorsed and substantiated, Malone's assertion that

1. Arber, II, p. 648.   2. See Chambers, *op. cit.*, vol. I, pp. 545–7.

3. For the readings in question see the textual notes on ll. 24, 31, 50, 125, 126, 1182, 1335, 1350.

4. See C. J. Sisson, *New Readings in Shakespeare* (Cambridge 1956), vol. I, pp. 207–8. The variants occur in three formes: inner B (six), outer I (two), and outer K (one). Those on I are obvious corrections of misprints (ll. 1182 and 1335), as that on K may also be (l. 1350). Those on B are deliberate alterations, of which only one (l. 50) is a legitimate correction; the 'uncorrected' readings probably represent what Shakespeare wrote.

5. Sidney Lee dissents (*op. cit.*, pp. 48–51).

in Shakespeare's time the correctors of the press (that is, the stewards or managers of the printing-house, where his plays and poems were printed,) who revised the sheets of the various editions as they were reprinted, altered the text at random according to their notion of propriety and grammar.[1]

This process is indeed suggested by an examination of the later Quartos of *Venus and Adonis* and *Lucrece*. The new readings can all be accounted for as either (*a*) compositor's errors or (*b*) editorial 'improvements'. Errors are often corrected wrongly by guess, either by compositor or editor; in other cases compositor or editor may correct such errors rightly, but equally by guesswork (or sometimes by reference to an earlier edition).

Examples may first be given of compositor's errors of various types, but all of the kind that can escape immediate detection because they can pass for sense at a glance or with a slight effort. Omission or addition of the *s* varies the number in *Lucr.*, ll. 13, 491, and 1721. Haplography gives 'sheathed' for 'she sheathed' in *Lucr.*, l. 1723. Words are caught from nearby positions above, below, or in the same line, in *Ven.*, ll. 75, 353, 700, 724, 990, 1054, and *Lucr.*, ll. 993, 1308. A word is assimilated to a like word in the same line in *Ven.*, ll. 62, 712, 1002, and *Lucr.*, ll. 308, 791, 1829. Vulgarization or the use of compositor's synonyms accounts for variants in *Ven.*, ll. 160, 203, 397, 447, 484, and 522.

Such errors can be seen corrected by guesswork in *Ven.*, l. 990, and *Lucr.*, l. 791. Similar cases of progressive corruption are found in *Ven.*, ll. 469, 547, 1073, and *Lucr.*, l. 1205.

The clue to the new readings in the early Quartos is thus provided when we have in mind corrections or 'improvements' by compositors or editors. In many cases we should not find the new readings unsatisfactory if we had not the readings of the First Quartos with which to compare them; but in such a comparison we find that the changes always tend towards the commonplace and the facile. In order to provide detailed evidence, we may turn to some of the early editions, noting how new readings could come, go, or remain, as chance or choice guided printers and editors.

The second edition of *Venus and Adonis* was published in 1594 by John Harrison, senior, the new owner of the copyright, and printed, like the first, by Richard Field.[2] It gives nine new readings which clearly represent either the compositor's errors, or his or an editor's 'notion of propriety and grammar'. In l. 56 'feather' for 'feathers' tidies up the disparity between the plural and the two

1. Ed. 1821. See R. B. McKerrow, *Prolegomena for the Oxford Shakespeare* (Oxford, 1939), pp. 14–16.

2. There are four known copies (British Museum, Bodley, Huntington, Yale).

singulars that immediately follow it. In l. 123 'be' for 'are' smooths
the sound of the line. In l. 156 'shouldst' for 'should' is better
grammar. In l. 353 'tender' for 'tendrer' smooths and weakens the
sense: the earlier reading is true to the hyperbolical fancy of the
poem and its striving after epigrammatic point, and the punctuation (the significant pause of the comma after 'cheek') supports it.
In l. 397 'seekes' for 'sees' is either a vulgarization or an 'improvement'; it dislocates the sense, which is carried on by the visual contrast between flesh and sheets and by the 'glutton eye'. In l. 484
'world' for 'earth' loses the vowel alliteration between 'all' and
'earth' and the other musical effect of the two 'th's'. In l. 1113
'would' for 'did', and in l. 1116 'his' for 'the', show an attempt to
improve the sense or the force of the phrase, with the usual dubious
results: 'would' anticipates the boar's motive, given clearly enough
in the next line; the second 'his', referring to a different 'he', gives
l. 1116 a positive clumsiness.

The only surviving copy of Q3 (actually the first octavo edition)
lacks the opening pages.[1] It was perhaps printed in 1595, by Richard Field for John Harrison, and is based upon Q2. Some of its new
readings are obvious mistakes (see ll. 644 and 1162). Others are
plausible, and tend to stick (as in ll. 447, 668, and 911). One ('as'
for 'are' in l. 1031) has been widely accepted, and Malone called it
'manifestly an improvement'. But the couplet remains clumsy in
spite of it: the eyes are now both 'murdred with the view' and 'like
stars asham'd of day', and we feel that something may still be wrong.

Q4 was printed from Q3 in 1596, by Richard Field for John
Harrison[2]; most of its new readings are obvious errors, though they
enjoyed some favour. Two of its corruptions (ll. 317 and 1021) have
flourished in modern editions; most appear again only in Q5
(ll. 700, 765, 990, 1002, 1051, 1052), while others come and go
(ll. 522, 668, 712). In l. 896 'sore dismaid' for 'all dismayd' became
established, and was given a special blessing by Malone as 'doubtless the author's correction'.[3] Yet 'sore-dismay'd' has just the
quality of commonplace that pleases printers and editors. This
alone would tell against it, but it also introduces an ugly clash of
sibilants.

With the transfer of the poems to a new publisher, who employed
a new printer, comes a striking illustration of the hazards to which
the text was exposed. Q5 was printed in 1599 by Peter Short[4] for

1. It is now in the Folger Library.
2. There are two copies (British Museum, Bodley).   3. Ed. 1821.
4. The only known copy of Q5 is in the Huntington Library. Farr wrote that
'though no printer's name appears in the imprint the ornaments used in the
volume leave no doubt that it came from the press of Peter Short' (op. cit., p. 228).

William Leake, to whom Harrison had assigned the copyright in
1596.[1] Q5 seems to have been based on Q4, but it contains a larger
proportion of mere errors than any previous edition. Some were
too obvious to survive (ll. 190, 213, 350, 424, 460, 464, 500, 506,
680, 704, 794, 863, 901, 1099, 1136, 1160). When Q6 was printed
for Leake by a new printer, Richard Bradocke, also in 1599, these
mistakes were removed, presumably with the help of Q4, or some
other earlier edition.[2] But some of the new readings in Q5, though
of no intrinsic merit, were allowed to stand; several were reproduced in all the later quartos (ll. 281, 593, 654, 705, 760, 851), and
these and others were accepted by many editors (ll. 315, 325).

Four more editions of *Venus and Adonis* (of which three survive)
were printed between 1599 and the year of Shakespeare's death;
but to run through them would add little to the outline already
given of the nature of the new readings. The early quartos of
Lucrece can provide more, and sometimes more striking, evidence.

The second edition of *Lucrece*, Q2 (an octavo), was printed by
Peter Short for John Harrison in 1598.[3] It derives from Q1 and
follows it closely. Some of its new readings are glaring errors (ll.
738, 1214, 1254, 1547). One of its mistakes (l. 1214) is amended by
guess in Q3 and affects many later editions; and another is repeated
only once (l. 1854). Those of its new readings which find most
favour are of the usual type, blatant or unobtrusive 'improvements' (see ll. 21, 1254, 1519, 1640, 1661, 1781).

Q3 was based upon Q2, and printed by the younger John Harrison in 1600.[4] Two of its new readings are mere errors (ll. 185 and
274). Conscious mind may have been at work in the others;
among these some were eventually rejected (see ll. 48, 978, and
1842), while others were either endorsed or passed unnoticed (as in
ll. 490, 871, 903, 1299, 1583, 1702, 1838).

Q4, which was printed for the same publisher by the same
printer and in the same year as Q3, is based upon Q3 and follows it
in page-arrangement and even ornament; yet it offers a great contrast in accuracy.[5] It occupies the place among reprints of *Lucrece*
that is occupied by Q5 among reprints of *Venus and Adonis*, and its
mass of careless and presumptuous readings illustrates even better
the way in which these texts lay at the mercy of printers and proof-
readers. A selection from its long list of misprints may be seen in
ll. 47, 314, 347, 400, 450, 453, 487, 606, 613, 630, 639, 704, 783, 809,

1. Arber, III, p. 65.
2. The only known copy of Q6 is in the Folger Library.
3. The only known copy is in the Library of Trinity College, Cambridge.
4. The only known copy is in the Folger Library.
5. There are two copies, both in the Bodleian.

1151, 1200, 1220, 1268, 1386, 1451, 1507, 1529, 1551, 1712. Most of these mistakes were not perpetuated; it appears that, as in the case of Q5 of *Venus and Adonis*, an edition as bad as this was soon judged, and that if it was used as a basis for a subsequent edition, which does not seem likely, care was taken to supplement it. But the printer of Q4 only brings an exceptional personal ineptitude to his acknowledged task. Since we are interested in the workings of the system we may watch with gratification while he 'amends' no less freely than he botches. Examples of his more or less plausible results occur in ll. 24, 73, 82, 205, 269, 368, 462, 492, 543, 628, 782, 808, 1006, 1107, 1248, 1361, 1498, 1588, 1633.

The next surviving edition, Q5, appeared in 1607, printed by Nicholas Okes for John Harrison[1]; it is not based only on Q4, though some of Q4's new readings reappear in it (as in ll. 1190, 1200, 1207, 1515, 1648, 1712, 1755, 1765, 1784, 1851). A copy of Q4 was probably available for reference, and may inadvertently have been used too often in setting up some parts of the text.[2] But Q5 must have been based for the most part on one or more of the editions previous to Q4, and may well have been eclectic in its use of earlier editions. However, the greater amount of editing that must have gone into Q5 did not exclude new readings of the usual types. Some are easily detected errors (ll. 321, 1308, 1383). Others are hardly less obvious and yet reappear later (see ll. 282, 993, 1375, 1614, 1721). Other new readings which persist are clearly of the same origin, but are either not easily detectable (as in ll. 651 and 807) or are introduced and accepted as improvements (as in ll. 1083 and 1105). In l. 879 'points' for 'poinst' may be an assimilation of the last two letters to 'plots' in the same line; yet it brings 'thou points' into line with 'Thou sets' in the previous line, and is an emendation such as a modern editor might make.

It is, however, the next edition of *Lucrece*, Q6, published in 1616, that provides the best illustration of the liberties taken with these texts by printers and publishers.[3] John Harrison, junior, who had published all the editions up to this point, in 1614 transferred the copyright to Roger Jackson.[4] Jackson, with a new printer, Thomas Snodham, presented the poem with various improvements and embellishments, which justify the words 'Newly Revised' on the title-page. The title becomes *The Rape of Lucrece*, and Shakespeare's name appears on the title-page for the first time. The text is en-

1. There are two copies (Huntington; Trinity College, Cambridge).

2. The readings taken over by Q5 from Q4 occur in two sigs. only.

3. There are four copies (British Museum, Bodley, Huntington, New York Public Library).

4. Arber, III, p. 542.

livened by frequent italics, which persist in the three subsequent seventeenth-century editions. The amount of italicization varies considerably, apparently according to the degree of attention given it by the printer. The following lines show its greater incidence:

> So shall these *slaves* be *King*, and thou their *slave*:
> Thou *nobly base*, they basely *dignified*:
> Thou their *faire life*, and they thy *fouler grave*:
> Thou lothed in their *shame*, they in thy *pride*,
> The *lesser thing* should not the *greater* hide.
>   The *Cedar* stoops not to the base *shrubs* foot,
>   But low *shrubs* wither at the *Cedars root*.
>   (ll. 659–65)

The following stanza, not much farther on, has a much lighter application:

> So fares it with this fault-full Lord of Rome,
> Who this accomplishment so hotly chased;
> For, now against himselfe he sounds this doome,
> That through the length of *times* he stands disgraced:
> Besides, his soules faire temple is defaced:
>   To whose weake *ruines* muster troopes of *cares*,
>   To ask the spotted *Princesse* how she fares.
>   (ll. 715–21)

On A3^v the printer added the following list, under the heading of '*The Contents*':

1 LUCRECE praifes for chafte, vertuous, and beautifull, enamoreth *Tarquin*.
2 *Tarquin* welcomed by *Lucrece*.
3 *Tarquin* overthrowes all difputing with wilfulneffe.
4 He puts his refolution in practife.
5 *Lucrece* awakes and is amazed to be fo furprifed.
6 She pleads in defence of Chaftity.
7 *Tarquin* all impatient interrupteth her, and ravifheth her by force.
8 *Lucrece* complaines on her abufe.
9 She difputeth whether fhe fhould kill her felfe or no.
10 She is refolved on her felfe-murther, yet fendeth firft for her Husband.
11 *Colatinus* with his friends returne home.
12 *Lucrece* relateth the mifchiefe: they fweare revenge, and fhe to exafperate the matter killeth her felfe.

Twelve marginal notes to the text correspond (with some discrepancies) to the headings of the list of contents (the fourth head-ing is omitted, and the last two notes are not numbered).

A text presented with such adornments is not likely to be care-lessly printed, and none of the new readings are obvious errors. Even 'feeded' for 'seeded' (l. 603) and 'other' for 'others' (l. 1238) may be attempts to 'correct' what were felt to be awkward expressions.

Most of the new readings in Q6 were to commend themselves to seventeenth- and eighteenth-century editors precisely because they had been introduced for their 'correctness'. A conscious ideal can be seen at work. When 'shuts' is substituted for 'stows' (l. 119), it is to eliminate a 'low' expression. A hankering after facility or commonplace in phrase and rhythm is shown in such changes as 'star' for 'stars' in l. 13, 'if' for 'is' in l. 24, 'if once' for 'I, if' in l. 239, 'too' for 'ful' in l. 370, 'breasts' for 'brest' in l. 439, 'pretty' for 'petty' in l. 649, 'fowle' for 'prone' in l. 684, 'these' for 'the' in l. 1504, and 'But' for 'Both' in l. 1595. Notions of metrical regularity bring about the change from 'mother' to 'sad source' in l. 117. The same dislike of an 'inverted' stress appears in l. 26, together with disapproval of the recession of accent in 'expir'd'. The forcefulness of

> An expir'd date canceld ere well begunne

is transformed into the almost eighteenth-century glibness and balance of

> A date expir'd: and canceld ere begunne.

Similar intimations of Augustanism may be traced in 'recites' for 'retires' (l. 303) and 'ever' for 'mute and' in l. 1123.

In crucial passages the guess of an editor working to such prin-ciples may often be as good as another's, and in l. 135,

> That what they have not, that which they possesse

puts on the passable sense of:

> That oft they have not that which they possesse.

However, it is plain that the editor of Q6 had the same conception of his task as Gildon, who substituted 'reign' for 'raine' in l. 392 of *Venus and Adonis*.

Q6 was published in the year of Shakespeare's death, and it is theoretically possible that he intervened in its production, as in that of previous editions both of *Lucrece* and *Venus and Adonis*. It is equally a possibility that MS. material was made available to the publish-ers, both before and after Shakespeare's death. Yet nothing in the readings we have considered makes it necessary to take these possibilities seriously. Even those few readings that are really improvements can be explained by the workings of the system—the more or less intelligent printer and his assistants working from previous editions. Moreover, if Shakespeare went to the trouble of inserting the very small number of new readings that can be described as good, how are we to explain why he did not eliminate the far greater number of those that are gratuitous, inferior, or downright bad?

Since we are now weighing evidence external to the texts, we must bear in mind Shakespeare's situation in the twenty years following the first appearance of these poems. He was already a successful playwright when they were published. His financial interest in them probably ceased with the sum for which he sold them to the booksellers, and the amounts he received from Lord Southampton as the dedicatee. As long as the theatres were open, much bigger money offered itself to him from the writing of two plays a year. Can we suppose that in the astonishing creative activity of the fifteen years from about 1595 to about 1610, and in the press of personal and business interests in which he became involved, Shakespeare cared to follow the fortunes of these early works, which had served their immediate purpose? The booksellers were free to sell the copyright to whom they chose, and each new bookseller could choose a new printer. Can we imagine Shakespeare, in the midst of his unflagging career as a successful dramatist, pursuing these texts from publisher to publisher and printer to printer, and all for the sake of an aesthetic ideal—the perfection of every detail of the verse? And if we can imagine this, can we go on to imagine that he would fail so completely in his purpose, by overlooking more blemishes than he introduced improvements?

Both the evidence of the early editions, and what we know and can conjecture of Shakespeare's poetic career, point to the conclusion that he was directly responsible only for the texts of the First Quartos of *Venus and Adonis* and *Lucrece*.

Variants given in the present edition have been chosen in the light of this conclusion. New readings are given from the early Quartos (up to and including Q9[1] of *Venus and Adonis* and Q6 (1616) of *Lucrece*) if they are more than unique misprints or changes in spelling and punctuation. Where such new readings pass into later Quartos this is indicated.[2]

1. Q9 bears the date 1602, but it was probably printed in 1607/8 (see p. xii, n. 2, above). It is the last surviving edition printed before Shakespeare's death. Q10 appeared in 1617.

2. Q16 of *Venus and Adonis* was printed in 1675, Q9 of *Lucrece* in 1655. The 18th-century editors before Malone based their texts on these last quartos.

(iv)

Of the three early editions of *The Passionate Pilgrim* the first exists only in a fragment of two sheets, which form part of the copy in the Folger Library. The remainder of this volume, which lacks a title-page, is made up of sheets from the second edition.[1] The first edition sheets (the Folger fragment) in this book will be referred to as Q1, although they are in octavo, like the other early editions. They give the text of eight poems, numbered as follows in the present edition: I, II, III, IV, V, XVI, XVII, XVIII.

Q1 has eleven leaves, without signatures, but belonging to quires A and C, which were probably signed on the initial leaves now missing. The poems are printed on the recto only of each leaf, a poem to each leaf, until we get to XVII, which begins on C3^r, continues on C3^v, and ends on C4^r. Similarly XVIII is printed on both recto and verso, beginning on C5^r and ending on C7^r.

The earliest surviving complete edition is the second, of which two copies exist (in addition to those sheets included in the Folger copy); one is in the Library of Trinity College, Cambridge, the other in the Huntington Library. The volume is an octavo:

Q2. THE / PASSIONATE / PILGRIME. / *By W. Shakespeare.* / [Ornament] / *AT LONDON* / Printed for W. Iaggard, and are / to be fold by W. Leake, at the Grey- / hound in Paules Church-yard. / 1599. /

The title-page is A2^r. The poems are printed on twenty-eight leaves; in the first twenty-five the text is printed on the recto only, but in the last three (D5–D7) it is on both recto and verso. There is a second title-page on C3^r:

SONNETS / To fundry notes of Muficke. / [Ornament as on A2^r] / *AT LONDON* / Printed for W. Iaggard, and are / to be fold by W. Leake, at the Grey- / hound in Paules Churchyard. / 1599. /

Bibliographical analysis of the fragmentary first and the second editions shows that the second was set up from the first, and that the second title-page was first inserted in the second edition. The printer of the second edition departed from the method of the first edition, in which poems began only on rectos, but could be continued on versos. The printer of the second edition printed poems on rectos only, whether they were continued or not, until he reached D5^r; at this point he found that if he proceeded in the same way

1. The relationship between the fragmentary first edition and the second was first set out in 1939 in the Introduction to the Folger Shakespeare Library facsimile of *The Passionate Pilgrim* [1599], edited by J. Q. Adams. Rollins in 1938 gave a complete list of the variant readings, but left open the question of which edition was the first (*Poems*, p. 526).

to the end of the text, he would have to take another sheet, E. In order to avoid this, he printed the two remaining poems (XIX and XX) on both rectos and versos of D from D5^r to D7^v.[1]

A third edition, with additional matter, came out in 1612:

Q3. THE / PASSIONATE / PILGRIME. / OR / *Certaine Amorous Sonnets,* / *betweene* Venus *and* Adonis, / *newly corrected and aug-* / *mented.* / By W. Shakefpeare. / The third Edition./ VVhere-unto is newly ad- / ded two Loue-Epiftles, the firft / from *Paris* to *Hellen,* and / *Hellens* anfwere backe / againe to *Paris.* / Printed by W. Iaggard. / 1612. /

There are two copies extant, one in the Folger Library, the other in the Bodleian; the latter, which once belonged to Malone, has, in addition to the above, a second title-page, omitting the ascription to Shakespeare.

Neither of the two title-pages in the Bodleian copy gives an accurate account of the contents, for the two epistles mentioned are followed by another seven poems. These pieces, nine in all, were taken from Thomas Heywood's *Troia Britanica, or Great Britaines Troy,* printed by Jaggard in 1609. Heywood was indignant at this misuse of his poems, and also at the badness of the printing in *Troia Britanica;* and he added to his *Apologie for Actors* (1612) an epistle to his new printer, in which he spoke of his own irritation and also of Shakespeare's resentment at what Jaggard had done.[2] It seems likely that Shakespeare's displeasure caused Jaggard to cancel the original title-page to Q3 and substitute one without Shakespeare's name. An earlier protest by Shakespeare at the ascription to him of the whole of the first edition may have led to the insertion of the second title-page in the second edition; it is true that this title-page is placed immediately before a poem by Shakespeare, and after several pieces which are probably not his, and one (VIII) which is by Barnfield; but Jaggard may have hoped that it would make some amends by indicating, though obscurely, that the whole volume was not to be regarded as by Shakespeare.[3]

1. See Introduction, Folger Library facsimile, ed. Adams, pp. xxx–xxxi.

2. 'Here likewise, I must necessarily insert a manifest injury done me in that worke [*Troia Britanica*], by taking the two Epistles of *Paris* to *Helen,* and *Helen* to *Paris,* and printing them in a lesse volume [*The Passionate Pilgrim,* 1612], under the name of another [Shakespeare], ... but as I must acknowledge my lines not worthy his patronage, under whom he [Jaggard] hath publisht them, so the Author [Shakespeare] I know much offended with M. *Jaggard* (that altogether unknowne to him) presumed to make so bold with his name.' See the Introduction to the Folger Library facsimile of *The Passionate Pilgrim, 1612,* edited by H. E. Rollins (1940), pp. xxvii–xxviii; see also *Poems,* ed. Rollins, p. 535.

3. See Introduction to Folger Library facsimile of *The Passionate Pilgrim* [1599], p. xxxvi.

Of the twenty poems in *The Passionate Pilgrim*, five are known to be by Shakespeare (I, II, III, V, and XVI), and others are known to be by other writers (VIII, XIX, XX).[1] There is no evidence to prove the rest to be by Shakespeare, and the piratical processes by which the book came into being do not favour the supposition. Moreover, the quality of the unassigned poems is such that there is little temptation to try to establish Shakespeare as their author. 'Crabbed age and youth' (XII) is alone among them in having a beauty and energy which make us regret that we have no means of determining its origin. An ugly and stupid poem like XVIII confirms the general impression that Jaggard had to eke out his few genuine Shakespearian pieces with whatever inferior stuff he could find.[2]

The present text is based on the earliest surviving editions, i.e. Q1 for the poems numbered I, II, III, IV, V, XVI, XVII, XVIII, and Q2 for the remainder.[3]

(v)

The Phoenix and Turtle was first printed in a book by Robert Chester published in quarto in 1601[4]:

LOVES MARTYR: / OR, / ROSALINS COMPLAINT. / *Allegorically ſhadowing the truth of Loue,* / in the conſtant Fate of the Phoenix / *and Turtle.* / A Poeme enterlaced with much varietie and raritie; / *now firſt tranſlated out of the venerable Italian* Torquato / Cæliano, by ROBERT CHESTER. / With the true legend of famous King *Arthur*, the laſt of the nine / Worthies, being the firſt *Eſſay* of a new *Brytiſh* Poet, collected / out of diuerſe Authenticall Records. / *To theſe are added ſome new compoſitions, of ſeuerall moderne Writers* / *whoſe names are ſubſcribed to their ſeuerall workes, upon the* / *firſt Subject: viz. the* Phoenix *and* Turtle. / *Mar:—Mutare dominum non poteſt liber notus.* / [Ornament] / LONDON / Imprinted for F.B.

4°: A–Aᵃ⁴, Bᵇ².

Y⁴ is followed by a separate title-page, on Z¹, announcing the compositions already mentioned:

HEREAFTER / FOLLOVV DIVERSE / Poeticall Eſſaies on the

1. MS. versions of I, IV, VI, VII, XI, and XVIII are found in three early MS. miscellanies now in the Folger Library (Folger MS. 1.112, Folger MS. 1.8, and Folger MS. 2071.7). These versions are reproduced in the facsimile edition by J. Q. Adams, pp. lv–lxiii.

2. For details of attribution and MS. versions see the notes to individual pieces.

3. It should be clear that this edition of *The Passionate Pilgrim* is committed to giving 'bad' texts of some poems of which other and perhaps better texts exist (e.g. I, II, III, V, XVI, and XIX). Its purpose is not to recover what Shakespeare or Marlowe really wrote, but to give an accurate text of the pirated version.

4. There are copies in the Folger Library and the Huntington Library.

former Sub- / iect; viz: the *Turtle* and *Phoenix*. / *Done by the beſt and chiefeſt of our* / moderne writers, with their names fub- / fcribed to their particular workes: / *neuer before extant.* / And (now firſt) confecrated by them all generally, / *to the loue and merite of the true-noble Knight,* / Sir Iohn Salisburie. / *Dignum laude virum Muſa vetat mori.* / [Device] / MDCI.

The group of poems which follows is made up of two pieces signed 'Vatum Chorus', one signed 'Ignoto', one signed 'William Shake-speare', one signed 'John Marston', one signed 'George Chapman', and two signed 'Ben Johnson'.

In 1611 the old sheets of Chester's book were reissued by a new publisher, Matthew Lownes, with a new title-page[1]:

[Ornament] / THE / Anuals of great / Brittaine. / OR, / A MOST EXCEL- / lent Monument, wherein may be / *feene all the antiquities of this King-* / dome, to the fatisfaction both of the / Vniuerfities, or any other place ftir- / red with Emulation of long / continu-ance. / *Excellently figured out in a worthy Poem.* / [Device, Mc-Kerrow 310] / LONDON / Printed for MATHEW LOWNES. / 1611. /

  4°: [Title] B–A^a4, B^b2.

The third appearance of Shakespeare's poem was in Benson's *Poems Written by Wil. Shake-speare. Gent.*, in 1640; from this source it passed into the eighteenth-century editions, until in Malone's edition of 1780 it was reproduced from *Loves Martyr.* Malone print-ed it, however, as Poem XX of *The Passionate Pilgrim*, and it thus ap-peared in many later editions as an item in that collection.

The text of 1601, unchanged in 1611, is the sole authority for the poem.

II. THE POEMS

(i)

'In Shakespeare's *poems*,' wrote Coleridge, 'the creative power and the intellectual energy wrestle as in a war embrace. Each in its excess of strength seems to threaten the extinction of the other. At length in the DRAMA they were reconciled, and fought each with its shield before the breast of the other.'[2] Fervid imagery increases the real difficulty offered by Coleridge's thought; yet his criticism of *Venus and Adonis* and *Lucrece* nevertheless first provided the point

1. The only known copy is in the British Museum.

2. *Biographia Literaria*, vol. II (Oxford, 1907), p. 19. A somewhat fuller version was given in the *Literary Remains*, vol. II, pp. 53–60. Coleridge began his lectures on Shakespeare with this analysis, showing Shakespeare as a poet generally, and assuming that the narrative poems were written before any of the plays. But this too easy view hardly affects the value of what he has to say.

of view from which it is most profitable to examine these poems. His appreciation of *Venus and Adonis* shows indeed that he fully felt its intrinsic beauty; but he was wise to make his criticism serve the larger purpose of illuminating Shakespeare the dramatist. Nothing else was likely then, or is likely even now, to win an attentive reading of these poems. For one thing, their eroticism is hardly more acceptable than it was in Coleridge's day; few English or American readers nowadays will respond to such happily wanton fancies as *Venus and Adonis*. The guilty and tormented passions of *Lucrece* are perhaps more to the taste of our time; but the poem is in itself much less readable than its predecessor. Moreover, both poems must compete with a body of dramatic work which is immensely superior in poetic achievement, and which offers endless opportunities, or temptations, for research and speculation.

The two narrative poems have nevertheless a unique distinction: they were the only works Shakespeare published in which he claims the status of a professional poet. The poems are given signed dedications to a noble patron, and presented with as much care as Spenser gave to his books. It is ironical that these works, so put forward by their young author, should be among those of his productions which have been least valued by posterity. But their later fortunes cannot detract from their value as evidence: evidence both of Shakespeare's ambition (no doubt transient) to be taken for a 'real' poet, and of the powers he could in fact bring to non-dramatic poetry. Here we can see Shakespeare as a literary artist, a craftsman seeking to shape a completed aesthetic whole on the written page; we can criticize his success or failure in a medium which does not involve us in the uncertainties and ironies of drama. In this respect even the Sonnets are less useful; for the unity of even the most carefully and consciously composed 'sonnet sequences' (and Shakespeare's is not one of these) is not comparable to the unity required in short idyllic or narrative poems.[1]

In order, then, to extract their full value from *Venus and Adonis* and *Lucrece*, we must first consider the intrinsic merits of each poem, its final artistic effect; in this undertaking it will not be difficult to argue that *Venus* is a complete artistic success, despite some flaws or weaker passages, while *Lucrece* is undoubtedly as a whole an artistic

1. Professor C. S. Lewis defines *Venus and Adonis* (but apparently not *Lucrece*) as an 'epyllion'. But the term, at least in his interpretation of it, seems to hinder appreciation of the poem. By insisting on the exclusion of humour from the 'erotic epyllion' Professor Lewis renders himself incapable of enjoying *Venus and Adonis*; *Hero and Leander* is for him the perfect Elizabethan example of the form (see *English Literature in the Sixteenth Century* (Oxford, 1954), pp. 486-7 and 498-9). See p. xxxii below.

failure, despite the magnificence of many of its parts. A comparison between the two poems may then indicate the underlying forces which determine success or failure. And finally, it should be possible to set the two pieces in their place among Shakespeare's works, where they represent a phase in his development, and indicate the capacities and problems of his genius.

(ii)

Despite the presentation of *Venus and Adonis* and *Lucrece* as the works of a conscious artist, Shakespeare probably sat down to write them in the hope that they would bring him some immediate practical reward. It has sometimes been suggested that *Venus* was written in the 1580's, perhaps before Shakespeare came to London.[1] However, its appearance in 1593, and that of *Lucrece* in the following year, coincided with a difficult period for the London theatres: they were closed in August 1592, when the plague broke out with violence, and remained closed throughout 1593. Shakespeare's own description of the poem as the 'first heir' of his 'invention' offers an apparent difficulty, since he had already begun to make his name as a playwright; but Lord Southampton would not have been flattered, and might even have been annoyed, by a reference to the vulgar dramatic successes of the young writer: such works were not considered to fall into the category of literature. If *Venus*, and *Lucrece* a year later, are taken to be a result of the enforced idleness of the London players in 1592–3, their motives being to compensate in part for the disastrous financial losses of that time, we have an explanation both of why the rising young dramatist turned to 'narrative' verse, and of why he chose first such a subject as that of *Venus and Adonis*.

The theme was wanton, and was to be made witty. That Shakespeare gauged the taste of his readers as successfully as he had been gauging that of his audiences is proved by the many editions of the poem in his own time and by frequent allusions to its somewhat disreputable popularity.[2] But wantonness and wit were to be found elsewhere. The finer interest of the poem lies in its demonstration that for Shakespeare these are only manifestations of an intenser activity: they become the adjuncts of an almost intoxicating poetic vision. Verse and language, though of wonderful beauty, may be compared to their disadvantage with Marlowe's style in *Hero and Leander*, and with Shakespeare's own unequalled later achieve-

1. See Rollins, p. 390.
2. In *The Returne from Parnassus*, Part i (1600), the booby Gullio wishes to sleep with *Venus and Adonis* under his pillow.

ments[1]; but no other Elizabethan, not even Spenser, had yet shown such a gift for poetic eloquence. In its general quality, above all in its capacity for both opulent delicacy and fresh, blunt, colloquial statement, the language of the poem is characteristically Elizabethan; but the range may be seen very clearly here because here it corresponds to Shakespeare's rejuvenation of his theme, the sensual mythological tale of the youth and the goddess being suffused with the familiar freshness of English landscape, and the savour and the harshness of country sports.

The lordship of language, the conscious, self-delighting artistry of these poems, have generally been recognized, even by those who have been able to take little pleasure in the display. In *Lucrece* pleasure may well lag behind admiration; success there is not attained, for reasons which must be considered later. But in *Venus and Adonis* all things work together. We must acknowledge the magic of single lines or images such as the often quoted:

> Leading him prisoner in a red rose chain: (l. 110)

or:

> Full gently now she takes him by the hand,
> A lily prison'd in a gaol of snow, (ll. 361–2)

or:

> O fairest mover on this mortal round, (l. 368)

or:

> Which bred more beauty in his angry eyes: (l. 70)

But to praise only such beauties is proper only in assessing a work of confused intricacy, like Keats's *Endymion*, where unity of effect has not been achieved. To go further, and point out the full splendour of single stanzas, is perhaps to be on the right track; for we can hardly feel their force without glimpsing the power of the whole. Coleridge chose several such examples for admiration:

> With this he breaketh from the sweet embrace
> Of those fair arms which bound him to her breast,
> And homeward through the dark laund runs apace;
> Leaves love upon her back deeply distress'd.
>> Look how a bright star shooteth from the sky,
>> So glides he in the night from Venus' eye;
>>> (ll. 811–16)

Here he commented on 'the flight of Adonis in the dusk of the

---

1. See Douglas Bush, *Mythology and the Renaissance Tradition*, pp. 146–7. M. C. Bradbrook thinks it probable 'that Shakespeare knew Marlowe's poem before he composed his own... The unmanageable horse, symbol of the conquest of reason by passion, is the adopted "impresa" of both poets' (*Shakespeare and Elizabethan Poetry* (London, 1951), pp. 65–6). See *Ven.*, l. 3 n.

evening', and particularly on the image of the shooting star: 'How many images and feelings are here brought together without effort and without discord, in the beauty of Adonis, the rapidity of his flight, the yearning, yet hopelessness of the enamoured gazer, while a shadowy ideal character is thrown over the whole!'[1] Such stanzas helped to illustrate his definition of poetic imagination as 'the power by which one image or feeling is made to modify many others, and by a sort of fusion to force many into one'. He gave as further instances the first stanza of the poem, ll. 31 to 36, and:

> Lo here the gentle lark, weary of rest,
> From his moist cabinet mounts up on high,
> And wakes the morning, from whose silver breast
> The sun ariseth in his majesty;
>   Who doth the world so gloriously behold
>   That cedar tops and hills seem burnish'd gold.
>
> (ll. 853–8)

And he could easily have added a dozen others, such as ll. 67–72, ll. 85–90, and the airy grace of the final lines:

> Thus weary of the world, away she hies,
> And yokes her silver doves, by whose swift aid
> Their mistress mounted through the empty skies,
> In her light chariot quickly is convey'd,
>   Holding their course to Paphos, where their queen
>   Means to immure herself and not be seen.
>
> (ll. 1189–94)

The concentrated, leaping lightness of these passages is enhanced by their occurring most often at turning-points: many begin with 'By this' or 'With this', or some other abrupt phrase indicating movement or the passing of time. They contribute to our impression that this poetry spurts forth like the jet of a fountain, recovering with a brilliant swiftness whenever its energy seems momentarily to falter.

Flashing or glowing speed is thus the dominating quality of the verse. Today we have an appreciation of Elizabethan English which should enable us to enjoy the beauty of the style more easily than the eighteenth-century reader, offended by what was too concrete and familiar, and over-conscious of grammatical freedoms,[2]

1. *Literary Remains*, vol. II, pp. 55–6.

2. The emendations of Lintott and Gildon and some other 18th-century editors are worth notice for the light they throw on contemporary taste. The best single illustration of their attempt to 'refine' the style is Gildon's substitution of 'a leathern reign' for 'a leathern rein' in *Ven.*, l. 392. Sewell's 'shrine' for 'shine' in l. 728 is another instance; and there are numerous attempts to 'regularize' the grammar and smooth the verse. Even Malone was not unaffected by the 18th-

or than the nineteenth-century reader, who may have craved for sensuous delights in poetry, but preferred them to be veiled by Tennysonian delicacy of expression or fermented by such linguistic excesses as those of Swinburne. Shakespeare is both explicit and light in his touch; he has his eye on the object, but he never fails in a cleverness delightful in itself.

It is the brilliance of treatment, the variety and swiftness of expression, the vivid details of rhythm and phrase, which after all determine our reaction to the material. In the language, the poetry, the poet lives one life, and in his vision of the subject he lives another. He creates the poem in a kind of double consciousness, in two concurrent lives, made possible by intense activity of mind and feeling. We who read can share this double consciousness; indeed such a detached yet intense participation in the imagined life of beings other than ourselves is the end of all art. Try to explain it, and you initiate an explanation of human consciousness itself, with all that may be entailed.

Thus Coleridge's theory of the imagination is a part of his theory of the universe, his metaphysics and theology; and seeing Shakespeare's youthful poetic imagination at work in *Venus and Adonis*, he is able to claim for it a sublime emancipation, to assert that 'though the very subject cannot but detract from the pleasure of a delicate mind, yet never was poem less dangerous on a moral account'.[1] Whether or not one accepts Coleridge's sense of the indelicate, or his theory of the imagination completed by his metaphysics, one can see what he finds in Shakespeare's treatment of the subject: 'It is throughout as if a superior spirit more intuitive, more intimately conscious, even than the characters themselves, not only of every outward look and act, but of the flux and reflux of the mind in all its subtlest thoughts and feelings, were placing the whole before our view; himself meanwhile unparticipating in the passions, and actuated only by that pleasureable excitement, which had resulted from the energetic fervour of his own spirit in so vividly exhibiting, what it had so accurately and profoundly contemplated.'[2] Coleridge sees that this is the dramatist's gift: 'His "Venus and Adonis" seem at once the characters themselves, and the whole representation of those characters by the most consummate actors. You seem to be told nothing, but to see and hear everything.'[3]

By thus simply giving of the full energy of his imagination, Shakespeare produced a poem which was unique in its own time, and which in its own kind was never to be equalled. The poem has

century feeling for what was 'low' or 'mean' in language (see *Ven.*, l. 74 n.).
1. *Biographia Literaria*, vol. II, p. 16.   2. *Op. cit.*, p. 15.   3. *Ibid*·

predecessors and analogues among contemporary Elizabethan and other sixteenth-century pieces; the tradition of this witty and sensuous re-telling of mythological stories went back through Italian literature to Ovid.[1] The Elizabethans idolized their Ovid, and they did not need to know much Italian to absorb the intention and the methods of the numerous Italian poets who set out to expand and modernize the same type of material. Most Elizabethan poets or prose writers needed little but general examples; Shakespeare needed less. As Douglas Bush sums it up: 'The luxuriant Italianate manner had been naturalized in England, and no immediate foreign contacts were necessary. Not only was every poetical device at hand, there was also Elizabethan fiction. If in Shakespeare's poems action bears to rhetoric much the same proportion as bread to sack in Falstaff's bill, we may remember the technique of Pettie, Lyly, and Greene in their prose tales.'[2] Shakespeare therefore set out to invent no new form, but turned out a poem different and superior only by its brilliant efficiency, by the fire of a poetic genius in its prime.

The style of *Venus and Adonis* is something that can only be appreciated by a certain application, a deliberate savouring of its texture and verbal music. But it must be realized, before the poetry can be read aright, that here we have the spirit of comedy—of a romantic, that is to say, a Shakespearian, comedy. The death of Adonis might seem to make this impossible: but Shakespeare has endeavoured, as he has done with all else in the poem, to keep it at some distance from reality. The fate of a youth who, having been slain by a wild boar, evaporates into air, and whose blood turns into a flower, to be plucked and worn by a goddess in her bosom, is not intended to rouse tragic emotion. The retention of this fairy-tale detail from

1. The direct sources of *Venus and Adonis* are the passages from Ovid's *Metamorphoses* given in Appendix I. No Italian poem is discoverable, which might have had a direct influence. The Latin and Neo-Latin background is dealt with by T. W. Baldwin in *On the Literary Genetics of Shakespeare's Poems and Sonnets* (Urbana, University of Illinois Press, 1950). The best summary of the effect of Ovid on *Venus and Adonis* is by Geoffrey Bullough, *Narrative and Dramatic Sources of Shakespeare* (London, 1957), vol. 1, pp. 161–5.

2. *Op. cit.*, p. 143. Pooler commented on the resemblance of these poems to Elizabethan novels: 'Elizabethan novels and Elizabethan narrative poems are precisely similar. In both, the plot is of the slightest. The few incidents are held apart by soliloquies, or by debates or conversations usually confined to two persons, and consisting of set speeches. Soliloquies and speeches alike are for the most part *loci communes*, their subjects being love, time, death, friendship, etc.' (*Shakespeare's Poems*, 1911, p. xxvii). Lodge's *Glaucus and Scilla* is sometimes cited as a forerunner of *Venus and Adonis*; Miss M. C. Bradbrook's estimate of it in *Shakespeare and Elizabethan Poetry* is very indulgent (pp. 55–7). See also C. S. Lewis, *op. cit.*, pp. 488–9.

Ovid is only the most obvious of Shakespeare's innumerable devices to make his story light as a bubble and to keep it floating. The texture and tone of the language, the use of imagery and simile, all contribute to a half-sympathetic, half-mocking manner, in which Mercutio or Berowne or Theseus might have recounted this tale of love's misfortunes. Venus, frustrated in her wooing and cheated of her idol's presence by his flight, spends the night singing laments of love's power and love's folly. Her behaviour is that of a very unworthy immortal, and sufficiently detaches her situation from deep pathos. Shakespeare's comment on the tedious nature of her song makes clear the irony with which he shows these amorous frenzies; and his simile for the echoes which repeat her words clinches the careless poetical humour of the whole:

> For who hath she to spend the night withal,
> But idle sounds resembling parasites,
> Like shrill-tongu'd tapsters answering every call
> Soothing the humour of fantastic wits?
>   She says " 'Tis so," they answer all " 'Tis so,"
>   And would say after her, if she said "No."
>
> (ll. 847–52)

Later, her terror at the sound of the hunt, and her frantic pursuit, her wildly alternating hopes and fears, are depicted with vividness and yet with a sort of intent calm, which seems to comment 'Poor fool!'[1] The exquisite and much-praised simile of the frightened snail serves the same purpose, for it applies to her shrinking as she suddenly comes upon Adonis lying dead:

> Which seen, her eyes as murder'd with the view,
> Like stars asham'd of day, themselves withdrew.
>
> Or as the snail, whose tender horns being hit,
> Shrinks backward in his shelly cave with pain,
> And there all smother'd up in shade doth sit,
> Long after fearing to creep forth again:
>   So at his bloody view her eyes are fled
>   Into the deep dark cabins of her head.
>
> (ll. 1031–8)

Only Shakespeare could have contrived this fusion of sympathy and humour, crystallized in the homely image of the snail, and that other comparison, of the sulking Adonis to a dabchick.[2]

The imaginative unity of the poem lies here—in its view of elemental and human passions as a feast for the mind and the spirit: as sometimes moving, and sometimes amusing, but always offering an

---

1. See ll. 875–6 n.   2. Ll. 85–7.

absorbing living spectacle.[1] This is the indulgent mood of Shakespeare's comedies, with their delight in human energies and emotions, their keen savour of everyday life mixed with abundant
poetry, and their undertones of deeper seriousness. Venus is both a
romantic lover and an object of sympathetic irony; and it is she
who is the focus of the situation throughout. Adonis is an appropriate focus for *her* emotions; but as seen by us he is 'a man of wax',
a beautiful but self-centred and baffling creature. The unsuccessful
entreaties of the goddess, her frustrated attempts at seduction, are
the essential matter for enjoyment.[2] And these, it may be noticed,
are Shakespeare's own, both in substance and in treatment: in
Ovid, and in ancient mythology in general, there is no indication
that Adonis was not in fact the willing lover of Venus,[3] though the
emphasis is always on the love of the goddess for the youth. Shakespeare's view of the goddess and of her situation relates her to
several of his dramatic characters: she has a kinship with Cleopatra,
and even with Falstaff. We may think that there is more of Shakespeare himself in these three characters than there is in Adonis,
Prince Hal, or Antony.

The fusion of romance and humour in *Venus and Adonis* sets it
apart in Elizabethan poetry even of this kind. Marlowe's *Hero and
Leander*, also permeated with wit and humour, is more obviously in
the Ovidian mode of licentious artifice, and perhaps for this reason
has found readier appreciation among critics. C. S. Lewis, for example, is prepared to devise an elaborate explanation of why we
enjoy Marlowe's poem; but he rejects *Venus and Adonis* as unsuccessful, unable to decide whether it is 'a poem by a young moralist,
a poem against lust', or an 'epyllion',—that is, a poem in the
Ovidian and Alexandrian tradition of delicate sensuality.[4] The

1. 'The poem is . . . a pictorial and psychological study of the physical and
emotional attitudes of wooing and revulsion, lust and coyness, pursued with a
voluptuous delight . . . which is extended after Adonis's death to the goddess's
anguish. . .' Bullough, *op. cit.*, p. 164.

2. The detachment with which Shakespeare always mingles his delight in
romantic passion is to be seen also in the presentation of Romeo and Juliet—
Romeo chidden by Friar Lawrence for his unmanly paroxysms, Juliet tormented
by the Nurse's slowness. Prospero's tender irony towards Miranda, as she is drawn
to Ferdinand, is another example (*Tp.*, III. i. 31).

3. The wooing of the reluctant Adonis is generally attributed to a combination
by Shakespeare of Ovid's tale of Venus and Adonis with his tale of Salmacis and
Hermaphroditus (see Baldwin, *op. cit.*, pp. 84–7, and Bullough, *op. cit.*, and
Appendix I). But it may be added that a disdainful Adonis had already appeared
in several English works (*Hero and Leander*, I. 12–14, *Faerie Queene*, Book III. i,
and Greene's *Never Too Late*); see A. T. Hatto, ' "Venus and Adonis"—and the
Boar', *Modern Language Review*, vol. XLI, p. 355.

4. *Op. cit.*, pp. 498–9.

details of Mr Lewis's objections show that he has been unable to accept the more physical aspects of Shakespeare's treatment of the subject[1]; he has even refused to respond to the powerful colloquialism which goes with it. Yet Shakespeare has but given his own unique vividness of realization to a kind of poem which includes *Hero and Leander* and Donne's *Elegies*, and continues through Ben Jonson's verse into that of Herrick and other Caroline poets. Can the depreciation of *Venus and Adonis* be due to a feeling that Shakespeare should not so whole-heartedly indulge in a species of poem which is felt to be minor, when permissible at all? Or is the failure of appreciation due to the very presence of the qualities which redeem the poem from coarse frivolity—to its intelligence, wit, and humour, its living sensibility? For the element of humour, the comic spirit, is always more difficult to appreciate than tragedy or romance. If we look at modern criticism of Shakespeare, we find a far smaller proportion devoted to the Comedies than to any other section of his work; those who teach can confirm that an appreciation of comedy or satire is one of the most long-delayed results of the study of literature. As for the modern critical exaltation of 'wit' in poetry, this has only been possible because wit has been made into a *solemn* activity, licensed in the name of psychological or emotional health, and accepted as a method of self-improvement. If *Venus and Adonis* is to be placed among Shakespeare's comedies, if its motive is a spontaneous and personal blend of sensuous enjoyment, wit, and humour, it is not surprising that it has received less than its due from modern criticism.

(iii)

All that has been said of Shakespeare's gift for language as it appears in *Venus and Adonis* is confirmed by the style of *Lucrece*. Here are many passages which are quite different in mood and content, yet which in richness and power of expression equal or surpass anything in the previous poem. The best sustained passages of this kind are Lucrece's long tirade against Opportunity and Time (ll. 876–994), and the description of the pictures of the siege and fall of Troy (ll. 1366–1561). Everywhere there stand out ingenious fancies, dexterous thoughts and phrases, vividly felt emotions and actions and images; and an unfailing rhythmic power throbs through the verse. Yet it is only too obvious that the poem, as a whole, is a fail-

---

1. M. C. Bradbrook points out this carnal quality: 'The early part of the poem is full of feeling presented in terms of flesh: its moistness, its texture, Adonis's sweating palm, his rose-cheeks, his panting breath upon Venus's skin' (*op. cit.*, p. 63). Less convincingly she adds: 'Sometimes in violent contrast Shakespeare will adopt the heraldic manner for relief' (see ll. 361–4n.).

ure. Shakespeare's skill of expression is self-defeating. 'From end to end of the poem,' says Legouis, 'the reader is exasperated by the poet's very talent, his fancy and eloquence.'[1] To account for this failure, rather than to linger over the more obvious beauties of the poem, would seem to be the most rewarding task offered by *Lucrece* to the literary critic.

It is generally accepted that *Lucrece* is the 'graver labour' which Shakespeare promised Southampton when he dedicated *Venus and Adonis* to him. The kinship between the two poems is as plain as the contrast.[2] *Venus and Adonis* treats sexual desire in the spirit of romantic comedy; *Lucrece* does so in the spirit of tragedy. *Venus and Adonis* had no serious moral purpose—rather did it delight in its release from such restraints; *Lucrece* is therefore to have a positively obsessive moral purpose, to present an example of 'lust in action' and enforce a terrible lesson.

Lucrece, narrative in form, is in substance a tragedy.[3] And the comparison with its serio-comic predecessor bears out what Dr Johnson says concerning Shakespeare's aptitude for these two modes of writing: 'His disposition, as *Rhymer* has remarked, led him to comedy. In tragedy he often writes with great appearance of toil and study, what is written at last with little felicity; but in his comick scenes, he seems to produce without labour, what no labour can improve. In tragedy he is always struggling after some occasion to be comick, but in comedy he seems to repose, or to luxuriate, as in a mode of thinking congenial to his nature. In his tragick scenes there is always something wanting, but his comedy often surpasses expectation or desire. His comedy pleases by the thoughts and the language, and his tragedy for the greater part by incident and action. His tragedy seems to be skill, his comedy to be instinct.'[4]

Johnson shrank from Shakespearian tragedy even at its most magnificent, and we cannot acquiesce in his view of the great tragedies; but what he says of the poet's natural bent carries conviction. It is a critical summary which easily sweeps *Lucrece* into its scope, pointing to its faults, and enabling us to look at them in the light of the poet's other achievements. For if *Lucrece* is a tragedy, it

1. *History of English Literature*, 1924, p. 203.

2. *Lucrece* is 'a companion piece to the other, for, having described desire unaccomplished against reluctance, Shakespeare now gives desire accomplished by force' (Bullough, *op. cit.*, p. 179).

3. 'In this poem and *Titus Andronicus* he seems to be trying to indicate the blind senseless horror of purely physical outrage, which constituted for the moment his idea of tragedy. . . Tragedy is something that slaps you in the face: it is tragedy in the newspaper sense' (M. C. Bradbrook, *op. cit.*, p. 115). See *Lucrece*, ll. 52–70 n.

4. *Preface to Shakespeare*, 1765.

is of course a tragedy by the author of *Titus Andronicus*, and not by
the author of *Lear* or *Othello*. We think of the failure of the poem
most readily in terms of its treatment, for its excesses of rhetoric are
glaringly obvious. But the true weakness lies in the subject, as it
does in *Titus Andronicus*: there is 'an original sin' in it, as Hazlitt said
of *Measure for Measure*, and this reveals itself ever more disastrously
as the poem proceeds.

In spite of its length and over-elaboration, its apparent excess,
there is indeed 'something wanting' in *Lucrece*. We remember from
it images such as the 'pale swan in her watery nest', or Collatine's
suppressed grief compared to the tide rushing through the arch of
a bridge.[1] Various living pictures are imprinted on our minds:
Tarquin creeping through the dark house; Lucrece weeping with
her maid or blushing in the presence of her groom; her reddened
eyes surrounded by 'blue circles'; and the 'watery rigol' which
separates itself from her 'black blood'. Typical of such nightmarish
impressions is the image of Tarquin's hot hand, 'smoking with
pride', placed upon his victim's naked breast:

> Whose ranks of blue veins, as his hand did scale,
> Left their round turrets destitute and pale.
>
> (ll. 440–1)

But these and many other powerful effects are isolated from one
another by long passages which may be coherent and magnificent
in themselves, like the picture of the fall of Troy, or full of brilliant
or tormented force, like Tarquin's deliberations before the crime or
Lucrece's endless tirades after it; but which confuse the total impression. It is remarkable that, while the digressions in *Venus and
Adonis* strengthen the whole, those in *Lucrece* consistently weaken it.
In *Venus and Adonis* the episode of the lustful stallion, and the description of the hunted hare, bring movement and perspective, give
a sense of air and freedom, add a strong fresh savour of natural
appetites and physical energy; Shakespeare's 'instinct' for comedy
never served him better.[2] But in *Lucrece* all his 'skill' cannot achieve
a corresponding balance, though the digression into the 'matter of
Troy' comes nearer to it than anything else in the poem.[3]

Success in a poem constructed with such wanton exuberance
must always no doubt be a matter of 'touch and go'; but there are

1. L. 1611 and ll. 1667–70.

2. These episodes recall how constantly in Shakespeare's hands comedy makes
use of a rustic element, or setting. *Venus and Adonis* is a poem of the open air.

3. Much may depend on the speed with which the poet can carry through his
discursive passages; in this respect *Venus* has the advantage, for the six-line stanza
is swifter than the rhyme royal of *Lucrece*.

several possible reasons for Shakespeare's failure here. In the first place, the poem offers, in turn, two centres of interest. Until the crime is committed, Tarquin is the focus of our attention, and convinces us that he is a tragically complex character. After the deed, Lucrece becomes the tragic heroine; but we are never wholly convinced that she deserves the part, and the more we ponder the more clearly we can see why she does not. Not only is she a less *interesting* character than Tarquin: she is forced to express herself in a way which dissipates the real pathos of her situation.

The tragedy of Lucrece is in fact unsuited to direct 'dramatic' presentation; it should be related in the true narrative manner of Ovid or Chaucer, not in the semi-dramatic, semi-rhetorical manner of Shakespeare's poem.[1] If the story is treated at length, and above all if the heroine is given great powers of self-expression, her sufferings become sensational and not tragic. Her part is not wholly passive, since it ends in a heroic act of self-sacrifice. But this final positive action, which alone can give significance to her fate, should be presented with as few preliminaries as possible. It should come as a startling revelation of the final dimension of her character, the depth of her feeling, and the strength of her determination. The greatest weakness of Shakespeare's Lucrece is therefore her remorseless eloquence. In Ovid Lucrece does not even plead with Tarquin; but Shakespeare makes her start an argument which might have continued indefinitely, if the ravisher had not cut it short.[2] After her violation, Lucrece loses our sympathy exactly in proportion as she gives tongue.

The most moving passages are those in which she is silent, or nearly so: the interviews with the maid and with the groom. Here we are shown her grief momentarily from without, or indirectly, checked by social circumstance. These scenes are, like much in *Venus and Adonis*, a true equivalent in narrative form of Shakespeare's dramatic vision, a fusion of dialogue, action, and description.[3] Lucrece's lengthy self-expression in other passages is *apparently* dramatic, but the conditions of the stage would soon have revealed its absurdity.

When we look at the poem in this way we may be inclined to think that Shakespeare had a clear vision neither of his subject nor of the treatment which would have fitted it. We may further doubt whether *any* tragic theme could have been treated successfully in

---

1. Ovid's version of the story in the *Fasti* was Shakespeare's chief source, though he also used Livy's version, and certainly knew Chaucer's, which is indebted to both Ovid and Livy. For the texts see Appendix II. Bullough lucidly summarizes Shakespeare's expansion of these materials (*op. cit.*, pp. 179–83).

2. See l. 667.   3. The best example in *Venus and Adonis* is ll. 337–54.

the fashion of these 'narrative' poems; and the end of all our analysis
may be that the whole thing was simply an artistic miscalculation,
a misuse of remarkable, yet immature, talents.

Yet there is another way of looking at *Lucrece*, and measuring its
value to our interpretation of Shakespeare. Does the poem not convey after all, fully and unmistakably, the poet's vision of his subject? From this point of view the artistic effect may be the same, but
the critical interest is much enhanced. We may still be irritated by
the poem's faults of taste and wearied by its length and emphasis;
but if we look upon it all as Shakespeare's projection of his own
immature spirit, it has much to tell us. This is a young man's idea
of tragedy, and the imagination of the young man in question is a
curious blend of health and morbidity, a bundle of self-contradic-
tory impulses. The youthful idea of tragedy reveals itself in the
physical and moral violence of the theme: the contrast between
vile evil and ideal virtue, the presentation of a sexual crime, accompanied by physical force and cruelty, and resulting in the bloody
death of the victim. The subject is less nightmarish than *Titus
Andronicus* only because its horrors are less elaborately redoubled
and drawn out, and because drama is necessarily more violent in
effect than narrative. In both works there is the fascinated contemplation of lust and bloodshed and violated virtue.[1] This is indeed a conception of tragedy which is not only youthful, but vulgar;
it is crude in its craving for sensation, and vulgar because the physical suffering is over-emphasized.

The subject sufficiently accounts for the painful, half-real and
half-unreal, oppressiveness of the poem; since the poet's vision is
itself nightmarish, he has perhaps found a true equivalent for it in
the clotted fancies, the agonizingly insistent cleverness of the long
'metaphysical' tirades. There is madness in Shakespeare's method,
but it is a madness appropriate to something which lurks in Tarquin's lust and Lucrece's wounded chastity. It is not enough to
judge, with Dr Johnson, that the young poet is forcing himself to
feel and write in a self-consciously tragic manner, and that we are
made aware of the strain by his lapses and faults of judgement. We
must go further, and see the whole imaginative process as a phase
in Shakespeare's vision of reality, something that was later to be
transformed into the vision of the great tragedies.

In *Venus and Adonis* and *Lucrece* Shakespeare both identifies himself with the various characters and remains detached from them.

1. There are obvious affinities between the story of *Lucrece* and the plot of *Titus
Andronicus*. There are references to Lucrece in *Tit.*, ii. i. 108, iv. i. 64, and iv. i. 95.
Passages resembling one another are *Tit.*, v. iii. 171, *Lucr.*, l. 577; ii. iii. 25–6 and
ll. 579–80; iii. i. 37–42 and ll. 592–4; and iv. iii. 45 and ll. 664–5.

He identifies himself in imagination with both the uncontrollable physical desire of Venus and the coldness of Adonis, both with her persuasions to love and with his condemnation of lust. In *Lucrece* he is similarly divided between a sense of the irresistible force of Tarquin's desires and of the beauty of virtue in Lucrece. This double or divided consciousness is indeed the secret of poetic genius; but to have it in the intense degree in which Shakespeare had it is to come close, at times, to delirium or mental instability. Comedy was the easier, safer, form for Shakespeare, because he could there remain at a certain distance from reality, moving in a familiar range between laughter, wit, sensuality, and pathos. In tragedy he was compelled to come closer to the seamy side of things, and to try to grasp the full reality of human crimes and passions. The instability latent in his genius then led him into strange aberrations: *Titus Andronicus* and *Lucrece* are there to show what dangers lay in wait for this youthful imagination, more rashly responsive both to physical desire and physical horror than it would be a few years later.

The morbidity of *Lucrece*, however, is but an earlier manifestation of that tragic disgust and revulsion which appear in various forms in *Hamlet*, *Lear*, and *Timon*, and underlie so much of Shakespeare's later work. An amazing process of development lies between the early poem and the plays of even only a few years later; and yet there are constant elements in this poetic growth. The murk of *Macbeth* is not without its reminiscence of Tarquin stalking his prey,[1] and in *Cymbeline* Iachimo's penetration of Imogen's bedchamber becomes almost a deliberate allusion to the early work.[2] These are incidental and external parallels, but they indicate the deeper continuity of Shakespeare's sensibility, concerning which *Lucrece* has more to tell us than many more pleasing pieces of work.

(iv)

The Phoenix and Turtle is not usually thought of as having a literary source, although Chaucer's *Parlement of Fowles* is sometimes mentioned in this connection, presumably because this is also a poem about birds by a great English poet.[3] But it would be well if we

1. ii. ii. 49–56. See M. C. Bradbrook, *op. cit.*, pp. 112–13.   2. ii. i. 12–14.
3. T. W. Baldwin writes: 'In *The Phoenix and the Turtle*, Shakespeare has taken his pattern from Ovid, *Amores* ii, 6, some material eventually from Lactantius, and has put the whole into the setting of a contemporary funeral' (*op. cit.*, p. 363). Ovid's mock-heroic elegy for Corinna's dead parrot may well have influenced Shakespeare's assembly of mourning birds; but this assembly was a common elegiac device in Elizabethan verse, appearing (for example) in *An Elegie, or friends passion, for his Astrophill* (*Spenser's Minor Poems* (Oxford, 1920), p. 357; see Baldwin, *op. cit.*, pp. 373–4).

could fix firmly in our minds that Shakespeare's 'subject' has a source, and that source is Chester's fantastic compilation. In 1878 Grosart edited *Loves Martyr* for the New Shakespeare Society. A summary by Pooler conveys the nature of the work:

> It contains interspersed in the allegory of the Phoenix and Turtle other matters, viz. a description of the Nine Female Worthies, a chronicle history of King Arthur, a bestiary, and treatises on birds, on plants and their uses, on precious stones, etc. The argument is as follows: Dame Nature at a council of the Roman gods described the beauty of the Arabian Phoenix, and expressed a fear that she would die without offspring. Jove answered that Nature would find in Paphos Isle 'true Honors lovely Squire' who would meet the Phoenix on a high hill,
>
> > And of their Ashes by my doome shal rise
> > Another Phoenix her to equalise.
>
> The meeting, postponed while Nature and the Phoenix discuss English history and medieval science (pp. 16–129), took place by the arrival of a turtle-dove, sorrowing for his turtle that is dead, and was the signal for Nature's departure. The Phoenix and the Turtle decided to die together, 'in a manner sacrificingly' and for posterity's sake, and gathered sweet wood for their pyre. After some striving of courtesies the Turtle entered the fire first, and was consumed. The Phoenix followed. A pelican which happened to be present was permitted to watch and report 'their love that she did see'.[1]

Little time need be spent on the motives and effect of *Loves Martyr*.[2] It is true that the most recent survey of its background and estimate of its significance, that by Mr G. Wilson Knight in *The Mutual Flame*,[3] leaves an impression that every part of the book is charged with mysterious meaning; but Mr Wilson Knight has been able so to charge it only by seeing it in the light of his own analysis of Shakespeare's Sonnets and *The Phoenix and Turtle*. The Phoenix in Shakespeare's poem he relates to the emotional experience which dominates the Sonnets; and, since Shakespeare took his Phoenix from *Loves Martyr*, Mr Wilson Knight sweeps that work into the same world of symbols. Yet even he can only proceed in a way which indirectly damages his claims for the book: he tries to prove the presence of a specific kind of love-experience by showing how

1. *Shakespeare's Poems* (London, 1911), pp. lxxxvii–lxxxviii.

2. M. C. Bradbrook flatters *Loves Martyr* when she quotes a passage from the description of the Phoenix, and adds: 'This is the Idea of a woman: yet it is also a real person' (*op. cit.*, p. 33). In fact Chester's Phoenix succeeds in being neither one nor the other.

3. London, 1955. See Part II, *Phoenix and Turtle*, I and II.

much confusion of feeling, how much imprecision of reference, how much abortive poetic vision, pervades the plan and the writing. Little that is positive or definite comes out of the demonstration; and it would be more profitable to admit that *Loves Martyr* is rubbish, though rubbish of a frustrated poetical intensity such as scarcely any but the Elizabethan period could have produced. We may understand Mr Wilson Knight's claim that 'the age was an age of human idealism from which many most potent, wonderful, and even transcendental personal experiences could mature, and such are the experiences behind the "Phoenix".'[1] But, while Shakespeare's Sonnets and *The Phoenix and Turtle* convince us of the reality of such experiences, that is just what *Loves Martyr* fails to do; and what it cannot do for itself, its connection with Shakespeare cannot do for it.

The writing is indeed grotesquely incompetent and tedious. Grosart claimed to find in it (and therefore also in Shakespeare's poem) an elaborate political allegory concerning Elizabeth and Essex. We are asked to believe that an eccentric amateur, aspiring to poethood, but showing an incomplete control of verse, syntax, narrative, and sense, should have sustained a complex allegorical meaning throughout his apparently chaotic work.[2] The work as we have it would seem to have grown by a process of accumulation and accretion over a considerable period. The myth of the Phoenix and the Turtle which serves to hold it together, in a semblance of shape, was the author's final bright idea. The final section of small anagrammatic love-poems, '*Cantoes Alphabet-wise to faire Phoenix* made by the Paphian Dove', is attached to the rest chiefly by its title; many of these tasteless knicknacks have no specific reference to Phoenix or Turtle, and some contain an element of indecent innuendo which is in startling contrast to the chastity of the main story.

What could have induced Shakespeare, and indeed Ben Jonson and the other reputable 'moderne Writers', to contribute their occasional verses to Chester's book? No doubt a chapter of social history is involved. But this is of less critical interest than the suspicion of irony which hangs about the whole publication, or at least about the contributions of Chester's literary friends. Jonson, Chapman, Marston, and Shakespeare seem to have felt not only the quaint, half-accidental charm of Chester's myth, but also the

1. *Op. cit.*, p. 205.
2. A recent investigation of these possible personal allegories is Professor Heinrich Straumann's *Phönix und Taube* (Zürich, 1953). The background to *Loves Martyr* may be filled in from Carleton Brown's *Poems by Sir John Salusbury and Robert Chester* (printed for the Early English Text Society, 1914).

absurdity of his use of it. Such a critical perception seems to be
hinted in the two pieces signed by the *Vatum Chorus*, and especially
in the first, the *Invocatio*. This bears marks of Jonson's hand; and
could he, or even Chapman or Marston, have written some of these
lines without a smile?

> Good Fate, faire *Thespian Deities*,
> And thou bright God, whose golden Eies,
>> Serve as a Mirrour to the silver Morne,
>> When (in the height of Grace) she doth adorne
> Her Chrystall presence, and invites
>> The ever-youthfull *Bromius* to delights,
> Sprinckling his sute of Vert with Pearle,
> And (like a loose enamour'd Girle)
>> Ingles his cheeke; which (waxing red with shame)
>> Instincts the senslesse Grapes to do the same,
> Till by his sweete reflection fed,
>> They gather spirit, and grow discoloured.
>
> To your high influence we commend
> Our following Labours, and sustend
>> Our mutuall palmes, prepar'd to gratulate
>> An *honorable friend*: then propagate
> With your illustrate faculties
>> Our mentall powers: Instruct us how to rise
> In weighty Numbers, well pursu'd,
> And varied from the Multitude:
>> Be lavish once, and plenteously profuse
>> Your holy waters, to our thirstie *Muse*,
> That we may give a Round to him
>> In a *Castalian* boule, crown'd to the brim.[1]

The imagery of the first stanza hints at caricature. Apollo's
'golden Eies', the dalliance of the dawn with her lover, and the
blushing cheek and sympathetic grapes of the conclusion, form an
inept conglomeration. The oddity is heightened by the carefully
pompous language, with calculated lapses into familiarity.[2] In the
second stanza the irony is effected chiefly by diction of the inflated
Latinate kind Jonson held up to ridicule in *The Poetaster*.[3] Jonson's
method is apparent in the use of these Latinisms; most are correct,
but the incorrect or the less correct, such as 'propagate' or 'profuse',
are just prominent enough to topple the style unmistakably into
burlesque.

In the rest of the appended poems (excluding for the moment
Shakespeare's) it is more difficult to distinguish the ironic element.

1. *Loves Martyr*, ed. 1878, p. 179.   2. E.g. 'Sprinckling' and 'Ingles'.
3. v. i.

Marston's inflated style always hovers between turgidity and a parody of itself; Chapman's verse is too crabbed to have any delicacy of touch. Jonson's *Praeludium* is full of his own straightforward racy harshness, and the long moral ode which is the centre of his contribution is wholly and impressively noble. Perhaps in his last two lyrics we may trace a return to the consciously fantastic elevation which prevails elsewhere.[1]

These ambiguous undertones, the lurking impression that these poets were participating in a private joke, are worth seizing if they enable us to approach Shakespeare's contribution from a new side. High fantasy, verging on the nonsensical, has entered also into the making of this uniquely beautiful poem.[2] Shakespeare has given us what he saw in the subject, and the subject, it must be repeated, comes from the unreadable *Loves Martyr*. He has not troubled himself to master the details of Chester's invention; we need only look at Chester's pitiful picture of the self-immolation of the two birds[3] to measure the distance between such confused fancy and the unearthly simplicity of Shakespeare's effect. Yet Chester had stumbled upon a strangely effective emblem, the germ of a myth, in his tale of a union in death between the apparently ill-assorted Dove and Phoenix. And Shakespeare, however he came to be drawn into the venture, seized to the full the opportunity proffered by 'the first Subject'.[4]

In consequence, *The Phoenix and Turtle*, slight as it is, is a priceless addition to Shakespeare's lyrics. The magic of many of the songs in the plays is beyond praise, but we are fortunate in having here a somewhat longer, and independent, example of his powers of incantation.

But even the most potent of incantations must sometimes fail: indeed, the fact that they are ineffective at certain times, or with

1. Jonson's pieces may be found in Herford and Simpson, *Ben Jonson*, vol. VIII, pp. 107–13 and 364–5. For Chapman's poem, *Peristeros: or the male Turtle*, see *The Poems of George Chapman*, ed. Phyllis Brooks Bartlett (New York, 1941), p. 357.

2. William Empson has written: 'There is a suggestion that the author finds the convention fascinating but absurd... This seems to me intentional, very delightful...' (*Some Versions of Pastoral*, p. 139). A few lines earlier Mr Empson has pointed out that the poem 'depends on the same ideas as Donne's *First Anniversary*, but gets very different feelings out of them'.

3. *Loves Martyr*, pp. 131–9.

4. M. C. Bradbrook describes *The Phoenix and Turtle* as 'the one poem which [Shakespeare] wrote in a courtly kind' (*op. cit.*, pp. 32–4). She sees it as an emblem of the 'union of natures which is Platonic Love': 'Its concentration and simplicity show what can be achieved when the great artist finds the proper occasion to make full use of a great tradition' (i.e. the tradition of courtly and Platonic love-poetry).

certain temperaments, or in some states of mind, is itself an indication of their nature, telling us that they rely upon factors which are not often or easily brought together, or brought to bear with such purpose. All poetry is vulnerable to changes of thought, taste, and language, or to mere indifference, dullness, and spiritual deafness; this kind of poetry, because it is pure and concentrated, is more obviously vulnerable than most—unless we choose to say that it is the least vulnerable of any, because it is the least concerned to succeed or fail, or to offer anything but itself.

Shakespeare took the notion of the Phoenix and the Turtle from *Loves Martyr* and treated it as he might have treated a dramatic subject, projecting himself into it and giving what he saw. His poem falls into three divisions. It is an elegiac poem on the death of the two birds, and begins by summoning the other birds to a funeral pageant. This calling together of the birds passes into an 'Antheme' which they are to sing, describing the mutual love of the Phoenix and the Turtle. The anthem passes into a 'Threne', the final lyrical celebration of their identity in love and death. The poem shows unsurpassed musical imagination, in its passage from the quatrains of the first section to the tercets of the *Threnos*; as the mood is evoked and rises to its full intensity, the verse follows it, seems to climb and soar in flight.

The assembly of the birds, though it is but indirectly conveyed and takes up no more than twenty lines, is a wonderfully effective opening. Shakespeare did not need to think of the *Parlement of Foules*, though that poem is an evocation of a kindred image. The kingdom of the birds, their divisions and occupations, was a theme deeply rooted in European and Oriental folk-lore. The natural poetry of these fancies was bound to leave its mark on literature, as it had become involved with pagan religion and with popular superstition. John Masefield has said, in the idiom of his time:

> This poem gives to a flock of thoughts about the passing of truth and beauty the mystery and vitality of birds, who come from a far country, to fill the mind with their crying.[1]

And among the innumerable associations of Shakespeare's verses there is indeed to be found this ancient folk memory of the significance of birds, their suggestions of myth; a homeliness like that of the burial of Cock-Robin is fused with apprehensions of the mystery of death and the migration of the soul.

The identity in love of the two dead birds is celebrated with a display of scholastic terms which gives a vague impression that the

[1]. *Shakespeare and Spiritual Life*, Romanes Lecture (Oxford, 1924); quoted in Rollins, p. 564.

poem is 'metaphysical' in the manner of Donne. Nothing could in fact be further from the methods of Donne's love-poetry than the method of this poem. Shakespeare's use of analytic terminology here is free and rhapsodic, a kind of ethereal frenzy; in using it so lavishly, he may well have been influenced by fashion, and by the manner of his fellow-poets writing on this theme, which evidently to them suggested abstract sublimities and verbiage.[1] Donne's analytic procedures are indeed not his personal property, coming to him as they do from Italy and France, and coming to many other learned poets of his generation; but they are distinguished by the concentration and deliberation with which he applies them to sexual experience, and this quality is certainly not paralleled in *The Phoenix and Turtle*.

In this curious poem, sprung from as curious a set of circumstances, we see the imaginative power which charges one after another of Shakespeare's mature plays with inexhaustible suggestions of meaning. Nowhere else, however, have we an opportunity to see this power at work in isolation and in so small a compass. What we see in effect is Shakespeare's capacity for 'pure' poetry; and the poem must be placed in what may seem an ill-assorted company, which includes Poe's *Ulalume* and Mallarmé's *Prose pour des Esseintes*. It is only in the nineteenth century, and particularly in France, that we find the conscious attempt to cultivate poetry in a 'pure' state. But the theories of Baudelaire and Mallarmé derived from Poe, and it is in the English Romantic school that we find the first glimpses of a poetry that is 'pure' in this sense. *Kubla Khan*, some of Keats's Odes, some of Tennyson's lyrics, provide more familiar examples than Poe or Mallarmé, whose work is for different reasons unlikely to fit into our current scale of poetic appreciation. Yet perhaps the suggestions of self-caricature in Poe, the rigorous self-consciousness and irony of Mallarmé, may also help us to approach *The Phoenix and Turtle*. For this element of irony, hyperbole, and high fantasy is generally missing in the Romantic and Victorian poets, unless we include in our survey the nonsense of Edward Lear and Lewis Carroll: and it is precisely this element which gives the point of departure for Shakespeare's poem, and the convention which supports it throughout.

For after all, the beauty of the poem consists in a marriage between intense emotion and almost unintelligible fantasy. It is inexhaustible because it is inexplicable; and it is inexplicable because it is deliberately unreasonable, beyond and contrary to both reason and nature. When Middleton Murry wrote that 'the poem floats

---

1. See especially Marston's first poem, *Loves Martyr*, p. 185.

high above the plane of intellectual apprehension'[1] (and yet proceeded to gloss its significance with surprising success), he nevertheless failed to indicate the presence of this conscious self-caricature, and its use of a language 'bouffonne et égarée au possible'.[2]

Yet Murry's account perhaps gives the 'feel' of the poem in as
adequate terms as modern critical equipment has yet found:

> There is surely no more astonishing description of the highest
> attainable by human love. . . It is the direct embodiment,
> through symbols which are necessarily dark, of a pure, compre-
> hensive and self-satisfying experience, which we may call, if we
> please, an immediate intuition into the nature of things. It is
> inevitable that such poetry should be obscure, mystical, and
> strictly unintelligible: it is too abstract for our comprehension,
> too little mediated. . . And it necessarily hovers between the
> condition of being the highest poetry of all and not being poetry
> at all. But, wherever in the scale we place it, it gives us a clue to
> the nature of poetry itself.[3]

In *The Mutual Flame* Mr Wilson Knight goes further, and tries to
relate the poem, on the one hand, to the experience of passionate
friendship recorded in the *Sonnets*, and, on the other hand, to the
total pattern of the dramas, which he imagines to spring out of that
uniquely intense experience, as a kind of expansion and objecti-
fication of it. Nothing could be more convincing, as far as it goes,
than Mr Wilson Knight's exposition of the *Sonnets*: he grasps the
living emotional realities which run through them, and shows
Shakespeare's miraculous poetic gift at work to dominate and
transform those realities. But he is less successful in trying to tie *The
Phoenix and Turtle* closely to his main theme. Much special pleading
is required to prove that *Loves Martyr* and its appended poems are
inspired by 'sexual confusions and abnormalities', even if we agree
that *The Phoenix and Turtle* itself is 'in celebration of a mystical love-
union beyond sex, as we understand it, and all biological cate-
gories'.[4] Not that one would deny that this wonderful poem is an
expression of the same sensibility, the same play of passion and
thought, that led Shakespeare through the *Sonnets*; or that Shakespeare has here put into smaller compass the faith in disinterested
love, the admiration, the fervour, the irrational hope, which he had
struggled to win and to express. But these are things, as Mr Wilson

1. *Discoveries*, 1924: quoted in Rollins, pp. 565–6.
2. Rimbaud in *Une Saison en Enfer* so described the manner of his last lyrics, the
series of little songs in which he 'took farewell of the world'. Of these, *L'Eternité*
and *O saisons, ô châteaux* have something of the cryptic finality of Shakespeare's
poem.
3. *Op. cit.*, pp. 22–6, 43.   4. *Op. cit.*, p. 199.

Knight would admit, which Shakespeare could not but put into almost every serious poem he wrote. They may be in *The Phoenix and Turtle* because the poet had quite accidentally found a theme which drew them to itself. Such a possibility is suggested by Mr Wilson Knight himself, in discussing Shelley's *Epipsychidion*; he defines Emilia Viviani as a 'release-mechanism', and maintains that the ideals of love Shelley poured into the poem go far beyond the immediate realities of his situation.[1]

So it probably was with *The Phoenix and Turtle*. A chance conjunction of images precipitates a sudden intensity of emotion in the poet: thoughts and rhythms become the mysterious yet transparent expression of his deepest compulsions. The 'pure' poem is born, marked above all by its apparent remoteness from everyday experience. Many will always feel of such poetry that it is 'not poetry at all', or that, if it is, it is a minor variety, cut off from common life and thought. All one need reply is that a great poet may well allow himself to make an occasional dazzling excursion in this direction. Into *The Phoenix and Turtle*, fantastic as it is, Shakespeare has compressed all his feeling for pure passion and loyalty in human love.

1. *Op. cit.*, pp. 210–15.

VENUS AND ADONIS

VENUS AND ADONIS

Vilia miretur vulgus: mihi flavus Apollo
Pocula Castalia plena ministret aqua.

To the Right Honourable
Henry Wriothesley, Earl of Southampton,
and Baron of Titchfield.

Right Honourable,

I know not how I shall offend in dedicating my unpolished lines
to your Lordship, nor how the world will censure me for choosing
so strong a prop to support so weak a burden. Only, if your Honour
seem but pleased, I account myself highly praised; and vow to take
advantage of all idle hours, till I have honoured you with some
graver labour. But if the first heir of my invention prove deformed,
I shall be sorry it had so noble a godfather, and never after ear so
barren a land, for fear it yield me still so bad a harvest. I leave it to
your Honourable survey, and your Honour to your heart's content,
which I wish may always answer your own wish, and the world's
hopeful expectation.

Your Honour's in all duty,
William Shakespeare.

Dedication] In 'Shakespeare's Dedication', J. Middleton Murry constructs a theory of Shakespeare's relationship with Southampton, based upon this dedication and that of *Lucrece*, supported by occurrences of 'dedicate' and 'dedication' in the plays (*John Clare and Other Studies* (1950), pp. 45-57).

VENUS AND ADONIS

Even as the sun with purple-colour'd face
Had ta'en his last leave of the weeping morn,
Rose-cheek'd Adonis hied him to the chase;
Hunting he lov'd, but love he laugh'd to scorn.
   Sick-thoughted Venus makes amain unto him,   5
   And like a bold-fac'd suitor 'gins to woo him.

1. *purple-colour'd*] In Elizabethan English 'purple' often meant a colour ruddier and brighter than in modern usage. Pooler points out that Shakespeare often uses it of blood (*R2*, III. iii. 94; *R3*, IV. iv. 277; see also *John*, II. i. 322, and *Cæs.*, III. i. 158), though also of grapes (*MND.*, III. i. 170) and violets (*Per.*, IV. i. 16). The Latin *purpureus* was also applied to a variety of colours, since it originally expressed only extreme brightness of colour. However, there is no need to explain away the 'purple-colour'd face' of this rising sun. The epithet could be conventionally applied to dawn, as in Spenser's:

   Now when the rosy fingered morn-
     ing faire
   Weary of aged Tithones saffron bed,
   Had spred her purple robe through
     deawy aire   (*F.Q.*, I. ii. 7).

But Shakespeare's conceit has the touch which is to animate his whole poem: Spenser's frigid mythological colours are replaced by something fresher and livelier, an image *seen* as poetic and therefore given a touch of exaggeration.

2. *weeping*] Shakespeare's mythology is often a carefree variation on pagan lore. If dawn is personified in classical poetry her lover is always Tithonus, not the sun. But compare *3H6*, II. i. 21 f.:

See how the morning opes her
   golden gates
And takes her farewell of the
   glorious sun!

And for a fully developed Shakespearian myth of the same sort see Sonnet xxxiii.

3. *Rose-cheek'd Adonis*] The same words occur in Marlowe's *Hero and Leander*, I. 91–3:

The men of wealthy Sestos, every
   year,
For his sake whom their goddess
   held so dear,
Rose-cheek'd Adonis, kept a
   solemn feast.

Since the date of composition of the poem, left unfinished at Marlowe's death in 1593, is unknown, and it was not published until 1598, we can only conjecture that Shakespeare 'perhaps remembered' it (Malone). But *Hero and Leander* was very probably known to Shakespeare in manuscript; no other narrative poem of these years shows a combination of wit and sensuous beauty comparable to that we find in *Venus and Adonis*.

hied him] hastened. The verb could be used either with the reflexive pronoun, as here and in *Pilgr.*, XII. 11, or without it, as in *Rom.*, III. ii. 138.

5. *Sick-thoughted*] love-sick.

makes amain] hastens. 'Amain' meant originally 'with all one's strength', but

3

"Thrice fairer than myself," thus she began,
    "The field's chief flower, sweet above compare;
    Stain to all nymphs, more lovely than a man,
    More white and red than doves or roses are: 10
        Nature that made thee with herself at strife,
        Saith that the world hath ending with thy life.

"Vouchsafe, thou wonder, to alight thy steed,
    And rein his proud head to the saddle-bow;
    If thou wilt deign this favour, for thy meed   15
    A thousand honey secrets shalt thou know.
        Here come and sit, where never serpent hisses,
        And being set, I'll smother thee with kisses.

"And yet not cloy thy lips with loath'd satiety,
    But rather famish them amid their plenty,   20
    Making them red, and pale, with fresh variety:
    Ten kisses short as one, one long as twenty.
        A summer's day will seem an hour but short,
        Being wasted in such time-beguiling sport."

---

19. satiety] sacietie *Q1–5;* satietie *Q6.*   24. time-beguiling] *Q1–4;* time-beguilding *Q5.*

came to convey the idea of speed. The past and the historic present are used indifferently throughout the poem, as in this stanza; the predominance of the latter contributes to its vividness and speed.

8. *above compare*] This originally meant 'without or above compeer or rival', but, in association with the verb 'compare', it suggested a new substantive, as in Sonnet xxi, ll. 5–6:

Making a couplement of proud compare
With sun and moon, with earth and sea's rich gems.

9. *Stain*] Superior beauty or excellence is thought of as casting a stain or shadow on what it surpasses. Pooler quotes Lyly, ed. Bond, III, p. 142:

My Daphne's brow inthrones the Graces,
My Daphne's beauty staines all faces

and Sidney's 'sun-stayning excellencie' (*The Countess of Pembrokes Arcadia,* ed. A. Feuillerat (Cambridge, 1912),

p. 7). The feminine quality of Adonis' beauty is stressed by Shakespeare.

11–12. *Nature . . . life*] Nature strove to surpass herself in making Adonis, and having achieved perfection intends to let the world die with him. The hyperbole is repeated, with a similar conceit, in ll. 953–4.

13. *alight*] alight from.

14. *rein . . . saddle-bow*] i.e. to curb the horse, so that it might not stray.

16. *honey*] sweet. See also ll. 452, 538.

18. *set*] seated.

20. *famish them*] Malone compares *Ant.,* II. ii. 241–3.

21. *red, and pale*] Adonis' lips will be alternately stung to redness by the 'ten kisses short as one', and drained of their colour by the 'one long as twenty'.

24. *wasted*] spent; often used in no depreciatory sense, as in *Mer.V.,* III. iv. 12:   companions
That do converse and waste the time together.

With this she seizeth on his sweating palm,   25
The precedent of pith and livelihood,
And trembling in her passion, calls it balm,
Earth's sovereign salve to do a goddess good:
    Being so enrag'd, desire doth lend her force
    Courageously to pluck him from his horse.   30

Over one arm the lusty courser's rein,
Under her other was the tender boy,
Who blush'd and pouted in a dull disdain,
With leaden appetite, unapt to toy:
    She red and hot as coals of glowing fire,   35
    He red for shame, but frosty in desire.

The studded bridle on a ragged bough
Nimbly she fastens—O how quick is love!—
The steed is stalled up, and even now
To tie the rider she begins to prove: 40
    Backward she push'd him, as she would be thrust,
    And govern'd him in strength, though not in lust.

32. her] *Q1;* the *Q7–16.*

25. *sweating palm*] A moist palm was reckoned a sign of a sensuous disposition; see *Oth.*, III. iv. 36–9, cited by Malone, and *Ant.*, I. ii. 52 f.: 'if an oily palm be not a fruitful prognostication, I cannot scratch mine ear'. See also ll. 143–4 below. Adonis' coldness is all the more distressing to Venus because he has the physical marks of an ardent lover.

26. *precedent*] sign, example, proof; Shakespeare's meaning hovers between these senses, as in *Lr.*, II. iii. 13:

    The country gives me proof and
      precedent
    Of Bedlam beggars.

And *Tit.*, v. iii. 44:

    A reason mighty, strong, and
      effectual;
    A pattern, precedent, and lively
      warrant.

pith and livelihood] strength and energy. 'Pith' means 'marrow', the full development of which signifies maturity and hence strength. Compare *H5*, III, Prologue, 21:

    Guarded with grandsires, babies,
      and old women
    Either past or not arrived to pith or
      puissance.

29. *enrag'd*] roused by desire.

30. *pluck*] pull.

34. *leaden appetite*] heavy senses.

unapt to toy] unwilling or unfit for love's play.

37. *ragged*] rough. 'Ragged' is used by Shakespeare where we would use 'rugged'. See *Gent.*, I. ii. 121:

Unto a ragged, fearful-hanging rock also *R2*, v. v. 20–2; and *R3*, IV. i. 101–2. One 'ragged bough' here conveys the whole scene, the goddess and the youth reclining in the shade of some trees. The picture is suggested by Ovid, *Metam.*, x. 555–9 (see Baldwin, *op. cit.*, p. 13).

39. *stalled up*] tethered as in a stall.

40. *prove*] try, test. See *Ado*, I. iii. 75: Shall we go prove what's to be done? and *1H6*, II. ii. 58. See also l. 608 below.

So soon was she along as he was down,
Each leaning on their elbows and their hips;
Now doth she stroke his cheek, now doth he frown,   45
And 'gins to chide, but soon she stops his lips,
    And kissing speaks, with lustful language broken,
    "If thou wilt chide, thy lips shall never open."

He burns with bashful shame, she with her tears
Doth quench the maiden burning of his cheeks;   50
Then with her windy sighs and golden hairs
To fan and blow them dry again she seeks.
    He saith she is immodest, blames her miss;
    What follows more, she murders with a kiss.

Even as an empty eagle, sharp by fast,   55
Tires with her beak on feathers, flesh and bone,
Shaking her wings, devouring all in haste,
Till either gorge be stuff'd or prey be gone:
    Even so she kiss'd his brow, his cheek, his chin,
    And where she ends she doth anew begin.   60

Forc'd to content, but never to obey,

54. murders] *Q3;* murthers *Q1,2,4–6;* smothers *Q7–16.*   56. feathers] *Q1;*
leather *Q2,4,5.*

43. *So soon . . . down*] He was no
sooner stretched out than she was lying
at his side.
47. *with lustful language broken*] Her
words are broken by the kisses with
which she mingles them. Compare
Ovid, *Metam.,* x. 559:
    Sic ait, ac mediis interserit oscula
        verbis.
47, 48. *broken, open*] Similar imperfect rhymes are found in ll. 451, 453,
ll. 565, 567, and in *Lucr.,* ll. 1357, 1358.
53. *miss*] misbehaviour. Pooler refers to Lyly, *Woman in the Moone,* IV. i.
151:
    Pale be my lookes to witness my
        amisse
and Malone to Sonnet xxxv:
    Myself corrupting, salving thy
        amiss.
But 'miss' is not a contraction of
'amiss', since it occurs frequently in

Middle English and later (see O.E.D.).
55. *sharp by fast*] her appetite keen
from fasting.
56. *Tires*] tears ravenously. Nares
explains: 'A term in falconry; from
tirer, French, to drag or pull. The hawk
was said to tire on her prey, when it
was thrown to her, and she began to
pull at it and tear it'. Verity compares
3H6, I. i. 268 f.: like an empty eagle
    Tire on the flesh of me and of my
        son!
The animation of Shakespeare's image
is very striking. See *Lucr.,* l. 543 n.
61. *Forc'd to content*] Malone,
Steevens, R. H. Case, and others have
tried to determine whether 'content' is
a substantive meaning 'acquiescence',
or a verb, and if a verb, whether active
('to content Venus') or passive ('to
content himself'). Other passages show
that the word had not been limited to

Panting he lies and breatheth in her face.
She feedeth on the steam as on a prey,
And calls it heavenly moisture, air of grace,
    Wishing her cheeks were gardens full of flowers,   65
    So they were dew'd with such distilling showers.

Look how a bird lies tangled in a net,
So fasten'd in her arms Adonis lies;
Pure shame and aw'd resistance made him fret,
Which bred more beauty in his angry eyes: 70
    Rain added to a river that is rank
    Perforce will force it overflow the bank.

Still she entreats, and prettily entreats,
For to a pretty ear she tunes her tale.
Still is he sullen, still he lours and frets,   75
'Twixt crimson shame and anger ashy pale.
    Being red, she loves him best, and being white,
    Her best is better'd with a more delight.

62. breatheth] *Q1*; breathing *Q5*.   74. ear] *Q1*; care *Q13*; air *conj. Malone*.
75. still he] *Q1*; still she *Q4–6*.

the meanings of 'happy or happiness, satisfied or satisfaction', but could carry the idea of submission or passivity. See *Oth.*, III. iv. 120:

> So I shall clothe me in a forced
>   content.

63. *prey*] 'That which is procured or serves as food' (O.E.D.).

64. *grace*] A free gift or act of mercy by God.

66. *So they were*] provided that they were. See Abbott, § 133.

distilling] forming from mist or steam.

67. *Look how*] just as. 'Look' emphasizes 'the correspondence of relative and antecedent', here 'how' and 'so' (O.E.D.). See also ll. 289, 299, 925, and *Lucr.*, ll. 372, 694. But *Ven.*, l. 529, and *Lucr.*, l. 1548, show Shakespeare modifying this ancient idiom. Compare Sonnet xxxvii. 13:

> Look what is best, that best I wish
>   in thee.

69. *aw'd*] intimidated.

70.] Malone compares *Tw. N.*, III. i. 157 f.:

> O! what a deal of scorn looks beau-
>   tiful
> In the contempt and anger of his lip.

71. *rank*] full to overflowing. Compare *John*, v. iv. 54, and Drayton, *Polyolbion*, ix. 139:

> And with stern Aeolus' blasts, like
>   Thetis waxing rank,
> She only over-swells the surface of
>   her bank.

72. *Perforce . . . force*] For the tag 'force perforce', which underlies this phrase, see *John*, III. i. 142, and elsewhere.

74. *ear*] Malone yielded to the taste of his time in suggesting that this was a mistake for 'air'. Shakespeare's freedom to refer to such physical, even homely, details as Adonis' ears gives his poem life.

76.] He alternately blushes for shame and turns pale with rage.

78. *more*] greater in degree. O.E.D. quotes Heywood, 2nd Pt *Iron Age*, IV. i:

> Lets flye to some strong Cittadell,
> For our more safety.

Look how he can, she cannot choose but love;
And by her fair immortal hand she swears,   80
From his soft bosom never to remove
Till he take truce with her contending tears,
　　Which long have rain'd, making her cheeks all wet:
　　And one sweet kiss shall pay this comptless debt.

Upon this promise did he raise his chin,   85
Like a dive-dapper peering through a wave,
Who being look'd on, ducks as quickly in:
So offers he to give what she did crave,
　　But when her lips were ready for his pay,
　　He winks, and turns his lips another way.   90

Never did passenger in summer's heat
More thirst for drink than she for this good turn.
Her help she sees, but help she cannot get;
She bathes in water, yet her fire must burn.
　　"Oh pity," 'gan she cry, "flint-hearted boy,   95
　　'Tis but a kiss I beg, why art thou coy?

82. take] *Q1;* takes *Q5,6.*　　　84. comptless] *Q1–6;* countless *Q7–16.*　　　94. her]
Q1; in *Q7–16.*

82. *take truce*] make peace, come to
terms. Compare *John,* III. i. 17:
　　With my vex'd spirits I cannot take
　　　a truce.
contending tears] tears making war on
him.
84. *comptless*] inestimable. This is the
Latinized spelling common in the 16th
and 17th cents.; but see also *Tit.,* v. iii.
159:
　　O were the summe of these that I
　　　should pay
　　Countlesse and infinit, yet would
　　　I pay them.
86. *dive-dapper*] Another name for
the dabchick, or little grebe (*podiceps
minor,* according to Harting, *Orni-
thology of Shakespeare,* p. 258). Di-
dapper is the form in some dialects
(see Wright, *English Dialect Dictionary,*
vol. II, pp. 67 and 94).
87. *Who*] Frequently used where we
would use 'which'. See ll. 306, 630, 857,
891, 956, 968, 984, etc.; and Abbott,
§ 264.

ducks as quickly in] Note the colloquial
quality here.
89. *his pay*] What he is to pay
her.
90. *winks*] 'Wink' is 'here akin to
wince, formerly also *winch,* . . . to start
aside' (Wyndham). The word vividly
combines two meanings: that Adonis,
having screwed up his resolution for
the kiss, flinches at the last moment;
and that as he does so, he blinks and
averts his face. In l. 121 the word
means simply to close the eyes, its usual
Elizabethan sense. See *Lucr.,* l. 375, and
Cym., v. iv. 195, II. iii. 27 and iv. 89.
91. *passenger*] traveller, wayfarer.
93–4.] The myth of Tantalus, up to
his chin in water, yet unable to drink
(see *F.Q.,* II. vii. 57–60) may have
been in Shakespeare's mind when he
thought of the offered kiss which at
the last moment flees from Venus'
lips. Malone's interpretation of the
'water' as Venus' tears seems nonsense.

"I have been woo'd as I entreat thee now,
Even by the stern and direful god of war,
Whose sinewy neck in battle ne'er did bow,
Who conquers where he comes in every jar;   100
    Yet hath he been my captive and my slave,
    And begg'd for that which thou unask'd shalt have.

"Over my altars hath he hung his lance,
His batter'd shield, his uncontrolled crest;
And for my sake hath learn'd to sport and dance,   105
To toy, to wanton, dally, smile and jest,
    Scorning his churlish drum and ensign red,
    Making my arms his field, his tent my bed.

"Thus he that overrul'd I oversway'd,
Leading him prisoner in a red rose chain: 110
Strong-temper'd steel his stronger strength obey'd,
Yet was he servile to my coy disdain.
    Oh be not proud, nor brag not of thy might,
    For mast'ring her that foil'd the god of fight!

"Touch but my lips with those fair lips of thine—   115
Though mine be not so fair, yet are they red—
The kiss shall be thine own as well as mine.
What see'st thou in the ground? hold up thy head,
    Look in mine eye-balls, there thy beauty lies:
    Then why not lips on lips, since eyes in eyes?   120

106. toy] *Q1;* coy *Q4–16.*   119. there] *Q1;* where *Q5–16.*   120. in] *Q1;* on *Q7–16.*

100. *jar*] fight, trial of strength. Compare *Err.,* I. i. 11.

104. *uncontrolled crest*] his helmet which had never bowed in submission.

107. *churlish*] The adjective conveys the rough or rude 'speech' of the drum as well as its associations with violence.

110.] Malone compared this famous line to a passage from Ronsard, itself an imitation of Anacreon:

Les Muses lieront un jour
De chaisnes de roses Amour
        (Livre xiv, Ode xxiii)

and suggested that this and other odes by Anacreon may have been translated into English, and echoed by Shakespeare here and elsewhere (for example in *Tim.,* IV. iii. 439–45). Sidney Lee took the supposed relationship further in *The French Renaissance in England* (1910), p. 221. But Shakespeare's habit of transforming all such neo-classical imagery by a personal energy makes it difficult to demonstrate such 'debts', or to regard them as of any great significance.

113. *nor brag not*] Double negatives are frequent in Shakespearian English. See Abbott, § 406.

114. *foil'd*] overthrew. Compare *AYL.,* II. ii. 13–14: the wrestler
    That did but lately foil the sinewy Charles.

118.] Compare 'the murye wordes

"Art thou asham'd to kiss? then wink again,
And I will wink; so shall the day seem night.
Love keeps his revels where there are but twain;
Be bold to play, our sport is not in sight.
    These blue-vein'd violets whereon we lean   125
    Never can blab, nor know not what we mean.

"The tender spring upon thy tempting lip
Shows thee unripe; yet mayst thou well be tasted.
Make use of time, let not advantage slip;
Beauty within itself should not be wasted.   130
    Fair flowers that are not gather'd in their prime
    Rot, and consume themselves in little time.

"Were I hard-favour'd, foul, or wrinkled old,
Ill-nurtur'd, crooked, churlish, harsh in voice,
O'erworn, despised, rheumatic and cold,   135
Thick-sighted, barren, lean, and lacking juice,
    Then mightst thou pause, for then I were not for thee;
    But having no defects, why dost abhor me?

---

123. are] *Q1;* be *Q2,4–16.*   126. not] *Q1;* they *Q7–16.*   134. Ill-nurtur'd]
Q1; Ill natur'd *Q9,10.*

of the Host to Chaucer', *Cant. Tales,*
B. 1885–7.

  121. *wink*] See l. 90 n.

  126. *blab*] tell tales, betray. Compare *Tw. N.,* I. ii. 61, and *2H6,* III. i. 154:

Beaufort's red sparkling eyes blab
  his heart's malice.

  127. *The tender spring*] the down that will become a beard. See l. 487.

  129–30.] These lines introduce a topic relating *Venus and Adonis* to the first group of Shakespeare's Sonnets (i–vi). See M. C. Bradbrook, *op. cit.,* pp. 61–2. A commonplace of Greek and Roman lyric poetry, the exhortation to enjoy beauty and youth while time allowed became even more frequent in French and Italian poetry of the 16th cent., and consequently in Elizabethan poetry.

  advantage] opportunity.

  133–6.] With this catalogue compare *Err.,* IV. ii. 19–21:

He is deformed, crooked, old and
  sere,
Ill-fac'd, worse-bodied, shapeless
  everywhere;
Vicious, ungentle, foolish, blunt,
  unkind.

  133. *hard-favour'd*] hard-featured. See l. 931 and *Lucr.,* l. 1632.

  foul] ugly. Compare *Oth.,* II. i. 141–2:

There's none so foul and foolish
  thereunto
But does foul pranks which fair and
  wise ones do.

  135. *O'erworn*] worn out with age. Compare Sonnet lxiii:

With Time's injurious hand crush'd
  and o'erworn.

  rheumatic] The accent is on the first syllable, as in *MND.,* II. i. 105.

  136. *Thick-sighted*] with bad eyesight. Compare *Cæs.,* v. iii. 21:

My sight was ever thick.
  lacking juice] See l. 25 n.

"Thou canst not see one wrinkle in my brow,
  Mine eyes are grey and bright and quick in turning.   140
  My beauty as the spring doth yearly grow,
  My flesh is soft and plump, my marrow burning.
    My smooth moist hand, were it with thy hand felt,
    Would in thy palm dissolve, or seem to melt.

"Bid me discourse, I will enchant thine ear,   145
  Or like a fairy trip upon the green,
  Or like a nymph, with long dishevell'd hair,
  Dance on the sands, and yet no footing seen.
    Love is a spirit all compact of fire,
    Not gross to sink, but light, and will aspire.   150

"Witness this primrose bank whereon I lie:
  These forceless flowers like sturdy trees support me.
  Two strengthless doves will draw me through the sky
  From morn till night, even where I list to sport me.

142. plump] *Q1;* plumbe *Q5,6;* plum *Q7–10,12.*   152. These] *Q1;* The *Q9–11, 13–16.*

140. *grey*] Most commentators agree with Malone: 'What we now call *blue* eyes were in Shakespeare's time called *grey* eyes, and were considered as eminently beautiful'. Compare l. 482, and *Rom.,* II. iv. 47:
  Thisbe, a grey eye or so, but not to the purpose.
143. *My smooth moist hand*] See l. 25 n.
145. *enchant*] The word has its full meaning of 'to charm by means of song'.
148. *footing*] footprint. Compare *Tp.,* v. i. 34:
  And ye that on the sands with printless foot
  Do chase the ebbing Neptune,
and Ben Jonson, *The Vision of Delight* (Herford and Simpson, *Works,* vol. VII, p. 470):
  And thence did *Venus* learne to lead
  Th' *Idalian* Braules, and so ⟨to⟩ tread
  As if the wind, not she did walke;
  Nor prest a flower, nor bow'd a stalke.

149. *compact*] composed. Compare *AYL.,* II. vii. 5:
  If he, compact of jars, grow musical,
  We shall have shortly discord in the spheres.
All living things were believed to be composed of the four 'elements', fire, air, water, and earth, in varying proportions. Compare *Ant.,* v. ii. 291:
  I am fire, and air; my other elements
  I give to baser life.
150. *gross to sink*] heavy and so bound to sink.
aspire] rise up, float.
151. *Witness this primrose bank*] Let this bank bear witness. Compare *MND.,* I. i. 215.
152. *forceless*] frail, strengthless.
154. *list*] wish. O.E. *lystan* was an impersonal transitive verb used with accusative or dative; this survived into the 16th cent., as in *F.Q.,* I. vii. 35. But the personal construction Shakespeare uses also became common. Compare Milton, *P.L.,* VIII. 75.
to sport me] to take my pleasure.

Is love so light, sweet boy, and may it be   155
That thou should think it heavy unto thee?

"Is thine own heart to thine own face affected?
Can thy right hand seize love upon thy left?
Then woo thyself, be of thyself rejected;
Steal thine own freedom, and complain on theft.   160
    Narcissus so himself himself forsook,
    And died to kiss his shadow in the brook.

"Torches are made to light, jewels to wear,
Dainties to taste, fresh beauty for the use,
Herbs for their smell, and sappy plants to bear: 165
Things growing to themselves are growth's abuse.
    Seeds spring from seeds, and beauty breedeth beauty;
    Thou wast begot, to get it is thy duty.

156. should] *Q1;* shouldst *Q2,4–16.*   160. on] *Q1;* of *Q4–16.*   168. wast]
Q1; wert *Q5–16.*

156. *heavy*] tiresome.

157. *to . . . affected*] in love with.

158. *seize . . . left*] take possession of love by taking hold of your left hand. 'Seize' and 'seizure' are often used of clasping hands. See *John*, III. i. 241, and *Rom.*, III. iii. 35:

> more courtship lives
> In carrion-flies than Romeo; they
>   may seize
> On the white wonder of dear Juliet's
>   hand.

160. *on*] of.

161–2.] Sidney Lee objected that Narcissus did not drown himself; but drowning is implied in the passage he quoted from Marlowe's *Hero and Leander* (I. 74–6):

> [he] leapt into the water for a kiss
> Of his own shadow, and despising
>   many,
> Died ere he could enjoy the love of
>   any.

It appears also in earlier poetry (see Baldwin, *op. cit.*, pp. 18–21), and *Lucr.*, ll. 265–6. Golding (III. 522–4) was certainly known to both Marlowe and Shakespeare:

> like a foolish noddie
> He [Narcissus] thinks the shadow

that he sees, to be a lively bodie.

> Astraughted like an ymage made of
>   Marble stone he lyes,
> There gazing on his shadow still
>   with fixed staring eyes.

For 'shadow' meaning reflection or image see *R3*, I. i. 264, and *John*, II. i. 498:

> The shadow of myself formed in her
>   eye.

166. *to themselves*] for themselves. Compare l. 1180, and Sonnet xciv:

> The summer's flower is to the
>   summer sweet,
> Though to itself it only live and
>   die.

168. *Thou . . . duty*] This and the following lines repeat the theme of the first seventeen Sonnets, that 'fairest creatures' have a duty to reproduce their kind. Pooler quotes a parallel from Sidney (*The Last Part of the Countesse of Pembrokes Arcadia* [1593], ed. A. Feuillerat, p. 80):

> Thy father justly may of thee
>   complaine,
> If thou doo not repay his deeds for
>   thee,
> In granting unto him a grandsires
>   gaine.

"Upon the earth's increase why shouldst thou feed,
　Unless the earth with thy increase be fed? 170
By law of nature thou art bound to breed,
That thine may live when thou thyself art dead;
　　And so in spite of death thou dost survive,
　　In that thy likeness still is left alive."

By this the love-sick queen began to sweat, 175
For where they lay, the shadow had forsook them;
And Titan, tired in the mid-day heat,
With burning eye did hotly overlook them,
　　Wishing Adonis had his team to guide,
　　So he were like him and by Venus' side. 180

And now Adonis with a lazy sprite,
And with a heavy, dark, disliking eye,
His louring brows o'erwhelming his fair sight,
Like misty vapours when they blot the sky:
　　Souring his cheeks, cries, "Fie, no more of love! 185
　　The sun doth burn my face, I must remove."

"Ay me," quoth Venus, "young, and so unkind!
What bare excuses mak'st thou to be gone!
I'll sigh celestial breath, whose gentle wind

Thy common-wealth may rightly grieved be,
Which must by this immortall be preserved,
If thus thou murther thy posteritie.

169. *increase*] fruits or other natural products. Compare Sonnet i, l. 1.

177. *Titan*] the sun-god.

tired] Shakespeare's mythology is seldom satisfactory to pedants, and Boswell suggested that this meant 'attired'. Other commentators have been more liberal, and Pooler says: 'Shakespeare may have remembered the difficulties of the sun's course as enumerated in Ovid, *Metamorphoses* bk. ii, but more probably he fancifully represented it as feeling what it inflicts'.

178. *overlook*] survey, look down on.

180. *So*] For this construction see also ll. 65–6.

183. *louring*] frowning. See l. 75.

sight] eyes or gaze. The brows drawn down over the eyes are clearly pictured here and in the next line.

185. *Souring his cheeks*] Compare *R2*, II. i. 169:
　　made me sour my patient cheek
　Or bend one wrinkle on my
　　sovereign's face.
Malone quotes *Cor.*, IV. vi. 58 f., 'some news is come that turns their countenances'; but what is meant here is the expression of somebody tasting something sour, which first affects the lines of mouth and cheek.

187. *young, and so unkind*] Compare *Lr.*, I. i. 108:
　　So young, and so untender?
Both phrases have a proverbial ring.

188. *bare*] inadequate, poor. See *1H4*, III. ii. 13:
　　Such poor, such bare, such lewd,
　　such mean attempts.

Shall cool the heat of this descending sun.   190
　　I'll make a shadow for thee of my hairs;
　　If they burn too, I'll quench them with my tears.

"The sun that shines from heaven shines but warm,
　　And lo I lie between that sun and thee:
　　The heat I have from thence doth little harm,   195
　　Thine eye darts forth the fire that burneth me;
　　　　And were I not immortal, life were done,
　　　　Between this heavenly and earthly sun.

"Art thou obdurate, flinty, hard as steel?
　　Nay more than flint, for stone at rain relenteth;   200
　　Art thou a woman's son and canst not feel
　　What 'tis to love, how want of love tormenteth?
　　　　O had thy mother borne so hard a mind,
　　　　She had not brought forth thee, but died unkind.

"What am I that thou shouldst contemn me this,   205
　　Or what great danger dwells upon my suit?
　　What were thy lips the worse for one poor kiss?
　　Speak, fair, but speak fair words, or else be mute.
　　　　Give me one kiss, I'll give it thee again,
　　　　And one for int'rest, if thou wilt have twain.   210

"Fie, lifeless picture, cold and senseless stone,
　　Well-painted idol, image dull and dead,
　　Statue contenting but the eye alone,
　　Thing like a man, but of no woman bred!

190. heat] *Q1;* heart *Q5.*　　198. and] *Q1;* and this *Q8,12.*　　203. hard] *Q1;*
bad *Q2–4,16.*　　211. lifeless] livelesse *Q1.*　　213. contenting] *Q1;* contemning
Q5.

199. *obdurate*] The accent is on the
second syllable. See *Lucr.,* l. 429, and
Tit., II. iii. 160, *2H6,* IV. vii. 122, *3H6,*
I. iv. 142.

200. *relenteth*] grows soft.

201. *a woman's son*] Compare
Sonnet xli:

　And when a woman woos, what
　　woman's son
　Will sourly leave her, till she have
　　prevail'd?

204. *unkind*] Commonly used of
women who refused to make love; see
l. 310. Efforts to extract some further
meaning are misguided. Venus' argument is another commonplace for
wooers. Compare *All's W.,* IV. ii. 9 f.:

　now you should be as your mother
　　was
　When your sweet self was got.

205. *this*] thus. This form occurs in
Middle English and later, but this
would appear to be the latest recorded
instance (see O.E.D.).

Thou art no man, though of a man's complexion,   215
For men will kiss even by their own direction."

This said, impatience chokes her pleading tongue,
And swelling passion doth provoke a pause.
Red cheeks and fiery eyes blaze forth her wrong;
Being judge in love, she cannot right her cause.   220
   And now she weeps, and now she fain would speak,
   And now her sobs do her intendments break.

Sometime she shakes her head, and then his hand,
Now gazeth she on him, now on the ground.
Sometime her arms infold him like a band: 225
She would, he will not in her arms be bound.
   And when from thence he struggles to be gone,
   She locks her lily fingers one in one.

"Fondling," she saith, "since I have hemm'd thee here
Within the circuit of this ivory pale,   230
I'll be a park, and thou shalt be my deer:
Feed where thou wilt, on mountain or in dale;
   Graze on my lips, and if those hills be dry,
   Stray lower, where the pleasant fountains lie.

223, 225. Sometime] *Q1*; Sometimes *Q4–16*.   230. the] *Q1*; this *Q8,12.*
231. a] *Q1*; the *Q4–16.*   deer] deare *Q1.*   232. on] *Q1*; in *Q8,12.*

215. *complexion*] outward appearance. 'Complexion' meant in the first place 'temperament' or 'natural disposition', supposed to be determined by the combination of the 'four humours' (blood, bile, phlegm, melancholy). This 'natural disposition' showed in a person's face and physique. See *Wiv.*, v. v. 9: 'You were also, Jupiter, a swan for the love of Leda: O omnipotent love! how near the god drew to the complexion of a goose!'

217. *pleading*] There is a play upon the legal sense, which develops into the conceit of l. 220.

219. *blaze forth*] proclaim; originally 'to proclaim with a trumpet', but this becomes fused with the associations of a flaming fire, as in *Cæs.*, II. ii. 31:
   The heavens themselves blaze forth
     the death of princes.

220. *Being . . . cause*] A paradox is intended: 'she is judge in all disputes of love, yet she cannot obtain justice in her own cause.'

222. *intendments*] what she intends to say.

229. *Fondling*] foolish one. Pooler quotes Lyly, *Woman in the Moone*, II. i. 230:
   But fondling as I am why grieve
     I thus?

hemm'd] enclosed: more often used with adverbial extension, *in, round,* or *about*; see l. 1022. Compare *P.L.*, IV. 979.

230–1.] Waller adapts the conceit in the lines *On a Girdle*:
   The pale which held that lovely
     deer.
The word-play on 'deer' was hackneyed.

pale] fence. The 'ivory pale' is Venus' linked arms.

"Within this limit is relief enough,   235
   Sweet bottom grass and high delightful plain,
   Round rising hillocks, brakes obscure and rough,
   To shelter thee from tempest and from rain:
      Then be my deer, since I am such a park,
      No dog shall rouse thee, though a thousand bark."   240

At this Adonis smiles as in disdain,
   That in each cheek appears a pretty dimple;
   Love made those hollows, if himself were slain,
   He might be buried in a tomb so simple,
      Foreknowing well, if there he came to lie,   245
      Why there love liv'd, and there he could not die.

These lovely caves, these round enchanting pits,
   Open'd their mouths to swallow Venus' liking:
   Being mad before, how doth she now for wits?
   Struck dead before, what needs a second striking?   250
      Poor queen of love, in thine own law forlorn,
      To love a cheek that smiles at thee in scorn!

Now which way shall she turn? what shall she say?
   Her words are done, her woes the more increasing;
   The time is spent, her object will away,   255

247. these] *Q1*; those *Q7–13*.   253. she say] *Q1*; we say *Q5,6*.

235–40.] Even Adonis could not but smile at this and the preceding stanza (l. 241), and it was this sort of witticism which made *Venus and Adonis* so popular with the genteel readers of its day. The passage was often quoted by contemporaries; see Heywood, *Fair Maid of the Exchange* (Pearson, ii. 55).

235. *this limit*] this precinct.

relief] pasture. Pooler quotes *Master of Game* (Reprint 1909, p. 14, n.): 'Relief, which denoted the act of arising and going to feed, became afterwards the term for the feeding itself.'

236. *bottom*] valley. See *AYL.*, iv. iii. 79.

237. *brakes*] thickets.

240. *rouse*] drive from cover. The word was a technical term in hunting, but the examples quoted by Pooler show that such 'terms of venery' were more loosely used than such scholars as Wyndham would admit: 'So in Shakespeare, "rouse" is used of the lion [*1H4*, i. iii. 198]; of the panther, [*Tit.*, i. ii. 21]; and ... of the night-owl ... [*Tw. N.*, ii. iii. 60].'

242. *That*] so that. See Abbott, § 283.

243. *if himself were slain*] so that if he himself were slain.

245–8.] Echoed by Crashaw in *Love's Horoscope* (*The Delights of the Muses*, 1646).

248. *liking*] desire.

251. *in thine own law forlorn*] unhappy in a matter supposedly under your own rule.

253. *what ... say?*] Compare the last words of Book II of *Troilus and Criseyde*: 'O mighty god, what shal he seye?'

255. *her object*] Adonis.

And from her twining arms doth urge releasing.
"Pity," she cries, "some favour, some remorse!"
Away he springs, and hasteth to his horse.

But lo from forth a copse that neighbours by,
A breeding jennet, lusty, young and proud,   260
Adonis' trampling courser doth espy,
And forth she rushes, snorts and neighs aloud:
    The strong-neck'd steed being tied unto a tree,
    Breaketh his rein, and to her straight goes he.

Imperiously he leaps, he neighs, he bounds,   265
And now his woven girths he breaks asunder;
The bearing earth with his hard hoof he wounds,
Whose hollow womb resounds like heaven's thunder;
    The iron bit he crusheth 'tween his teeth,
    Controlling what he was controlled with.   270

His ears up-prick'd, his braided hanging mane
Upon his compass'd crest now stand on end;
His nostrils drink the air, and forth again
As from a furnace, vapours doth he send;

266. girths] *Q1–4;* girts *Q5–16.*   269. crusheth] *Q1;* crushes *Q6–16.*   his]
Q1; hir *Q2.*   272. stand] *Q1;* stands *Q7–16.*

257. *remorse*] mercy, tenderness. See
Lucr., ll. 269 and 562.
    259. *neighbours by*] lies nearby.
    260. *jennet*] a small Spanish horse.
O.E.D. quotes *Sqr. of lowe Degre,* ll.
749–50.
    Iennettes of Spayne, that ben so
        wyght,
    Trapped to the ground with velvet
        bright.
    267. *bearing*] Pooler compares *1H4,*
v. iv. 92:
        this earth that bears thee dead
    Bears not alive so stout a gentleman.
See also *H5,* Prol., ll. 26 f.:
    Think, when we talk of horses, that
        you see them
    Printing their proud hooves i' th'
        receiving earth.
wounds] Compare *R2,* III. ii. 7:
    Though rebels wound thee with
        their horses' hoofs.
263–70.]   Marlowe's   *Hero   and*

Leander, II. 141–5, provides another
spirited horse as an image of the violence of sexual desire:
    For as a hot proud horse highly
        disdains
    To have his head controll'd but
        breaks the reins,
    Spits forth the ringled bit, and with
        his hooves
    Checks the submissive ground: so
        he that loves,
    The more he is restrained, the
        worse he fares.
    271. *braided*] divided into locks.
    mane] The use of singular noun with
plural verb in the next line has often
been pointed out (Malone, Bell,
Wyndham, and others). See l. 517
and n.
    272. *compass'd*] arched. '*A compass'd
cieling* is a phrase yet in use' (Malone).
Shakespeare has 'a compass'd window'
for 'a bow window' in *Troil.,* I. ii. 120.

His eye which scornfully glisters like fire   275
Shows his hot courage and his high desire.

Sometime he trots, as if he told the steps,
With gentle majesty and modest pride;
Anon he rears upright, curvets and leaps,
As who should say "Lo thus my strength is tried: 280
      And this I do to captivate the eye
      Of the fair breeder that is standing by."

What recketh he his rider's angry stir,
His flattering "holla" or his "Stand, I say"?
What cares he now for curb or pricking spur,   285
For rich caparisons or trappings gay?
      He sees his love, and nothing else he sees,
      For nothing else with his proud sight agrees.

Look when a painter would surpass the life
In limning out a well-proportion'd steed,   290
His art with nature's workmanship at strife,
As if the dead the living should exceed:
      So did this horse excel a common one,
      In shape, in courage, colour, pace and bone.

---

277. Sometime] *Q1;* Sometimes *Q5–16.*   281. this] *Q1;* thus *Q5–16.*   286.
trappings] *Q1;* trapping *Q5.*   293. this] *Q1;* his *Q8,10–16.*

275. *glisters*] glitters.
276. *courage*] sexual inclination, lust
(Onions).
277. *told*] counted. See l. 520.
279. *curvets*] 'A term of the manege
. . . from Italian *corvetta* = a curvet;
corvo = a raven. The horse was made
to rear and prance forward with his
hind legs together, and this action was
likened to the hopping of a raven'
(Wyndham).
280. *tried*] tested, proved.
282. *breeder*] female. See *3H6*, II. i.
41–2:
      Nay, bear three daughters: by your
            leave I speak it,
      You love the breeder better than the
            male.
283. *stir*] exertion, excitement.
Compare *Gent.*, v. iv. 13:
      What hallowing and what stir is
            this today?

See *Lucr.*, l. 1471, and *R2*, II. iii. 51.
      recketh] cares for. Compare Spenser,
Sheph. Cal., October, l. 29:
      What wreaked I of wintrye ages
            waste.
284. *holla*] Explained by Malone as
'a term of the manege', as in *AYL.*, III.
ii. 257: 'Cry "holla" to thy tongue,
I prithee: it curvets unseasonably'.
Wyndham adds: 'Holla = stop, as in
the pleasant Elizabethan ditty, "Holla,
my Fancy, whither wilt thou stray?"'
290. *limning out*] drawing, painting.
291.] See l. 9. Compare *Tim.*, I. i.
37 f.:
      It tutors nature: artificial strife
      Lives in these touches, livelier than
            life.
294. *bone*] frame. Compare *Troil.,*
III. iii. 172:
      High birth, vigor of bone, desert in
            service.

Round-hoof'd, short-jointed, fetlocks shag and long,   295
Broad breast, full eye, small head, and nostril wide,
High crest, short ears, straight legs and passing strong,
Thin mane, thick tail, broad buttock, tender hide:
　　Look what a horse should have he did not lack,
　　Save a proud rider on so proud a back.   300

Sometime he scuds far off, and there he stares;
Anon he starts at stirring of a feather.
To bid the wind a base he now prepares,
And where he run or fly, they know not whether,

296. eye] *Q1;* eyes *Q7–16.*   302. starts] *Q1;* stares *Q8,10–16.*

295–8.] Dowden speaks for those who are unable to enter into the spirit of the poem: 'This passage of poetry has been admired; but is it poetry or a paragraph from an advertisement of a horse sale? It is part of Shakespeare's study of an animal, and he does his work thoroughly.' Bush finds here 'the minute, self-defeating realism of the tyro' (*Mythology and the Renaissance Tradition,* p. 148). But the light, sharp details of this description are swept forward as swiftly as all else in this episode, and as the episode itself is swept forward in the poem. The most obvious literary source is Virgil's description of a well-bred horse in the *Georgics,* III. 75–94. As Baldwin points out (*op. cit.,* p. 24), the episode of the stallion and mare was probably suggested by a later passage in the same book (*Georgics,* III. 266–8). Elizabethan treatises on horsemanship, deriving in most cases from Italian originals, embodied an ideal of the horse's physique which derived both from the experience of centuries, and from the aesthetic conceptions of Greek and Roman and Renaissance art and poetry. Thus Shakespeare might have remembered the description in Blundeville's *The Fowre Chiefyst Offices belonging to Horsemanshippe* (1565), which derived from Federico Grisone, *Ordini di Cavalcare* (1550): 'Round hooves, short pasterns with long fewter lockes, Broade breast, great eies, short and slender head, wide nostrils, the creast rising, short ears, strong legs, crispe mane, long and bushy tail, great round buttocks' (quoted in *Shakespeare's England,* vol. II, p. 413). But there is nothing literary or dry in Shakespeare's picture; it is the work of someone who has studied horses, read the authorities, and discussed the points with true interest and enjoyment.

shag] rough, untrimmed. Compare *2H6,* III. i. 367:

Like a shag-hair'd crafty kern.

301. *scuds*] runs smoothly and swiftly.

stares] stands and stares. The idea of a fixed or searching gaze implies standing still.

302.] Compare *All's W.,* v. iii. 232: 'every feather starts you', and *R3,* III. v. 7.

303. *bid . . . a base*] challenge the wind to a chase. The reference is to a country game: 'it is played by two sides, who occupy contiguous "bases" or "homes"; any player running out from his "base" is chased by one of the opposite side, and, if caught, made a prisoner. . . *to bid base*: to challenge to a chase in this game. . .' (O.E.D.). Compare *Gent.,* I. ii. 97:

Indeed I bid the base for Proteus

and *Cym.,* v. iii. 19 f.

304. *where*] whether. Compare *Tp.,* v. i. 111, 122, and *Err.,* IV. i. 60. For 'whether' meaning 'which of the two' O.E.D. quotes Massinger, *Parlt. Love,*

For through his mane and tail the high wind sings,   305
Fanning the hairs, who wave like feather'd wings.

He looks upon his love, and neighs unto her:
She answers him, as if she knew his mind.
Being proud, as females are, to see him woo her,
She puts on outward strangeness, seems unkind,   310
   Spurns at his love, and scorns the heat he feels,
   Beating his kind embracements with her heels.

Then like a melancholy malcontent,
He vails his tail that like a falling plume
Cool shadow to his melting buttock lent;   315
He stamps, and bites the poor flies in his fume.
   His love perceiving how he was enrag'd,
   Grew kinder, and his fury was assuag'd.

His testy master goeth about to take him,
When lo the unback'd breeder, full of fear,   320
Jealous of catching, swiftly doth forsake him;
With her the horse, and left Adonis there:
   As they were mad unto the wood they hie them,
   Outstripping crows that strive to overfly them.

All swoln with chafing, down Adonis sits,   325
Banning his boist'rous and unruly beast.
And now the happy season once more fits
That love-sick love by pleading may be blest;

305. through] *Q1;* thogh *Q5.*   315. buttock] *Q1–4;* buttocks *Q5–7, Q9–16.*
317. was] *Q1;* is *Q4–16.*   319. goeth] *Q1;* goes *Q9–16.*   325. chafing] *Q1;*
chasing *Q5–8,12,16.*

i. v, 'I am troubled with the toothach,
or with love, I know not whether.'

310. *outward strangeness*] a show of
indifference. Pooler quotes Lyly,
Euphues (ed. Bond, i. 200): 'The
Gentlewoman . . . gave hym suche a
colde welcome that he repented that he
was come . . . he uttred this speach.
Faire Ladye, if it be the guise of *Italy*
to welcome straungers with strangnes,
I must needes say the custome is
strange and the countrey barbarous.'

314. *vails*] droops. See l. 956.
316. *fume*] irritation.

319. *testy*] angry, tetchy.
goeth about] tries.

320. *unback'd*] not broken to a rider.
321. *Jealous of catching*] afraid of
being caught.

323–4.] These two lines show mag-
nificently Shakespeare's concise evocation of landscape. See also ll. 813–16.

overfly] fly faster or farther. But the
word also gives an image of the crows
flying overhead, as the horses flee.

325. *swoln with chafing*] bursting with
rage.

326. *Banning*] cursing.

For lovers say, the heart hath treble wrong,
When it is barr'd the aidance of the tongue.   330

An oven that is stopp'd, or river stay'd,
Burneth more hotly, swelleth with more rage:
So of concealed sorrow may be said
Free vent of words love's fire doth assuage;
    But when the heart's attorney once is mute,   335
    The client breaks, as desperate in his suit.

He sees her coming, and begins to glow,
Even as a dying coal revives with wind;
And with his bonnet hides his angry brow,
Looks on the dull earth with disturbed mind,   340
    Taking no notice that she is so nigh,
    For all askance he holds her in his eye.

O what a sight it was, wistly to view
How she came stealing to the wayward boy!
To note the fighting conflict of her hue,   345
How white and red each other did destroy!
    But now her cheek was pale, and by and by
    It flash'd forth fire, as lightning from the sky.

Now was she just before him as he sat,
And like a lowly lover down she kneels;   350
With one fair hand she heaveth up his hat,

348. as] *Q1*; and *Q9–11,13–15.*   350. lowly] *Q1*; slowly *Q5.*

330. *barr'd*] forbidden.
aidance] help. See *2H6*, III. ii. 165.
331. *stopp'd*] stopped up, closed.
Compare *F.Q.*, I. ii. 34:
    He oft finds med'cine who his griefs
        imparts,
    But double griefs afflict concealing
        harts,
    As raging flames who striveth to
        suppresse
and *Tit.*, II. iv. 36 f.:
    Sorrow concealed, like an oven
        stopp'd,
    Doth burn the heart to cinders
        where it is.
334. *vent*] utterance.
335. *the heart's attorney*] the tongue.
'Attorney' for 'advocate' was not
used after Shakespeare's time (see

O.E.D.). Compare *R3*, IV. iv. 126 f.:
    Why should calamity be full of
        words
    Windy attorneys to their client
        woes.
336. *breaks*] goes bankrupt. The
word-play may be compared to *Rom.*,
III. ii. 57.
339. *bonnet*] hat. See l. 351.
342. *all askance . . . eye*] he watches
her only surreptitiously.
343. *wistly*] intently. See *Lucr.*,
l. 1355.
345–6.] Compare the lengthy conceit in *Lucr.*, ll. 52–73.
351. *heaveth*] lifts. The effort implied
in the modern use was not a necessary
accompaniment of this word; see
l. 482, and *Lucr.*, l. 111. Pooler quotes

Her other tender hand his fair cheek feels:
　His tend'rer cheek receives her soft hand's print,
　As apt as new-fall'n snow takes any dint.

Oh what a war of looks was then between them! 355
Her eyes petitioners to his eyes suing,
His eyes saw her eyes, as they had not seen them,
Her eyes woo'd still, his eyes disdain'd the wooing;
　And all this dumb play had his acts made plain
　With tears, which chorus-like her eyes did rain. 360

Full gently now she takes him by the hand,
A lily prison'd in a gaol of snow,
Or ivory in an alablaster band:
So white a friend engirts so white a foe.
　This beauteous combat, wilful and unwilling, 365
　Show'd like two silver doves that sit a-billing.

352. cheek] *Q1;* cheekes *Q7–16.*　353. tend'rer] tendrer *Q1;* tender *Q2–5.*
cheek] cheeke, *Q1–4;* cheeks *Q5–16.*　365. unwilling] *Q1;* willing *Q5,6.*
366. two] *Q1;* to *Q5,6,8,10–16.*

Middleton, *A Chaste Maid in Cheapside* (Works, ed. Bullen, v, p. 94), v. i. 16:
　Look up an't please your worship;
　heave those eyes.
354. *dint*] impression.
359–60.] This conceit of the dumb-show accompanied by a 'chorus' cannot be pressed for too precise a meaning. Any actor who commented on the action from without could be called a 'chorus' by the Elizabethans. Compare the 'chorus' in *Henry V* and *Pericles.*
　his] 'Its' did not replace 'his' until after Shakespeare began to write. See Abbott, § 228.
362–3.] Perhaps a reminiscence of Ovid's description of Salmacis bathing: see Golding, iv. 438:
　As if a man an Ivorie Image or a
　　Lillie white
　Should overlay or close with glasse.
According to M. C. Bradbrook: 'The lily, the snow, the ivory and the alabaster are all chosen for their chilly whiteness, which has nothing in common with that of flesh. They are all symbols of chastity. . . The ideas of

death and chastity are precisely the opposite to those suggested in this passage. Again there is a direct contrast to the warm flexuous restraint of Venus' melting palm in the *hardness* of the ivory and alabaster which *binds* it, in the idea of imprisonment in a *gaol*, and the besieging force *engirting* the enemy. The passage is built on sensuous opposites: it is a definition by exclusion' (*op. cit.*, p. 64). Miss Bradbrook finds this a deliberate use of 'the heraldic manner' (see also *Lucr.*, ll. 52–70 n.). But this interpretation is forced. The ivory, lily, snow, alabaster, had been used in similar contexts by scores of poets whose thoughts were far from death or chastity (see the description of the naked Angelica in *Orlando Furioso*, x. 96–8). These conventional hyperboles go back to Greek poetry. Shakespeare revivifies them by conceits; but they remain simple, not paradoxical, in effect.
　364. *engirts*] encloses. See *Lucr.*, l. 221.
　366. *Show'd*] looked, made a picture.

Once more the engine of her thoughts began:
"O fairest mover on this mortal round,
  Would thou wert as I am, and I a man,
  My heart all whole as thine, thy heart my wound!   370
    For one sweet look thy help I would assure thee,
    Though nothing but my body's bane would cure thee."

"Give me my hand," said he, "why dost thou feel it?"
"Give me my heart," saith she, "and thou shalt have it.
  O give it me lest thy hard heart do steel it,   375
  And being steel'd, soft sighs can never grave it.
    Then love's deep groans I never shall regard,
    Because Adonis' heart hath made mine hard."

"For shame," he cries, "let go, and let me go:
  My day's delight is past, my horse is gone,   380
  And 'tis your fault I am bereft him so.
  I pray you hence, and leave me here alone,
    For all my mind, my thought, my busy care,
    Is how to get my palfrey from the mare."

Thus she replies: "Thy palfrey as he should,   385
  Welcomes the warm approach of sweet desire.
  Affection is a coal that must be cool'd;
  Else, suffer'd, it will set the heart on fire.
    The sea hath bounds, but deep desire hath none;
    Therefore no marvel though thy horse be gone.   390

368. on] *Q1;* of *Q6,12;* in *Q8.*   371. thy] *Q1;* my *Q9–11,13–16.*   385. he]
Q1; she *Q9–10,11,13–15.*

367. *the engine of her thoughts*] her tongue. Compare l. 335, and *Tit.,* III. i. 82:

  O that delightful engine of her
    thoughts,
  That blabbed them with such
    pleasing eloquence,
  Is torn from forth that pretty hollow
    cage.

368. *mover . . . round*] living creature on earth. Compare *Cor.,* I. v. 45:

  See here these movers that do prize
    their hours
  At a crack'd drachme!

370. *thy heart my wound*] This ellipti-cal expression is more effective than 'thy heart with my wound', or 'thine with my wound' (which would have been metrically possible).

375. *steel*] turn to steel.

376. *grave*] engrave, cut into.

381. *bereft him*] deprived of him.

382. *hence*] go hence.

387. *coal*] ember. See l. 338.

388. *suffer'd*] left to burn. Compare *3H6,* IV. viii. 8:

  A little fire is quickly trodden out;
  Which, being suffer'd, rivers cannot
    quench.

389.] Compare *Rom.,* II. ii. 133–4.

"How like a jade he stood tied to the tree,
  Servilely master'd with a leathern rein!
  But when he saw his love, his youth's fair fee,
  He held such petty bondage in disdain,
      Throwing the base thong from his bending crest,   395
      Enfranchising his mouth, his back, his breast.

"Who sees his true-love in her naked bed,
  Teaching the sheets a whiter hue than white,
  But when his glutton eye so full hath fed,
  His other agents aim at like delight?   400
      Who is so faint that dares not be so bold
      To touch the fire, the weather being cold?

"Let me excuse thy courser, gentle boy,
  And learn of him, I heartily beseech thee,
  To take advantage on presented joy;   405
  Though I were dumb, yet his proceedings teach thee.
      O learn to love, the lesson is but plain,
      And once made perfect, never lost again."

---

391. the] *Q1*; a *Q6–16*.   392. rein] raine *Q1*; reign *Gildon*.   397. sees] *Q1*;
seekes *Q2–5*.

391. *jade*] an inferior or spiritless
horse.

393. *fee*] due reward. The word was
often used to mean something due as
by right, as in Herbert, *The Discharge*,
l. 21:

  Only the present is thy part and
    fee.

396. *Enfranchising*] setting free.

397. *in her naked bed*] undressed and
in bed. The phrase is common in 16th-
cent. English; well-known examples
are Hieronymo's line in *The Spanish
Tragedy*, II. v. 1:

  What out-cries pluck me from my
    naked bed?

and Edwardes's song:

  When going to my naked bed as one
    that would have slept.

O.E.D. says: 'Orig. used with reference to the custom of sleeping entirely
naked; in later use denoting the
removal of the ordinary wearing
apparel.'

398. *Teaching . . . white*] Compare
Rom., I. v. 48, and *Cym.*, II. ii. 15 f.:

                          fresh lily,
  And whiter than the sheets!

400. *agents*] senses or organs.

397–400.] Malone first referred to a
similar passage in *The Phoenix' Nest*,
1593 (ed. H. E. Rollins, p. 22):

  Who hath beheld faire Venus in
    hir pride,
  Of nakednes all Alablaster white,
  In Iuorie bed, straight laid by Mars
    his side,
  And hath not been enchanted with
    the sight . . .

405. *on*] Compare 'having some
advantage on' in *Cæs.*, v. iii. 6, and
Sonnet lxiv:

  When I have seen the hungry ocean
    gain
  Advantage on the kingdom of the
    shore.
  presented] offered.

407. *but plain*] only an easy one.

"I know not love," quoth he, "nor will not know it,
Unless it be a boar, and then I chase it.   410
'Tis much to borrow, and I will not owe it:
My love to love is love but to disgrace it,
 For I have heard, it is a life in death,
 That laughs and weeps, and all but with a breath.

"Who wears a garment shapeless and unfinish'd?   415
Who plucks the bud before one leaf put forth?
If springing things be any jot diminish'd,
They wither in their prime, prove nothing worth;
 The colt that's back'd and burden'd being young,
 Loseth his pride, and never waxeth strong.   420

"You hurt my hand with wringing, let us part,
And leave this idle theme, this bootless chat;
Remove your siege from my unyielding heart,
To love's alarms it will not ope the gate.
 Dismiss your vows, your feigned tears, your flatt'ry,   425
 For where a heart is hard they make no batt'ry."

"What, canst thou talk?" quoth she, "hast thou a tongue?
O would thou hadst not, or I had no hearing!

424. alarms] *Q1;* alarum *Q5;* alarm *Q6–16.*

411. *'Tis much . . . owe it*] 'To accept
(or bestow) love involves great obli-
gations, which I do not wish to undertake.'

412. *My love . . . disgrace it*] 'What I
feel towards love is only a strong desire
to scorn it.'

414. *and all but with a breath*] in the
same breath.

417. *springing*] growing.

419. *back'd*] broken in, saddled. See
l. 320.

being young] while yet young.

420. *waxeth*] grows.

421. *wringing*] squeezing. Com-
mentators say that the word conveyed
less force than it would to us; but
Adonis does not seem to think so.
Pooler quotes Guilpin's *Skialetheia,*
Ep. 38 (Reprint, p. 14):

He's a fine fellow . . .

Who piertly jets, can caper, daunce
    and sing,
Play with his mistris fingers, her
    hand wring.

422. *bootless chat*] useless discussion.

424. *alarms*] attacks.

426. *batt'ry*] Originally the word
meant no more than a violent *attempt*
to break into a military position, but it
acquired the associations of a successful entry. See *3H6,* III. i. 37:

Her sighs will make a battery in his
    breast

and *Per.,* V. i. 47:

She questionless with her sweet
    harmony
And other chosen attractions,
    would allure
And make a battery through his
    deafen'd ports
Which now are midway stopp'd.

Thy mermaid's voice hath done me double wrong;
I had my load before, now press'd with bearing: 430
  Melodious discord, heavenly tune harsh-sounding,
  Ears' deep sweet music, and heart's deep sore wounding!

"Had I no eyes but ears, my ears would love
That inward beauty and invisible;
Or were I deaf, thy outward parts would move   435
Each part in me that were but sensible:
  Though neither eyes nor ears, to hear nor see,
  Yet should I be in love by touching thee.

"Say that the sense of feeling were bereft me,
And that I could not see, nor hear, nor touch,   440
And nothing but the very smell were left me,
Yet would my love to thee be still as much;
  For from the stillitory of thy face excelling
  Comes breath perfum'd, that breedeth love by smelling.

"But oh what banquet wert thou to the taste,   445
Being nurse and feeder of the other four!
Would they not wish the feast might ever last,

---

432. Ears'] Eares *Q1–4;* Earths *Q5–16.*
16.   447. might] *Q1;* should *Q3–16.*

439. feeling] *Q1;* reason *Q9–11,13–*

429. *mermaid's voice*] alluring voice. See l. 777 and *Lucr.,* l. 1411. Many passages in Shakespeare associate dangerously seductive song with mermaids. Compare *MND.,* II. i. 150–4, and *Err.,* III. ii. 45–7:

O! train me not, sweet mermaid, with thy note,
To drown me in thy sister flood of tears:
Sing, siren, for thyself, and I will dote.

430. *press'd with bearing*] weighed down with carrying it. Compare *Oth.,* III. iv. 177:

I have this while with leaden thoughts been press'd.

431.] When Shakespeare uses rhetorical devices such as this oxymoron, he follows contemporary taste in laying them on pretty heavily. See *Lucr.,* l. 79.

433–50.] Wyndham points out that Chapman has a similar but lengthier treatment of the five senses in *Ovid's Banquet of Sense* (1595).

435. *parts*] limbs or features; but perhaps with a play on the meaning of 'parts' as 'accomplishments'.

436. *sensible*] sensitive, i.e. capable of receiving impressions.

441–4.] Compare l. 1178.

443. *stillitory*] a still. For the application of the word to a face see Chaucer, *Cant. Tales,* G. 580: 'his forhead dropped as a stillatorie.'

excelling] surpassingly beautiful.

444.] Compare Marlowe, *Hero and Leander,* I. 21 f.:

Many would praise the sweet smell as she past,
When 'twas the odour which her breath forth cast.

446. *the other four*] i.e. senses.

And bid suspicion double-lock the door,
  Lest jealousy, that sour unwelcome guest,
  Should by his stealing in disturb the feast?" 450

Once more the ruby-colour'd portal open'd,
Which to his speech did honey passage yield,
Like a red morn that ever yet betoken'd
Wrack to the seaman, tempest to the field,
  Sorrow to shepherds, woe unto the birds, 455
  Gusts and foul flaws to herdmen and to herds.

This ill presage advisedly she marketh:
Even as the wind is hush'd before it raineth,
Or as the wolf doth grin before he barketh,
Or as the berry breaks before it staineth, 460
  Or like the deadly bullet of a gun,
  His meaning struck her ere his words begun.

And at his look she flatly falleth down,
For looks kill love, and love by looks reviveth:
A smile recures the wounding of a frown. 465
But blessed bankrout, that by love so thriveth!
  The silly boy, believing she is dead,
  Claps her pale cheek, till clapping makes it red.

And all amaz'd brake off his late intent,
For sharply did he think to reprehend her, 470

455. to] *Q1;* to the *Q5,6.*   456. Gusts] *Q1;* Gust *Q6–16.*   460. staineth] *Q1;*
straineth *Q5.*   464. kill] *Q1;* kils *Q5.*   466. love] *Qq;* losse *conj. Walker.*
469. all amaz'd] *Q1;* all in a maze *Q5;* in a maze *Q6–11,13–15.*

448. *double-lock*] lock by two turns of
the key.
  452. *honey*] sweet.
  453–6.] This piece of weather-lore
is very ancient (see St Matthew xvi.
2–3). Verity refers to Chapman's
Hero and Leander, iii. 177 f.:
  And after it a foul black day befell,
  Which ever since a red morn doth
    foretell.
  456. *flaws*] blasts of wind.
  457. *advisedly*] attentively, consciously; see *Lucr.,* l. 1527.
  marketh] notes, observes.
  459. *grin*] bare his teeth.
  463. *flatly*] The literal sense is she

'falls flat'. But also present is the meaning 'without more ado', as in 'deny
flatly' or 'flatly refuse'.
  465. *recures*] remedies, heals. Pooler
quotes Lyly, *Woman in the Moone,* ii. i.
21:
  And this my hand that hurt thy
    tender side
  Shall first with herbes recure the
    wound it made.
  466. *love*] Walker conjectured 'loss'.
The meaning would then be that as
Venus collapses ('becomes bankrupt'),
her very collapse brings her profit, in
the attention she receives from Adonis.

Which cunning love did wittily prevent:
Fair fall the wit that can so well defend her!
    For on the grass she lies as she were slain,
    Till his breath breatheth life in her again.

He wrings her nose, he strikes her on the cheeks,   475
He bends her fingers, holds her pulses hard,
He chafes her lips; a thousand ways he seeks
To mend the hurt that his unkindness marr'd.
    He kisses her, and she by her good will
    Will never rise, so he will kiss her still.   480

The night of sorrow now is turn'd to day:
Her two blue windows faintly she up-heaveth,
Like the fair sun when in his fresh array
He cheers the morn, and all the earth relieveth;
    And as the bright sun glorifies the sky,   485
    So is her face illumin'd with her eye.

Whose beams upon his hairless face are fix'd,
As if from thence they borrow'd all their shine.

484. earth] *Q1*; world *Q2–5*.

471. *wittily*] ingeniously.

472. *Fair fall*] May good fortune follow. Compare *John*, I. i. 78:
    Fair fall the bones that took the
        pains for me!

475. *wrings*] See l. 421 n. No doubt the milder meaning appears here.

478. *To mend . . . marr'd*] A good example of Shakespearian 'portmanteau' English. It combines the meaning that Adonis tries 'to repair the damage that he caused by unkindness', with a popular jingle and antithesis between 'mend' and 'mar'.

479. *by her good will*] cheerfully, willingly.

480. *so*] if, on condition that.

482. *blue windows*] Are these Venus' eyes, or her eyelids? 'Window' occurs elsewhere in Shakespeare as a metaphor for both; see *LLL.*, v. ii. 848:
    Behold the window of my heart, my
        eye
and *Cym.*, II. ii. 22:

    the flame o' the taper
Bows toward her and would
    underpeep her lids,
To see the enclosed lights, now
    canopied
Under these windows, white and
    azure laced
With blue of heaven's own
    tinct.

But in these passages, and also in *Ant.*, v. ii. 319, we are left in no doubt as to which application is meant; here the scale is tipped in favour of 'eyelids' by 'blue', which provides a link with the lines in *Cymbeline*. For this interpretation see also 'Windows in Shakespeare', by Kathleen Tillotson, in G. Tillotson, *Essays in Criticism and Research*, p. 204; and compare the note to II. ii. 21–3 in New Arden *Cym.*, ed. J. M. Nosworthy.

up-heaveth] See l. 351.

488. *shine*] See also l. 728, for this word as a noun.

Were never four such lamps together mix'd,
Had not his clouded with his brow's repine;   490
    But hers, which through the crystal tears gave light,
    Shone like the moon in water seen by night.

"O where am I?" quoth she, "in earth or heaven?
Or in the ocean drench'd, or in the fire?
What hour is this, or morn, or weary even?   495
Do I delight to die, or life desire?
    But now I liv'd, and life was death's annoy;
    But now I died, and death was lively joy.

"O thou didst kill me, kill me once again!
Thy eyes' shrewd tutor, that hard heart of thine,   500
Hath taught them scornful tricks, and such disdain,
That they have murder'd this poor heart of mine;
    And these mine eyes, true leaders to their queen,
    But for thy piteous lips no more had seen.

"Long may they kiss each other for this cure!   505
Oh never let their crimson liveries wear,
And as they last, their verdour still endure,

500. Thy] *Q1;* The *Q5.*   506. never] *Q1;* neither *Q5.*   507. verdour] *Q1;*
verdure *Q5–16.*

490. *repine*] discontent, vexation.
See ll. 181–4.
    494. *drench'd*] plunged, immersed.
Compare *Gent.,* I. iii. 79:
    Thus have I shunned the fire for
        fear of burning
    And drench'd me in the sea where
        I am drown'd.
497–8.] Adonis showed nothing but
unkindness until Venus swooned.
    497. *annoy*] torment, pain. Compare
R3, V. iii. 156:
    Good angels guard thee from the
        boar's annoy.
    498. *lively*] living, life-giving.
    500. *shrewd*] sharp, harsh.
    505. *kiss each other*] Pooler quotes
Sidney, *Astrophel and Stella,* 1591,
xliii:
    With either lip he doth the other
        kisse.
    506. *crimson liveries wear*] red colours

wear out, or fade. Compare Sonnet
lxxvii:
    Thy glass will show thee how thy
        beauties wear.
See also *Mer. V.,* II. i. 2.
    507. *verdour*] freshness, fragrance:
the sense of 'greenery' or 'greenness'
had not yet ousted a number of other
applications. Shakespeare generally
uses the word in metaphor, as in *Tp.,*
I. ii. 87:
    The ivy that had hid my princely
        trunk
    And suck'd my verdure out on't.
Compare also *Gent.,* I. i. 49:
        The young and tender wit
    Is turn'd to folly . . .
    Losing his verdure even in the
        prime.
The spelling in Q1 indicates the Elizabethan pronunciation, which is essential to the music of the line.

To drive infection from the dangerous year:
That the star-gazers, having writ on death,
May say, the plague is banish'd by thy breath.   510

"Pure lips, sweet seals in my soft lips imprinted,
What bargains may I make, still to be sealing?
To sell myself I can be well contented,
So thou wilt buy, and pay, and use good dealing:
Which purchase if thou make, for fear of slips,   515
Set thy seal manual on my wax-red lips.

"A thousand kisses buys my heart from me,
And pay them at thy leisure, one by one,
What is ten hundred touches unto thee?
Are they not quickly told and quickly gone?   520
Say for non-payment that the debt should double,
Is twenty hundred kisses such a trouble?"

"Fair queen," quoth he, "if any love you owe me,

519. touches] *Q1; kisses Q7–16.*   522. hundred] *Q1; thousand Q4–6.*

508.] 'The poet evidently alludes to a practice of his own age, when it was customary, in time of the plague, to strew the rooms of every house with rue and other strong smelling herbs, to prevent infection' (Malone).

509. *the star-gazers, having writ on death*] compilers of almanacs who have prophesied an epidemic.

510. *the plague*] Epidemics of the plague in Shakespeare's time were common, and it is impossible to use this passage to establish the date of composition of the poem. However, Shakespeare brought out *Venus and Adonis* at a time when the theatres were closed, owing to the plague of 1592–3; and Wyndham has taken these lines to be a topical allusion: 'In 1592 . . . the theatres were closed on account of the Plague from July to December. . . It is probable therefore, that Shakespeare wrote the poem during the enforced idleness of the second half of the year 1592.'

511. *sweet seals*] Kisses are 'seals of love' in the song in *Meas.*, IV. i. Compare *Gent.*, II. ii. 7:

> And seal the bargain with a holy
>   kiss.

and *Shr.*, III. ii. 125:

> And seal the title with a lovely kiss!

515. *slips*] Examples are quoted by Pooler, of 'slips' for counterfeit money; see *Rom.*, II. iv. 51. But there is no need here for more than the ordinary sense of 'error'.

517. *buys*] Shakespeare constantly uses a singular verb with a plural subject; see Abbott § 333.

519. *touches*] touches of the lips.

520. *told*] counted. See l. 277.

521.] Malone explains that an established form of contract is meant: 'The poet was thinking of a conditional bond's becoming forfeited for non-payment; in which case, the entire penalty (usually the double of the principal sum lent by the obligee) was formerly recoverable at law.'

523. *owe*] bear. This sense of 'owe' is obsolete except in *to owe a grudge*.

Measure my strangeness with my unripe years.
Before I know myself, seek not to know me: 525
No fisher but the ungrown fry forbears;
    The mellow plum doth fall, the green sticks fast,
    Or being early pluck'd, is sour to taste.

"Look the world's comforter with weary gait
His day's hot task hath ended in the west; 530
The owl, night's herald, shrieks, 'tis very late;
The sheep are gone to fold, birds to their nest,
    And coal-black clouds that shadow heaven's light
    Do summon us to part, and bid good night.

"Now let me say good night, and so say you; 535
If you will say so, you shall have a kiss."
"Good night," quoth she, and ere he says adieu,
    The honey fee of parting tender'd is:
    Her arms do lend his neck a sweet embrace;
    Incorporate then they seem, face grows to face. 540

Till breathless he disjoin'd, and backward drew
The heavenly moisture, that sweet coral mouth,
Whose precious taste her thirsty lips well knew,
Whereon they surfeit, yet complain on drouth.
    He with her plenty press'd, she faint with dearth, 545
    Their lips together glued, fall to the earth.

Now quick desire hath caught the yielding prey,
And glutton-like she feeds, yet never filleth.
Her lips are conquerors, his lips obey,

533. And] *Q1*; The *Q5–16*.   544. drouth] *Q1*; drough *Q5*; droughth *Q6–8*.
547. the] *Q1*; his *Q5,6*; her *Q7–16*.

524. *strangeness*] coldness, diffidence;
see l. 310. The sense is, 'Account
for my diffidence by my unripe
years.'
    526. *fry*] young fish.
    529. *the world's comforter*] the sun.
Compare *Tim.*, v. i. 134:
    Thou sun, that comfort'st, burn.
See also l. 799.
    538. *tender'd*] offered.
    540. *Incorporate*] made into one body.
Compare *MND.*, iii. ii. 207:

As if our hands, our sides, voices,
    and minds,
Had been incorporate. So we grew
    together. . .
grows to] Compare *H8*, i. i. 9 f.:
                        they clung
In their embracement, as they
    grew together.
    544. *on*] of. See Abbott, § 181; and
l. 160.
    545. *press'd*] oppressed. See l. 430.
    546. *glued*] Compare *Tit.*, ii. i. 41.

Paying what ransom the insulter willeth;   550
    Whose vulture thought doth pitch the price so high
    That she will draw his lips' rich treasure dry.

And having felt the sweetness of the spoil,
With blindfold fury she begins to forage;
Her face doth reek and smoke, her blood doth boil,   555
And careless lust stirs up a desperate courage,
    Planting oblivion, beating reason back,
    Forgetting shame's pure blush and honour's wrack.

Hot, faint and weary with her hard embracing,
Like a wild bird being tam'd with too much handling,   560
Or as the fleet-foot roe that's tir'd with chasing,
Or like the froward infant still'd with dandling:
    He now obeys, and now no more resisteth,
    While she takes all she can, not all she listeth.

What wax so frozen but dissolves with temp'ring,   565
And yields at last to very light impression?
Things out of hope are compass'd oft with vent'ring,
Chiefly in love, whose leave exceeds commission:

560. with] *Q1;* by *Q8,12.*   564. While] *Q1;* Whiles *Q7,8.*

550. *insulter*] one who boasts his triumph. Compare *AYL.*, III. v. 36.

551. *vulture thought*] ravenous imagination. Compare *Lucr.*, l. 556.

pitch] set at a certain level or point.

553. *spoil*] plunder.

554. *forage*] eat greedily, or glut oneself. Compare *H5*, I. ii. 108–10:

Whiles his most mighty father on a hill

Stood smiling to behold his lion's whelp

Forage in blood of French nobility.

556. *careless*] reckless.

557. *Planting oblivion*] establishing oblivion. Compare *LLL.*, IV. iii. 349:

And plant in tyrants mild humility.

558. *wrack*] wreck.

559. *hard*] close.

562. *froward*] fretful, wilful.

564. *listeth*] wishes. See l. 154 n.

565. *temp'ring*] moulding, or working. According to Malone, 'It was the custom formerly to seal with soft wax,

which was *tempered* between the fingers, before the impression was made.' See *2H4*, IV. iii. 140: 'I have him already tempering between my finger and thumb, and shortly will I seal with him.' Pooler quotes also Lyly (ed. Bond, I. 187): 'the tender youth of a childe is lyke the temperings of new waxe apt to receive any form.'

567. *out of hope*] beyond hope.

compass'd] achieved.

568. *whose leave exceeds commission*] Pooler paraphrases: 'which intemperately exceeds its instructions, is given an inch and takes an ell'. But if this were the full meaning, Shakespeare might as well have written 'whose commission exceeds leave'. The phrase is too compressed to yield a single or wholly logical sense. Perhaps what is suggested is that 'venturing', active daring, usually succeeds in matters of love, because passivity ('leave'), the yielding to one's own or

Affection faints not like a pale-fac'd coward,
But then woos best when most his choice is froward.   570

When he did frown, O had she then gave over,
Such nectar from his lips she had not suck'd.
Foul words and frowns must not repel a lover;
What though the rose have prickles, yet 'tis pluck'd.
   Were beauty under twenty locks kept fast,   575
   Yet love breaks through, and picks them all at last.

For pity now she can no more detain him;
The poor fool prays her that he may depart.
She is resolv'd no longer to restrain him,
Bids him farewell, and look well to her heart,   580
   The which by Cupid's bow she doth protest
   He carries thence encaged in his breast.

"Sweet boy," she says, "this night I'll waste in sorrow,
For my sick heart commands mine eyes to watch.
Tell me, love's master, shall we meet tomorrow?   585
Say, shall we, shall we? wilt thou make the match?"
   He tells her no, tomorrow he intends
   To hunt the boar with certain of his friends.

"The boar," quoth she: whereat a sudden pale,

---

574. prickles] *Q1–5,12*; pricks *Q6–11,13–16*.   'tis] *Q1*; is it *Q6–15*; it is *Q16*.
582. thence] *Q1*; then *Q8,12*.

---

to another's desire, there plays so large a part.

569. *Affection*] desire.

570. *his choice*] the object of his choice.

froward] wilful, obstinate.

571. *had . . . gave over*] Compare l. 176, 'had forsook'.

573. *Foul*] hard, unpleasant.

575–6.] See O.D.E.P., p. 390.

578. *poor fool*] Malone compares Lear's remark 'And my poor fool is hang'd' (which he takes to refer to Cordelia) and explains that this 'was formerly an expression of tenderness'. Porter suggests that 'some scorn of him and envy of his chance speaks in this endearing term'.

581. *by Cupid's bow*] Compare *MND.*, I. i. 169:

   I swear to thee by Cupid's strongest bow.

583. *waste*] See note to l. 24.

584. *watch*] stay awake. Compare Sonnet lxi, ll. 13–14:

   For thee watch I whilst thou dost wake elsewhere,
   From me far off, with others all too near.

586. *make the match*] make an agreement or bargain. Compare *Mer. V.*, III. i. 46: 'There I have another bad match'.

589. *pale*] paleness. Malone cites the following from *The Shepheard's Song of Venus and Adonis* (H.C. in *England's*

Like lawn being spread upon the blushing rose,   590
Usurps her cheek; she trembles at his tale,
And on his neck her yoking arms she throws.
 She sinketh down, still hanging by his neck;
 He on her belly falls, she on her back.

Now is she in the very lists of love,   595
Her champion mounted for the hot encounter.
All is imaginary she doth prove;
He will not manage her, although he mount her:
 That worse than Tantalus' is her annoy,
 To clip Elizium and to lack her joy.   600

Even so poor birds deceiv'd with painted grapes
Do surfeit by the eye and pine the maw:

591. cheek] *Q1;* cheekes *Q5–16.* 593. by] *Q1;* on *Q5–16.* 598. manage
her] *Q1;* manage he *Q4,5.*

Helicon) in proof of Shakespeare's
knowledge of that poem:
> At the name of boare
> Venus seemed dying:
> Deadly-colour'd pale
> Roses overcast.

590. *Like lawn . . . rose*] Lawn was a
kind of fine linen, resembling cambric.
Herrick provides the closest parallel:
> Like to a twi-light, or that simpring
> dawn,
> That roses show, when misted o're
> with lawn.
>   (*To Anthea Lying in Bed*)
But these effects of white and red
especially delighted the Elizabethans.
Feuillerat quotes from Lodge, *Scillaes
Metamorphoses*, 1589:
> An Yuorie shadowed front . . .
> Next which her cheekes appeerd
> like crimson silk,
> Or ruddie rose bespred on whitest
> milk.

For the contrast of roses and lawn see
also *Lucr.*, ll. 258–9.

595. *lists*] strips of cloth marking off
the enclosed space where tournaments
or other contests were to be held: the
word was used to mean the ground or
space itself. The next line completes
the metaphor.

597–8.] The two lines must be taken
together if we are to find the right
meaning. As Kittredge says, 'All that
she experiences is mere imagination',
because Adonis will not do his part.

prove] experience.

manage her] ride her, put her
through her paces. The term is technical, and from the stable, like the
total metaphor here.

599–600.] Pooler compares *Romeus
and Juliet*, ll. 339–40 (see G. Bullough,
*Narrative and Dramatic Sources of Shake-
speare*, vol. I, p. 295):
> The lot of Tantalus is Romeus lyke
> to thine
> For want of foode amid his foode,
> the myser styll doth pine.

The punishment of Tantalus was,
however, one of the most used stories
from classical mythology; see *Lucr.*,
l. 858, and *F.Q.*, II. vii. 57–60.

annoy] torment.

clip] embrace, clasp.

601–2.] Malone notes: 'Our
authour alludes to the celebrated picture of Zeuxis, mentioned by Pliny':
Holland's Pliny translated the passage
as follows (vol. II, p. 535): 'Zeuxis for
proofe of his cunning, brought upon
the scaffold a table, wherein were

Even so she languisheth in her mishaps,
As those poor birds that helpless berries saw.
 The warm effects which she in him finds missing   605
 She seeks to kindle with continual kissing.

But all in vain; good queen, it will not be.
She hath assay'd as much as may be prov'd:
Her pleading hath deserv'd a greater fee;
She's love, she loves, and yet she is not lov'd.   610
 "Fie, fie," he says, "you crush me; let me go,
 You have no reason to withhold me so."

"Thou hadst been gone," quoth she, "sweet boy, ere this,
But that thou told'st me, thou wouldst hunt the boar.
Oh be advis'd, thou know'st not what it is,   615
With javelin's point a churlish swine to gore,
 Whose tushes never sheath'd he whetteth still,
 Like to a mortal butcher, bent to kill.

"On his bow-back he hath a battle set

616. javelin's] javelings *Q1–4*.   619. bow-back] *Q1*; bow back *Q2–5*.

clusters of grapes so lively painted
that the very birds of the air flew
flocking thither for to bee pecking at
the grapes'. This tale of artistic prow-
ess could have been read by Shakespeare in Tottel's *Miscellany*, Lodge's
Rosalynde, Greene's *Dorastus and
Fawnia*, and elsewhere.

pine the maw] starve their stomach.
For this active use of 'pine' see *R2*,
v. i. 77:
 towards the north
 Where shivering cold and sickness
 pines the clime.
604. *helpless*] affording no help.
Compare *Err.*, II. i. 38–9:
 So thou, that hast no unkind mate
 to grieve thee,
 With urging helpless patience
 wouldst relieve me:
and *R3*, I. ii. 13. See also *Lucr.*, l. 1027.
605. *effects*] There may be some confusion with 'affects', i.e. desires or
emotions; see *Lucr.*, l. 251. But 'effects'
is appropriate enough to Adonis'
situation.

608. *assay'd . . . prov'd*] Feuillerat
observes that 'these words have the
same meaning, that of putting a metal
to the test'. But the technical application is a mere shadow, and the sense
is really no more than 'she has tried
everything in her power'.
615. *be advis'd*] take heed.
616. *churlish*] rough, boorish. Compare *AYL.*, II. i. 7.
617. *tushes*] tusks. Compare Golding, VIII. 384:
 Among the greatest Oliphants in
 all the land of Inde
 A greater tush than had this Boare,
 ye shall not lightly finde.
618. *mortal*] deadly. See l. 953, and
Lucr., l. 364 and l. 724. Compare *R2*,
III. ii. 21:
 a lurking adder
 Whose double tongue may with
 a mortal touch
 Throw death upon thy sovereign's
 enemies.
bent] determined.
619. *bow-back*] hunched or arched

Of bristly pikes that ever threat his foes;   620
His eyes like glow-worms shine when he doth fret,
His snout digs sepulchres where'er he goes;
    Being mov'd, he strikes whate'er is in his way,
    And whom he strikes his crooked tushes slay.

"His brawny sides with hairy bristles armed   625
Are better proof than thy spear's point can enter;
His short thick neck cannot be easily harmed;
Being ireful, on the lion he will venture.
    The thorny brambles and embracing bushes,
    As fearful of him, part; through whom he rushes.   630

"Alas, he naught esteems that face of thine,
To which love's eyes pays tributary gazes;
Nor thy soft hands, sweet lips and crystal eyne,
Whose full perfection all the world amazes:
    But having thee at vantage—wondrous dread!—   635
    Would root these beauties as he roots the mead.

"Oh let him keep his loathsome cabin still!
Beauty hath naught to do with such foul fiends.

627. easily] *Q1;* easly *Q5,6.*   628. venture] venter *Qq.*   632. love's eyes] *Q1;*
loves eie *Q7–10.*

back. See Tennyson, *Princ.*, VI. 339.
    battle] fighting force drawn up.
Compare *1H4*, IV. i. 129:
    What may the king's whole battle
        reach unto?
The description of the boar was
thought by Malone to owe something
to Golding, VIII. 379–80:
    And like a front of armed Pikes set
        close in battle ray,
    The sturdy bristles on his back
        stoode staring up alway.
Baldwin tries to determine the exact
relationship to this and to the original
(*op. cit.*, pp. 33–6).
    621. *fret*] rage.
    623. *Being mov'd*] once roused to
anger. Compare *Rom.*, I. i. 7: 'I strike
quickly being moved'.
    626. *better proof*] stronger armour.
'Proof' was used of armour which had
been tested and found impenetrable.

Shakespeare uses it as a substantive:
see *Ham.*, III. iv. 38:
    If it be made of penetrable stuff,
    If damned custom have not brass'd
        it so
    That it be proof and bulwark
        against sense.
    631–3.] See Ovid, *Metam.*, x. 547–9.
    633. *eyne*] See also *Lucr.*, ll. 643,
1229.
    635. *having thee at vantage*] getting a
position of superiority over you. Compare *F.Q.*, III. vii. 51:
    Me seely wretch she so at vauntage
        caught.
    636. *root*] root up, or dig up with the
snout (used of swine).
    637. *cabin*] den or cave. O.E.D.
quotes Stanyhurst, *Aeneis*, I. 23:
    A cel or cabban by nature formed,
        is vnder.
    638. *fiends*] evil beings, enemies.

Come not within his danger by thy will:
They that thrive well, take counsel of their friends.   640
   When thou didst name the boar, not to dissemble,
   I fear'd thy fortune, and my joints did tremble.

"Didst thou not mark my face, was it not white?
Saw'st thou not signs of fear lurk in mine eye?
Grew I not faint, and fell I not downright?   645
Within my bosom, whereon thou dost lie,
   My boding heart pants, beats, and takes no rest,
   But like an earthquake, shakes thee on my breast.

"For where love reigns, disturbing jealousy
Doth call himself affection's sentinel;   650
Gives false alarms, suggesteth mutiny,
And in a peaceful hour doth cry 'Kill, kill!'
   Distemp'ring gentle love in his desire,
   As air and water do abate the fire.

"This sour informer, this bate-breeding spy,   655
This canker that eats up love's tender spring,

644. eye] *Q1;* eyes *Q3–5.*   653. in] *Q1;* with *Q5–16.*   654. do] *Q1;* doth *Q5–16.*   655. bate-breeding] *Q1;* bare-breeding *Q5,6.*

639. *within his danger*] within reach of his power to do harm. Compare *Mer. V.,* IV. i. 180:
  You stand within his danger, do you not?
641. *not to dissemble*] to tell the truth.
642. *fear'd*] feared for. Compare *Tit.,* II. iii. 305:
  Fear not thy sons; they shall do well enough.
643. *mark*] note.
645. *downright*] straightway, directly.
647. *boding*] foreboding.
649. *jealousy*] solicitude or anxiety.
651. *suggesteth*] incites. The word was often used of insinuating, or prompting to, evil. Compare *H5,* II. ii. 114, *Oth.,* II. iii. 358, and *Lucr.,* l. 37 n.
652. *Kill, kill!*] Malone first pointed out that this was the word given to an English army for a general assault on the enemy. See *Lr.,* IV. vi. 191, and *Cor.,* v. vi. 131. Pooler quotes Drayton, *The Battle of Agincourt:*
  Whilst scalps about like broken pot sherds fly,
  And kill, kill, kill, the conqu'ring English cry.
653. *Distemp'ring*] disturbing, diluting.
655. *bate-breeding*] mischief-making. 'Bate' for 'strife' survived only in this alliterative phrase; compare *2H4,* II. iv. 271: 'And breeds no bate with telling of discreet stories'.
656. *canker*] canker-worm or caterpillar. Compare *MND.,* II. ii. 3:
  Some to kill cankers in the musk-rose buds.
See also *Rom.,* II. iii. 30:
  Full soon the canker death eats up that plant.
spring] young shoot or bud. Malone compares *Err.,* III. ii. 3:

This carry-tale, dissentious jealousy,
That sometime true news, sometime false doth bring,
    Knocks at my heart, and whispers in mine ear,
    That if I love thee, I thy death should fear.   660

"And more than so, presenteth to mine eye
The picture of an angry chafing boar,
Under whose sharp fangs on his back doth lie
An image like thyself, all stain'd with gore;
    Whose blood upon the fresh flowers being shed,   665
    Doth make them droop with grief and hang the head.

"What should I do, seeing thee so indeed,
That tremble at th' imagination?
The thought of it doth make my faint heart bleed,
And fear doth teach it divination: 670
    I prophesy thy death, my living sorrow,
    If thou encounter with the boar tomorrow.

"But if thou needs wilt hunt, be rul'd by me:
Uncouple at the timorous flying hare,
Or at the fox which lives by subtlety,   675
Or at the roe which no encounter dare;
    Pursue these fearful creatures o'er the downs,
    And on thy well-breath'd horse keep with thy hounds.

668. tremble] *Q1*; trembling *Q4–16*.

Even in the spring of love, thy love-springs rot.

657. *carry-tale*] tale-bearer. Compare *LLL.*, v. ii. 464:

Some carry-tale, some please-man,
    some slight zany.

662. *angry chafing*] The two words are practically synonymous, but 'angry' is perhaps adverbial: 'angrily chafing'.

670. *divination*] Prophetic warnings of this sort are a common dramatic device. See *Rom.*, iii. v. 54–6, and *Ham.*, v. ii. 222–38.

672. *encounter with*] meet as an adversary.

673. *be rul'd by me*] take my advice.
674. *Uncouple*] loose your hounds. The term is found in hunting treatises

and also in common use; Pooler quotes Topsel, *Four-footed Beasts*, 1658. Compare *MND*, iv. i. 112–13:

My love shall hear the music of my
    hounds.
Uncouple in the western valley;
    let them go.

674–6.] See Ovid, *Metam.*, x. 537–9:

Hortaturque canes tutaeque
    animalia praedae,
Aut pronos lepores aut celsum in
    cornua cervum
Aut agitat dammas.

676. *dare*] Shakespeare often interchanges third person singular and plural forms of this verb. See Abbott, § 361.

677. *fearful*] timid.
678. *well-breath'd*] sound in wind.

"And when thou hast on foot the purblind hare,
　　Mark the poor wretch, to overshoot his troubles,　　680
　　How he outruns the wind, and with what care
　　He cranks and crosses with a thousand doubles;
　　　　The many musits through the which he goes
　　　　Are like a labyrinth to amaze his foes.

"Sometime he runs among a flock of sheep,　　　　685
　　To make the cunning hounds mistake their smell;
　　And sometime where earth-delving conies keep,
　　To stop the loud pursuers in their yell;
　　　　And sometime sorteth with a herd of deer:
　　　　Danger deviseth shifts, wit waits on fear.　　690

680. Mark] *Q1;* Make *Q5.*　　　684. to] *Q1;* t' *Q6–16.*　　　685. a] *Q1;* the *Q5–16.*

679. *on foot*] in motion.

purblind] The hare has weak sight. Pooler quotes from Topsel (ed. 1658, p. 208): 'The eyelids coming from the brows, are too short to cover their eyes and therefore this sense is weak in them; and besides their over-much sleep, their fear of Dogs and swiftness, causeth them to see the less.'

680. *overshoot*] Q1 'overshut' is said by O.E.D. to be an obsolete form of *overshoot,* 'to shoot or run beyond'. Pooler quotes Turbervile's *Booke of Hunting,* 1576: '[The hounds] are hote, and doe quickly overshoote the track or path of the chace which they undertake' (ed. Clarendon Press, 1908, p. 11).

682. *cranks*] twists, turns suddenly. Compare *1H4,* III. i. 98:

　See how this river comes me
　　　cranking in,
　And cuts me from the best of all
　　　my land
　A huge half-moon, a monstrous
　　　cantle out.

683. *musits*] gaps or round holes in a hedge or fence. 'A hare's muse (French *musse*) is still the common and only term for the round hole made in a fence through which a hare traces her run. *Musit* is from the Fr. diminutive *mussette*' (Wyndham). Pooler says that 'muse' and 'muset' 'were, however,

occasionally used of the hare's form and, figuratively, of any lurking place, as well as of the hole or short tunnel through which she passes', and cites Topsel, p. 212: 'a quick smelling Hound, which raiseth the Hare out of her muse.'

684. *amaze*] bewilder.

685–8.] Pooler quotes from Turbervile's *Booke of Hunting,* 1576: 'And I have seen hares oftentimes runne into a flock of sheepe in the field when they were hunted, and woulde never leave the flocke, untill I was forced to couple up my houndes, and folde up the sheepe or sometimes drive them to the Cote: and then the hare would forsake them. . . I have seene that would take the grounde like a Coney . . . when they have been hunted' (ed. 1908, p. 165).

687. *earth-delving conies*] rabbits that make burrows.

keep] dwell.

688. *in their yell*] i.e. in full cry. The hounds yelp most loudly when in full pursuit of the quarry.

689. *sorteth with*] keeps company with. Compare *LLL.,* I. i. 258: 'sorted and consorted . . . with a child of our grandmother Eve, a female'.

690. *shifts*] tricks, evasions. Compare *John,* IV. iii. 7:

"For there his smell with others being mingled,
  The hot scent-snuffing hounds are driven to doubt,
  Ceasing their clamorous cry, till they have singled
  With much ado the cold fault cleanly out;
      Then they do spend their mouths: echo replies,   695
      As if another chase were in the skies.

"By this, poor Wat, far off upon a hill,
  Stands on his hinder-legs with list'ning ear,
  To hearken if his foes pursue him still.
  Anon their loud alarums he doth hear;   700
      And now his grief may be compared well
      To one sore sick, that hears the passing bell.

700. their] *Q1;* with *Q4,5.*

If I get down and do not break my
  limbs,
I'll find a thousand shifts to get
  away.

waits on] attends, goes with. See
Lucr., l. 275.

693. *Ceasing their clamorous cry*]
Pooler quotes from *The Master of Game*
(circa 1406–11) to show that this was
'a sign of good hounds', and that
hounds were to be trained not to give
tongue except when they were on the
scent (Reprint, 1909, pp. 107 and
110).

singled] distinguished the scent from
that of other animals. Pooler again
refers to *Master of Game*, and to Turbervile (p. 35): 'there is difference
between the scent of a Harte and a
Hynde, as you may see by experience
that hounds do oftentimes single that
one from that other'.

694. *cold fault*] loss of scent. ' "Fault"
is defect *sc.* of scent, and strictly
speaking, it is the scent not the fault
which is cold, whether from being
mixed with that of other beasts than
"the chase", or from the nature of the
ground, or from the lapse of time.
Hounds were said to "fail" or to be "at
default" when they lost the scent'
(Pooler).

695. *spend their mouths*] yelp, give
tongue. Compare *Troil.,* v. i. 98, *Oth.,*

I. ii. 48, and *H5,* II. iv. 69:
                    coward dogs
Most spend their mouths when what
  they seem to threaten
Runs far before them.

695–6.] Compare *Tit.,* II. iii. 17–19,
and *MND.,* IV. i. 117–20:
              Never did I hear
Such gallant chiding; for, besides
  the groves,
The skies, the fountains, every
  region near
Seem'd all one mutual cry.

697. *Wat*] 'A familiar term among
sportsmen for a hare; why, does not
appear. Perhaps for no better reason
than *Philip,* for a sparrow, *Tom,* for a
cat, and the like' (Nares, *Glossary,*
1822). The first example in O.E.D.
dates from about 1500, the last from
1692.

698.] Pooler compares Topsel, p.
211: 'When she [the hare] hath left
both Hunters and Dogs a great way
behind her, she getteth to some hill or
rising of the earth, there she raiseth
herself upon her hinder legs, like a
Watch-man in his Tower, observing
how far or near the enemy approach-
eth.'

700. *Anon*] soon.

alarums] war-cries or battle-cries.

702. *passing bell*] 'The bell which
rings at the hour of departure, to

"Then shalt thou see the dew-bedabbled wretch
  Turn, and return, indenting with the way.
  Each envious briar his weary legs do scratch,   705
  Each shadow makes him stop, each murmur stay:
    For misery is trodden on by many,
    And being low, never reliev'd by any.

"Lie quietly, and hear a little more;
  Nay, do not struggle, for thou shalt not rise.   710
  To make thee hate the hunting of the boar,
  Unlike myself thou hear'st me moralise,
    Applying this to that, and so to so,
    For love can comment upon every woe.

"Where did I leave?" "No matter where," quoth he;   715
  "Leave me, and then the story aptly ends:
  The night is spent." "Why, what of that?" quoth she.
  "I am," quoth he, "expected of my friends,
    And now 'tis dark, and going I shall fall."
    "In night," quoth she, "desire sees best of all.   720

  "But if thou fall, oh then imagine this:

704.] indenting] *Q1*; intending *Q5*.   705. do] *Q1*; doth *Q5–16*.   712. my-
self] my selfe *Q1*; thy selfe *Q4–8,12*.

obtain prayers for the passing soul'
(Johnson).

  704. *indenting*] zigzagging. The
expression originated with the practice of drawing up a legal or business
document in duplicate and then dividing it into two pieces by a zigzag or
toothed line; the tallying or fitting of
the two sections was thought to guar-
antee the authenticity of the whole.
The metaphorical use is illustrated by
Pooler in quotations from Drayton's
Polyolbion, I. 158, and Topsel, p. 212:
'The Dogs . . . run along with a gallant cry, turning over the doubtful
footsteps; now one way, now another,
like the cuts of Indentures . . .' Compare also Golding, VII. 1016:
  [the fox] doubling and indenting
    still avoydes his enmies lipes.
  705. *envious*] spiteful.
  712. *moralise*] teach by example or

illustration, i.e. 'applying this to that'.
The idea of a didactic treatise is sus-
tained in 'comment' in l. 714. See also
Lucr., l. 104.
  715. *leave*] break off. Compare
Arden of Feversham, III. vi. 72:
  Do you remember where my tale
    did leave?
Compare also *3H6*, II. ii. 168:
  Yet know thou, since we have
    begun to strike,
  We'll never leave, till we have
    hewn thee down.
  716. *aptly*] suitably.
  718. *expected of*] expected by. See
Abbott, § 170.
  720.] Compare *Rom.*, III. ii. 8:
  Lovers can see to do their amorous
    rites
  By their own beauties.
See also *Hero and Leander*, I. 191:
  dark night is Cupid's day.

The earth in love with thee thy footing trips,
And all is but to rob thee of a kiss.
Rich preys make true men thieves; so do thy lips
    Make modest Dian cloudy and forlorn,   725
    Lest she should steal a kiss and die forsworn.

"Now of this dark night I perceive the reason:
Cynthia for shame obscures her silver shine,
Till forging nature be condemn'd of treason,
    For stealing moulds from heaven, that were divine;   730
    Wherein she fram'd thee, in high heaven's despite,
    To shame the sun by day and her by night.

"And therefore hath she brib'd the destinies
To cross the curious workmanship of nature,
To mingle beauty with infirmities   735
And pure perfection with impure defeature,
    Making it subject to the tyranny
    Of mad mischances and much misery:

"As burning fevers, agues pale and faint,
    Life-poisoning pestilence and frenzies wood,   740

724. true men] true-men *Q1*; rich-men *Q4*; rich men *Q5–16*.   738. mad] *Q1*; sad *Q7–16*.

722. *footing*] step. The word is used variously by Shakespeare: for 'footprint' (l. 148 above), for 'footfall' (*Mer. V.*, v. i. 24), for 'foot' or 'feet' in *2H6*, III. ii. 87.

724. *preys*] booty, spoils.

true men] honest men; generally used as the opposite of 'thieves' as in *Meas.*, IV. ii. 46: 'Every true man's apparel fits your thief', *LLL.*, IV. iii. 187, and *1H4*, II. ii. 102.

725. *cloudy*] gloomy, sullen. Compare *1H4*, III. ii. 83:

      such aspect
As cloudy men use to their
    adversaries.

The metaphorical sense is here combined with the literal image of the clouded moon in a way which carries out the half-jocular 'conceit' of the stanza. See also *Lucr.*, l. 1084.

726. *forsworn*] having broken her vow of chastity.

727–32.] Venus continues to pile up conceits and hyperboles, one growing out of another.

728. *shine*] See l. 488.

729. *forging*] counterfeiting. The word 'moulds' in the next line brings out the metaphor from forged money.

731–2.] 'She' in l. 731 is Nature; 'her' in l. 732 is the moon.

734. *cross*] thwart.

curious] cunning, elaborate.

736. *defeature*] disfigurement. Compare *Err.*, II. i. 98, and v. i. 299:

    And careful hours, with Time's
      deformed hand,
    Have written strange defeatures in
      my face.

739. *agues*] fevers, characterized by fits of shivering.

740. *wood*] mad. Pooler quotes Greene's *Orlando Furioso*, 'Franticke Companion, lunatick and wood'

The marrow-eating sickness whose attaint
Disorder breeds by heating of the blood;
    Surfeits, imposthumes, grief and damn'd despair,
    Swear nature's death, for framing thee so fair.

"And not the least of all these maladies   745
But in one minute's fight brings beauty under;
Both favour, savour, hue and qualities,
Whereat th' impartial gazer late did wonder,
    Are on the sudden wasted, thaw'd and done,
    As mountain snow melts with the midday sun.   750

"Therefore despite of fruitless chastity,
Love-lacking vestals and self-loving nuns,
That on the earth would breed a scarcity
And barren dearth of daughters and of sons,
    Be prodigal; the lamp that burns by night   755
    Dries up his oil to lend the world his light.

"What is thy body but a swallowing grave,

---

746. fight] *Q1;* sight *Q6–16.*   748. impartial] *Q1;* imperiall *Q5–16.*   754. dearth] *Q1;* death *Q5,6,8,12.*   sons] *Q2–16;* suns *Q1.*

(*Plays and Poems,* ed. Churton Collins (Oxford, 1905), vol. I, p. 249).

741. *marrow-eating sickness*] Either phthisis or syphilis may be meant. See *Troil.,* v. i. 19–23, and the article on 'Medicine' in *Shakespeare's England,* vol. I.

attaint] infection. Compare *H5,* IV. Chor. 39:

  But freshly looks and overbears attaint
  With cheerful countenance.

743. *Surfeits*] illnesses caused by excessive eating or drinking.

imposthumes] abscesses, or accumulations of poisonous matter. Compare *Troil.,* v. i. 20–8, where 'bladders full of imposthumes' are included among 'the rotten diseases of the south'.

744. *Swear nature's death*] vow to bring about Nature's death.

745–6.] Even the least serious of these ailments 'after a *momentary en-gagement* subdues beauty' (Malone).

747. *favour*] aspect or countenance.

hue] The word could mean 'shape' as well as 'colour'; see Sonnet xx, l. 7:

  A man in hue, all hues in his controlling.

748. *impartial*] indifferent, i.e. not swayed by desire.

late] lately.

749. *done*] destroyed. Compare *Lucr.,* l. 23.

751. *despite of*] in defiance of.

752. *vestals*] virgins or nuns: the word originally meant one of the priestesses who tended the sacred fire in the Temple of Vesta at Rome. See *Per.,* IV. v. 7:

  Shall's go hear the vestals sing?

755. *Be prodigal*] spend what you have. 'The lamp that burns by night' is an Ovidian witticism for beauty and love.

757–62.] The first group of the Sonnets (particularly iv–vi) plays with

Seeming to bury that posterity,
Which by the rights of time thou needs must have,
If thou destroy them not in dark obscurity?   760
    If so, the world will hold thee in disdain,
    Sith in thy pride so fair a hope is slain.

"So in thyself thyself art made away;
A mischief worse than civil home-bred strife,
Or theirs whose desperate hands themselves do slay,   765
Or butcher sire that reaves his son of life.
    Foul cank'ring rust the hidden treasure frets,
    But gold that's put to use more gold begets."

"Nay then," quoth Adon, "you will fall again
Into your idle over-handled theme.   770
The kiss I gave you is bestow'd in vain,
And all in vain you strive against the stream;
    For by this black-fac'd night, desire's foul nurse,
    Your treatise makes me like you worse and worse.

---

760. dark] *Q1*; their *Q5–16*.   765. do] *Q1*; to *Q4,5*.   766. butcher sire] *Q1*; butchers sire *Q5–11,13–16*.

the same ideas. Malone compares Sonnet iii, l. 7:

    who is he so fond will be the tomb
    Of his self-love, to stop posterity?

758, 760. *posterity, obscurity*] This loose kind of rhyme has drawn severe reprobation from some critics. Dodge (University of Wisconsin, *Sh. Studies*, 1916) remarks: 'What we have here is a bygone mode of rhyming so alien to our main traditions that we can hardly believe it was ever recognized by reputable moderns'. But see *Lucr.*, ll. 352, 354.

762. *Sith*] since.

764–6.] Compare *R3*, v. v. 25 f.:

    The father rashly slaughtered his own son;
    The son, compell'd, been butcher to the sire.

766. *reaves*] deprives. Compare *All's W.*, v. iii. 86:

    Had you that craft to reave her
    Of what should stead her most?

767. *frets*] eats away.

768.] Venus is recurring to commonplace arguments for enjoying beauty, her 'idle over-handled theme'. Her last metaphor had been used in *Hero and Leander*, I. 232–6:

    What difference betwixt the richest mine
    And basest mould, but use? for both, not us'd,
    Are of like worth. Then treasure is abus'd,
    When misers keep it: being put to loan,
    In time it will return us two for one.

Compare *Rom.*, III. v. 226.

769. *you will fall*] you are determined to fall.

773. *foul*] ugly as well as impure. For the conceit see also *Lucr.*, l. 674.

774. *treatise*] discourse. Compare *Mac.*, v. v. 12, and *Ado*, I. i. 317:

    But lest my liking might too sudden seem,
    I would have salved it with a longer treatise.

"If love have lent you twenty thousand tongues, 775
And every tongue more moving than your own,
Bewitching like the wanton mermaid's songs,
Yet from my heart the tempting tune is blown;
　For know, my heart stands armed in mine ear,
　And will not let a false sound enter there; 780

"Lest the deceiving harmony should run
Into the quiet closure of my breast,
And then my little heart were quite undone,
In his bedchamber to be barr'd of rest.
　No, lady, no; my heart longs not to groan, 785
　But soundly sleeps, while now it sleeps alone.

"What have you urg'd that I cannot reprove?
The path is smooth that leadeth on to danger.
I hate not love, but your device in love
That lends embracements unto every stranger. 790
　You do it for increase: O strange excuse,
　When reason is the bawd to lust's abuse!

"Call it not love, for love to heaven is fled,
Since sweating lust on earth usurp'd his name;
Under whose simple semblance he hath fed 795
Upon fresh beauty, blotting it with blame;
　Which the hot tyrant stains and soon bereaves,
　As caterpillars do the tender leaves.

779. mine] *Q1*; my *Q7-11,13-16*. 788. on to] *Q1*; unto *Q5-16*. 794.
usurp'd] usurpt *Q1*; usurpe *Q5*.

777. *the wanton mermaid's songs*] See
l. 429 n.
778. *blown*] blown away.
782. *closure*] enclosure. Compare
R3, III. iii. 11: 'the guilty closure of thy
walls', and Sonnet xlviii:
　Within the gentle closure of my
　　breast.
784. *barr'd of rest*] kept from rest.
787. *urg'd*] argued.
reprove] refute. Compare *2H6*, III. i.
40:
　Reprove my allegation, if you can:
　Or else conclude my words
　　effectual.

789. *device*] conduct, with a suggestion of ingenuity or cunning. In *AYL.*,
I. i. 174, 'full of noble device' illustrates
the innocent meaning of the word, as
'invention' or 'faculty of devising'.
791. *increase*] procreation, breeding.
795. *simple semblance*] innocent appearance.
797-8.] Compare *2H6*, III. i. 89 f.:
　Thus are my blossoms blasted in
　　the bud,
　And caterpillars eat my leaves
　　away.
bereaves] takes away.

"Love comforteth like sunshine after rain,
But lust's effect is tempest after sun;   800
Love's gentle spring doth always fresh remain,
Lust's winter comes ere summer half be done;
    Love surfeits not, lust like a glutton dies;
    Love is all truth, lust full of forged lies.

"More I could tell, but more I dare not say: 805
The text is old, the orator too green.
Therefore in sadness, now I will away;
My face is full of shame, my heart of teen,
    Mine ears that to your wanton talk attended
    Do burn themselves, for having so offended."   810

With this he breaketh from the sweet embrace
Of those fair arms which bound him to her breast,
And homeward through the dark laund runs apace;
Leaves love upon her back deeply distress'd.
    Look how a bright star shooteth from the sky,   815
    So glides he in the night from Venus' eye;

Which after him she darts, as one on shore
Gazing upon a late embarked friend,
Till the wild waves will have him seen no more,
Whose ridges with the meeting clouds contend: 820
    So did the merciless and pitchy night
    Fold in the object that did feed her sight.

---

813. laund] lawnd *Q1–4;* lawnes *Q5–15;* lanes *Q16.*   814. love] *Q1;* Love
Q4.

799–802.] Compare *Lucr.,* ll. 48–
9.

806. *green*] young, inexperienced.
Compare *John,* III. iv. 145:

How green you are and fresh in
    this old world.

See also *Pilgr.,* IV, l. 2.

807. *in sadness*] in earnest, truly. See
Rom., I. i. 205:

Tell me in sadness, who is that you
    love.

808. *teen*] vexation, sorrow. Compare *R3,* IV. i. 95:

Eighty odd years of sorrow have
    I seen,

And each hour's joy wrack'd with
    a week of teen.

810.] Compare *Cym.,* I. vi. 141, and
Ado, III. i. 107: 'What fire is in my
ears?'

813. *laund*] lawn, an open space of
untilled ground in a wood. Pooler
quotes Drayton, *Polyolbion,* XIII. 89:

And near to these our thicks the
    wild and frightful herds . . .

Feed finely on the launds.

815–16.] Coleridge's comment on
these lines is important in his appreciation of the poem. See p. xviii above.

819–20.] Compare *Oth.,* II. i. 12.

Whereat amaz'd, as one that unaware
Hath dropp'd a precious jewel in the flood,
Or 'stonish'd as night-wand'rers often are, 825
Their light blown out in some mistrustful wood:
    Even so confounded in the dark she lay,
    Having lost the fair discovery of her way.

And now she beats her heart, whereat it groans,
That all the neighbour caves, as seeming troubled, 830
Make verbal repetition of her moans;
Passion on passion deeply is redoubled:
    "Ay me," she cries, and twenty times, "Woe, woe,"
    And twenty echoes twenty times cry so.

She marking them, begins a wailing note, 835
And sings extemporally a woeful ditty:
How love makes young men thrall, and old men dote,
How love is wise in folly, foolish witty.
    Her heavy anthem still concludes in woe,
    And still the quire of echoes answer so. 840

825. *'stonish'd*] bewildered, confounded. See *H5*, v. i. 40.

826. *mistrustful*] fearful, rousing anxiety.

828. *fair discovery*] Steevens, Malone, and later commentators have taken this phrase to mean 'Adonis', and have therefore argued that the true reading is 'discoverer', or that 'discovery' could be used for 'discoverer', as 'divorce' for 'divorcer' (l. 932), or 'conduct' for 'body-guard' in *Tw. N.*, iii. iv. 265. The line is lighter and more attractive without this literal meaning. Adonis has been compared to a star, a jewel, and a lamp, all set against darkness and confusion, and all this is resumed in the word 'fair'. But the 'discovery of her way' evokes a path lit and opened up through surrounding darkness, and we lose this image, and the natural grace of the idiom, if we force an unusual construction on 'discovery'.

829–52.] This passage was probably suggested, as Pooler, Feuillerat, and Bullough point out, by Ovid's descrip-

tion of the lamentations of Narcissus repeated by Echo (*Metam.*, iii. 495–8):

    Quotiensque puer miserabilis
      [Narcissus] 'eheu'
    Dixerat, haec [Echo] resonis
      iterabat vocibus 'eheu';
    Cumque suos manibus percusserat
      ille lacertos,
    Haec quoque reddebat sonitum
      plangoris eundem.

832. *Passion*] lamentation, expression of deep emotion. Compare *John*, iii. iv. 38:

    O! that my tongue were in the
      thunder's mouth!
    Then with a passion would I shake
      the world,

and *Mer. V.*, ii. viii. 12:

    I never heard a passion so confus'd,
    So strange, outrageous, and so
      variable,
    As the dog Jew did utter in the
      streets.

833. *Ay me*] See *Ham.*, iii. iv. 51, and *Ant.*, iii. vi. 76.

837. *thrall*] captive.

Her song was tedious, and outwore the night,
For lovers' hours are long, though seeming short.
If pleas'd themselves, others they think delight
In such like circumstance, with such like sport.
   Their copious stories oftentimes begun,   845
   End without audience, and are never done.

For who hath she to spend the night withal,
But idle sounds resembling parasites,
Like shrill-tongu'd tapsters answering every call,
Soothing the humour of fantastic wits?   850
   She says " 'Tis so," they answer all " 'Tis so,"
   And would say after her, if she said "No."

Lo here the gentle lark, weary of rest,
From his moist cabinet mounts up on high,
And wakes the morning, from whose silver breast   855
The sun ariseth in his majesty;
   Who doth the world so gloriously behold
   That cedar tops and hills seem burnish'd gold.

Venus salutes him with this fair good-morrow,
"Oh thou clear god, and patron of all light,   860
From whom each lamp and shining star doth borrow
The beauteous influence that makes him bright:
   There lives a son that suck'd an earthly mother,
   May lend thee light, as thou dost lend to other."

843. others] *Q1;* other *Q8,12.*   851. says] *Q1;* said *Q5–16.*   863. There] *Q1;* Their *Q5.*

841. *outwore*] outlasted. Compare *F.Q.*, iii. xii. 29:
   All that day she outwore in wandering
   And gazing on that Chambers ornament.

844. *circumstance*] lengthy or deliberate or detailed affairs or descriptions.

847. *who . . . withal*] For this construction see Abbott, §§ 274 and 196. 'Withal' for 'with' is common when the preposition is not followed by its object and is placed at the end of the sentence.

849. *tapsters answering every call*] The comparison recalls the joke played on Francis in *1H4,* ii. iv.

854. *moist*] dewy.
   cabinet] dwelling, lodging. Pooler quotes Lyly, *Woman in the Moone,* iv. i. 162: 'For he hath thrust me from his cabinet', where a cottage is meant.

853–8.] The charm of the stanza has made it hackneyed, yet it must be admired as one of the poem's masterly transitions.

858.] Echoed by Dryden in *The State of Innocence,* Act v, l. 140.

863.] Shakespeare has chosen to forget the fabulous circumstances of Adonis' birth (Ovid, *Metam.,* x. 503–14).

This said, she hasteth to a myrtle grove,   865
Musing the morning is so much o'erworn,
And yet she hears no tidings of her love;
She hearkens for his hounds and for his horn.
 Anon she hears them chant it lustily,
 And all in haste she coasteth to the cry.   870

And as she runs, the bushes in the way,
Some catch her by the neck, some kiss her face,
Some twine about her thigh to make her stay;
She wildly breaketh from their strict embrace,
 Like a milch doe, whose swelling dugs do ache,   875
 Hasting to feed her fawn, hid in some brake.

By this she hears the hounds are at a bay,
Whereat she starts like one that spies an adder
Wreath'd up in fatal folds just in his way,
The fear whereof doth make him shake and shudder: 880
 Even so the timorous yelping of the hounds
 Appals her senses and her spirit confounds.

For now she knows it is no gentle chase,

868. his hounds] *Q1;* hounds *Q5.* 873. twine] *Q7–16;* twin'd *Q1–6.* 882.
Appals] *Q1;* Appales *Q5.*

866–7.] wondering that, although so much of the morning is passed, she hears nothing of her lover.

869. *chant it*] give tongue. The expression recalls 'the musical confusion' of baying hounds in *MND.*, iv. i. 112–24. For 'it' as an indefinite object see Abbott, § 226.

870. *coasteth*] approaches. 'Coast', among other meanings, seems to have associations with hunting. Pooler says: 'It is a favourite word of Turbervile's, often in the sense of running parallel with an animal in order to get ahead of it.' The implication of the word, in all uses, is that movement is sidelong, uncertain, or groping. Here such a sense is appropriate, since Venus moves towards the cry, her only guide, which is itself in movement.

874. *strict*] close, tight.
875–6.] 'Perhaps the most perfect

example of implied emotion in the poem is the description of Venus hurrying to save Adonis, driven by purely animal instinct' (Bradbrook, *op. cit.*, p. 64). Compare *AYL.*, ii. vi. 128 f.:
 Whiles, like a doe, I go to find my
  fawn
 And give it food.
See also *Lucr.*, l. 581 n.

877. *By this*] by this time.
at a bay] The situation when a hunted animal is driven to turn upon the hunters. A passage from Turbervile shows that it can be applied to either the quarry or the hounds: 'A great Bore ... wil sildome keepe houndes at a Baye, unless he be forced; and if he do stand at Baye, the huntsmen must ride in unto him' (Pooler).

883–5.] Root and Feuillerat refer this to Ovid, *Metam.*, x. 539–41:
 A fortibus abstinet apris

But the blunt boar, rough bear, or lion proud,
Because the cry remaineth in one place,   885
Where fearfully the dogs exclaim aloud;
     Finding their enemy to be so curst,
     They all strain court'sy who shall cope him first.

This dismal cry rings sadly in her ear,
Through which it enters to surprise her heart;   890
Who overcome by doubt and bloodless fear,
With cold pale weakness numbs each feeling part:
     Like soldiers when their captain once doth yield,
     They basely fly, and dare not stay the field.

Thus stands she in a trembling ecstasy,   895
Till cheering up her senses all dismay'd,
She tells them 'tis a causeless fantasy,
And childish error, that they are afraid;
     Bids them leave quaking, bids them fear no more,
     And with that word, she spied the hunted boar: 900

896. all dismay'd] *Q1*; sore dismaid *Q4–16*; sore-dismay'd *Malone*.   897.
them] *Q1*; him *Q7,8*.   899. bids] *Q1*; will's *Q9–11,13–16*.

Raptoresque lupos armatosque
     unguibus ursos
Vitat et armenti saturatos caede
     leones.
887. *curst*] malevolent, vicious.
Compare *Ado*, II. i. 25:
God sends a curst cow short horns.
888. *strain court'sy*] exaggerate polite-
ness, hold back to let another go first.
Hounds were said to 'strain courtesy'
when they shrank from closing with
the quarry: 'I haue seene Greyhounds
which . . . would not refuse the wilde
Bore, nor the Wolfe, and yet they
would streyen curtesie at a Foxe'
(Turbervile, *Noble Art of Venerie*, 1576,
ed. 1908, p. 188). The expression was
used sarcastically of anyone who hesi-
tated to take the lead in a dangerous
action. Pooler closely analyses the
term, giving examples of an opposite
sense, in which 'straining courtesy' is
applied to something which might be
taken as a breach of good manners. So
in *Rom.*, II. iv. 55, Romeo speaks of

having broken his appointment: 'Pardon, good Mercutio, my business was
great; and in such a case as mine a
man may strain courtesy'.
cope him] attack him, encounter him
as an opponent. Compare *Lucr.*, l. 99.
889. *dismal*] unlucky, boding misfortune.
892. *each feeling part*] senses and
sense-organs.
893–4.] M. C. Bradbrook points out
the resemblance to *Hero and Leander*,
I. 121–2 (*op. cit.*, p. 65).
894. *stay the field*] remain on the field
of battle, fight the battle out.
895. *ecstasy*] fit of emotion, loss of
self-control. The word retained its
Greek sense of 'being out of oneself'.
Compare *Err.*, IV. iv. 54, and *Ham.*, II.
i. 102:
This is the very ecstasy of love,
and II. i. 168:
That unmatch'd form and feature
     of blown youth
Blasted with ecstasy.

Whose frothy mouth bepainted all with red,
Like milk and blood being mingled both together,
A second fear through all her sinews spread,
Which madly hurries her she knows not whither.
This way she runs, and now she will no further, 905
And back retires, to rate the boar for murther.

A thousand spleens bear her a thousand ways,
She treads the path that she untreads again;
Her more than haste is mated with delays
Like the proceedings of a drunken brain, 910
Full of respects, yet naught at all respecting,
In hand with all things, naught at all effecting.

Here kennell'd in a brake she finds a hound,
And asks the weary caitiff for his master;
And there another licking of his wound, 915
'Gainst venom'd sores the only sovereign plaster.
And here she meets another sadly scowling,
To whom she speaks, and he replies with howling.

When he hath ceas'd his ill-resounding noise,
Another flap-mouth'd mourner, black and grim, 920
Against the welkin volleys out his voice;
Another and another answer him,
Clapping their proud tails to the ground below,
Shaking their scratch'd ears, bleeding as they go.

901. bepainted] *Q1;* be painted *Q5.*   909. mated] *Q1;* marred *Q9–11,13–16.*
911. respects] *Q1;* respect *Q3–16.*   913. she] *Q1;* he *Q4.*   919. hath] *Q1;*
had *Q7–16.*

903. *sinews*] Perhaps in the obsolete sense of 'nerves'.

906. *rate*] scold.

907. *spleens*] morbid fears, angers, or griefs.

909. *mated with*] checked, frustrated. The reference is to chess. Compare *Mac.,* v. i. 86: 'My mind she has mated, and amazed my sight'.

911.] 'Full of consideration, and yet really considering nothing' (Pooler). 'Respects' means 'matters seriously weighed or observed'. Malone comments: 'This is one of our authour's nice observations. No one affects more wisdom than a drunken man'.

912. *In hand with all things*] taking everything in hand, occupying himself with everything.

914. *caitiff*] wretch; used with affectionate contempt.

920. *flap-mouth'd*] with loose hanging lips. In *The Master of Game* 'great lips and well hanging down' are one of the points of 'a running hound' (Pooler).

921. *welkin*] sky. See *Lucr.,* l. 116 and n.

Look how the world's poor people are amazed   925
At apparitions, signs and prodigies,
Whereon with fearful eyes they long have gazed,
Infusing them with dreadful prophecies:
    So she at these sad signs draws up her breath,
    And sighing it again, exclaims on death.   930

"Hard-favour'd tyrant, ugly, meagre, lean,
Hateful divorce of love," thus chides she death:
"Grim-grinning ghost, earth's worm, what dost thou mean,
To stifle beauty and to steal his breath?
    Who when he liv'd, his breath and beauty set   935
    Gloss on the rose, smell to the violet.

"If he be dead,—O no, it cannot be,
Seeing his beauty, thou shouldst strike at it,—
O yes, it may, thou hast no eyes to see,
But hatefully at randon dost thou hit: 940
    Thy mark is feeble age, but thy false dart
    Mistakes that aim, and cleaves an infant's heart.

"Hadst thou but bid beware, then he had spoke,
And hearing him, thy power had lost his power.
The destinies will curse thee for this stroke: 945
    They bid thee crop a weed, thou pluck'st a flower.

---

940. randon] *Q1–6;* randome *Q7-16.*   946. pluck'st] pluckst *Q1–6;* plucktst
Q7,9–13,15; pluktst *Q8,14.*

928. *Infusing them*] As Pooler says, 'It may be doubted whether *them* denotes the world's poor people or the apparitions'. Warburton assumes the latter sense: 'Shakespeare was well acquainted with the nature of popular superstition. . . Here he plainly tells us that signs in the heavens gave birth to prophesies on the earth . . . by infusing fancies into the crazy imagination of the people. . .' It is doubtful whether here 'infusing' has such 18th-cent. precision.

930. *sighing it again*] letting her breath out again.

exclaims on] reproaches, denounces. Compare *1H6*, III. iii. 60:

Besides, all French and France
    exclaim on thee,
Doubting thy birth and lawful
    progeny.

931. *Hard-favour'd*] with a hard or ugly face.

933. *earth's worm*] There is no need to find the meaning 'serpent' in 'worm' as in *Ant.*, v. ii, and elsewhere. Death and worms went together. Shakespeare has perhaps given the association a new twist by a conceit, that Death is a kind of 'worm in the bud' to earth or earthly life. But this is not clear, and the expression is no less effective for its lack of definition.

Love's golden arrow at him should have fled,
And not death's ebon dart to strike him dead.

"Dost thou drink tears, that thou provok'st such weeping?
What may a heavy groan advantage thee?   950
Why hast thou cast into eternal sleeping
Those eyes that taught all other eyes to see?
    Now nature cares not for thy mortal vigour,
    Since her best work is ruin'd with thy rigour."

Here overcome, as one full of despair,   955
She vail'd her eyelids, who like sluices stopp'd
The crystal tide that from her two cheeks fair
In the sweet channel of her bosom dropp'd;
    But through the flood-gates breaks the silver rain,
    And with his strong course opens them again.   960

O how her eyes and tears did lend and borrow!
Her eye seen in the tears, tears in her eye:
Both crystals where they view'd each other's sorrow,
Sorrow that friendly sighs sought still to dry;
    But like a stormy day, now wind, now rain,   965
    Sighs dry her cheeks, tears make them wet again.

Variable passions throng her constant woe,
As striving who should best become her grief;
All entertain'd, each passion labours so,
That every present sorrow seemeth chief,   970
    But none is best: then join they all together,
    Like many clouds consulting for foul weather.

962. Her eye] *Q1*; Her eies *Q6–16*.   968. who] *Q1*; which *Q7–16*.   969.
passion labours] *Q1*; passions labour *Q5,6*.

947–8.] The dart of death was often
coupled with the dart of love in
Renaissance poetry and art. 'Ebon'
probably means no more than 'black',
though ebony wood could be used for
a bow, if not for an arrow: see *F.Q.*, I,
Prol. 3:

    Lay now thy deadly Heben bowe
        apart.

950. *advantage*] help, profit.

953. *mortal vigour*] deadly power.
Nature no longer cares how destruc-
tive Death may be.

956. *vail'd*] lowered. See l. 314.
Pooler quotes *Lust's Dominion*, I. iii. 4:
'vailing my knees to the cold earth'.

sluices] floodgates.

963. *crystals*] The conceit derives
from the notion of a magic crystal, 'in
which one in sympathy with another
could see the scene of his distress'
(Wyndham).

968. *striving*] competing.

969. *entertain'd*] received or admitted.

972. *consulting*] The conceit is that

By this, far off she hears some huntsman holla:
A nurse's song ne'er pleas'd her babe so well.
The dire imagination she did follow   975
This sound of hope doth labour to expel;
    For now reviving joy bids her rejoice,
    And flatters her it is Adonis' voice.

Whereat her tears began to turn their tide,
Being prison'd in her eye like pearls in glass;   980
Yet sometimes falls an orient drop beside,
Which her cheek melts, as scorning it should pass
    To wash the foul face of the sluttish ground,
    Who is but drunken when she seemeth drown'd.

O hard-believing love, how strange it seems   985
Not to believe, and yet too credulous!
Thy weal and woe are both of them extremes;
Despair and hope makes thee ridiculous:
    The one doth flatter thee in thoughts unlikely,
    In likely thoughts the other kills thee quickly.   990

Now she unweaves the web that she hath wrought:
Adonis lives, and death is not to blame;
It was not she that call'd him all to naught;

973. holla] *Malone;* hallow *Q1–4,6;* hollow *Q5,7–16.*   975. dire] *Q1;* drie *Q5–8,12.*   981. sometimes] *Q1;* sometime *Q6–16.*   988. makes] *Q1;* make *Q7–16.*   990. In] *Q1;* The *Q4,5;* With *Q6–16.*   991. hath] *Q1;* had *Q7–16.* 992. to] *Q1;* too *Q5–11,13.*

clouds gather and plot to cause a storm.

973. *By this*] See l. 877 n.

975. *The dire imagination*] The death of Adonis, which she was following, led by the sound of the hunt.

979. *turn their tide*] ebb.

980. *pearls in glass*] See ll. 362–3.

981. *orient*] Jewels were often called 'orient', with some confusion between their associations with the East and the literal meaning of the word applied to the rising sun. Pooler quotes Harrison's *Description of England*, 1577, III. xii: 'Pearls are called orient, because of the clearenesse, which resembleth the colour of the cleere aire before the rising of the sun'.

985–8.] The total meaning is obvious enough, but it is difficult to gloss the first two lines. Two alternatives appear: (i) 'O sceptical love, that seems so wary of believing, and yet is too credulous!' (ii) 'O sceptical love, that seems so wary of believing, and yet (too credulous!), thy weal and woe', etc. Compare *Hero and Leander*, II. 221 f.:

Love is too full of faith, too credulous,
With folly and false hope deluding us.

992. *to blame*] to be blamed, blameworthy.

993. *all to naught*] worthless, vile. Pooler points out that Swift uses the

Now she adds honours to his hateful name:
>   She clepes him king of graves, and grave for kings,   995
>   Imperious supreme of all mortal things.

"No, no," quoth she, "sweet death, I did but jest;
Yet pardon me, I felt a kind of fear
Whenas I met the boar, that bloody beast,
Which knows no pity, but is still severe: 1000
>   Then, gentle shadow,—truth I must confess,—
>   I rail'd on thee, fearing my love's decease.

" 'Tis not my fault, the boar provok'd my tongue:
Be wreak'd on him, invisible commander.
'Tis he, foul creature, that hath done thee wrong: 1005
I did but act, he's author of thy slander.
>   Grief hath two tongues, and never woman yet
>   Could rule them both, without ten women's wit."

Thus hoping that Adonis is alive,
Her rash suspect she doth extenuate;   1010
And that his beauty may the better thrive,
With death she humbly doth insinuate;
>   Tells him of trophies, statues, tombs, and stories
>   His victories, his triumphs and his glories.

"O love," quoth she, "how much a fool was I,   1015
To be of such a weak and silly mind,
To wail his death who lives, and must not die
'Till mutual overthrow of mortal kind!
>   For he being dead, with him is beauty slain,
>   And beauty dead, black Chaos comes again.   1020

994. honours] *Q1;* honour *Q6-16.*   996. Imperious] *Q1;* Imperiall *Q6-16.*
1000. no] *Q1;* not *Q8.*   1002. my] *Q1;* thy *Q4,5.*   decease] decesse *Q1.*

phrase in *Mrs Harris's Petition*: 'So she
roar'd like a Bedlam, as tho' I had
call'd her all to nought'. 'All to' may
be adverbial, intensifying the following word, as in 'all-to-torn' or 'all-to-
rent'.

995. *clepes*] names.
996. *supreme*] ruler. The accent is on
the first syllable. The word as a substantive occurs again in *Phoen.*, l. 51.
999. *Whenas*] when.
1001. *shadow*] spectre.

1004. *Be wreak'd*] be revenged.
1006. *author*] inventor, originator.
1010. *suspect*] suspicion.
1012. *insinuate*] flatter, insinuate
herself.
1013. *stories*] relates.
1018. *mutual*] common, as in 'a
mutual friend'.
1020.] With this hyperbole com-
pare *Rom.*, I. i. 222 f., and *Oth.*, III. iii.
91 f., as well as various lines in the
Sonnets. Here the cosmic application

"Fie, fie, fond love, thou art as full of fear
As one with treasure laden, hemm'd with thieves!
Trifles unwitnessed with eye or ear
Thy coward heart with false bethinking grieves."
    Even at this word she hears a merry horn,   1025
    Whereat she leaps that was but late forlorn.

As falcons to the lure, away she flies;
The grass stoops not, she treads on it so light,
And in her haste unfortunately spies
The foul boar's conquest on her fair delight: 1030
    Which seen, her eyes as murder'd with the view,
    Like stars asham'd of day, themselves withdrew.

Or as the snail, whose tender horns being hit,
Shrinks backward in his shelly cave with pain,
And there all smother'd up in shade doth sit,   1035
Long after fearing to creep forth again:
    So at his bloody view her eyes are fled
    Into the deep dark cabins of her head.

Where they resign their office and their light
To the disposing of her troubled brain,   1040
Who bids them still consort with ugly night

1021. as] *Q1;* so *Q4–16.*   1027. falcons] *Q1;* falcon *Q7–16.*   1031. as] *Q3–*
11,13–16; are *Q1,2,12.*   1040. her] *Q1;* their *Q8,12.*

---

of the conceit recalls the loose Platonic tradition within which Shakespeare wrote, best represented in English by Spenser's *Fowre Hymnes.* Baldwin devotes a chapter to this passage seen in relation to Neo-Latin poets, and to Shakespeare's reading of Golding's Ovid (*op. cit.,* pp. 49–72).

1022. *hemm'd*] surrounded. See l. 229 n.

1023. *unwitnessed with*] unconfirmed by.

1024. *bethinking*] the action of thinking, considering.

1026. *leaps*] jumps for joy. See Sonnet xcviii, l. 4, and *LLL.,* IV. iii. 148:

How will he triumph, leap and
    laugh at it!

1027. *lure*] A 'lure' was a term of fal-conry, usually meaning a bundle of feathers with bits of flesh attached, representing a bird, and used to train falcons or to tempt them to return to the falconer. It came also to mean the falconer's call or whistle to the bird to return.

1028.] Steevens first cited *Aeneid,* VII. 808 f. The lightness of Venus was a commonplace; see l. 148 n.

1032. *asham'd of day*] put to shame by day.

1033–4.] Compare *LLL.,* IV. iii. 338:

Love's feeling is more soft and
    sensible
Than are the tender horns of
    cockled snails.

1038. *cabins*] See l. 637 n.

1041. *still consort with*] always keep

And never wound the heart with looks again;
  Who like a king perplexed in his throne
  By their suggestion, gives a deadly groan.

Whereat each tributary subject quakes,   1045
As when the wind imprison'd in the ground,
Struggling for passage, earth's foundation shakes;
Which with cold terror doth men's minds confound.
    This mutiny each part doth so surprise
    That from their dark beds once more leap her eyes: 1050

And being open'd threw unwilling light
Upon the wide wound that the boar had trench'd
In his soft flank, whose wonted lily-white
With purple tears that his wound wept, was drench'd.
    No flower was nigh, no grass, herb, leaf or weed,   1055
    But stole his blood and seem'd with him to bleed.

This solemn sympathy poor Venus noteth;
Over one shoulder doth she hang her head.
Dumbly she passions, franticly she doteth:
She thinks he could not die, he is not dead.   1060
    Her voice is stopp'd, her joints forget to bow,
    Her eyes are mad, that they have wept till now.

Upon his hurt she looks so steadfastly
That her sight dazzling makes the wound seem three;

1051. light] *Q1*; night *Q4,5*; sight *Q7–16*.   1052. trench'd] trencht *Q1*;
drencht *Q4,5*.   1054. was] *Q7–11,13–16*; had *Q1–6*.

company with. Compare *MND.*, III.
ii. 387:
    They wilfully themselves exile from
        light,
    And must for aye consort with
        black-brow'd night.
    1046–8.] Subterranean wind was
supposed to be the cause of earth-
quakes. See *1H4*, III. i. 28–33. The
theory came from Aristotle and Pliny.
    1052. *trench'd*] cut. Compare *Mac.*,
III. iv. 27:
    With twenty trenched gashes on
        his head.
    1054. *purple tears*] See l. 1 n. for
purple'.

    1059. *passions*] suffers, expresses
passion. Compare *Gent.*, IV. iv. 174:
    Madam, 'twas Ariadne passioning
    For Theseus' perjury and unjust
        flight.
    1062.] Her eyes are distracted to
think that they have wept already,
now that they have true cause to
weep.
    1063–8.] These hallucinations are
convincing symptoms of extreme grief
or hysteria.
    1064. *dazzling*] Compare *3H6*, II. i.
25:
    Dazzle mine eyes, or do I see three
        suns?

And then she reprehends her mangling eye,   1065
That makes more gashes, where no breach should be.
  His face seems twain, each several limb is doubled,
  For oft the eye mistakes, the brain being troubled.

"My tongue cannot express my grief for one,
And yet," quoth she, "behold two Adons dead!   1070
My sighs are blown away, my salt tears gone;
Mine eyes are turn'd to fire, my heart to lead.
  Heavy heart's lead melt at mine eyes' red fire!
  So I shall die by drops of hot desire.

"Alas, poor world, what treasure hast thou lost!   1075
What face remains alive that's worth the viewing?
What tongue is music now? what canst thou boast
Of things long since, or any thing ensuing?
  The flowers are sweet, their colours fresh and trim,
  But true sweet beauty liv'd and died with him.   1080

"Bonnet nor veil henceforth no creature wear:
Nor sun nor wind will ever strive to kiss you.
Having no fair to lose, you need not fear:
The sun doth scorn you and the wind doth hiss you.
  But when Adonis liv'd, sun and sharp air   1085
  Lurk'd like two thieves to rob him of his fair.

"And therefore would he put his bonnet on,
Under whose brim the gaudy sun would peep:
The wind would blow it off, and being gone,
Play with his locks; then would Adonis weep,   1090

1073. eyes' red fire] eyes red fire *Q1*; eyes red as fire *Q4*; eies as red as fire *Q5*;
eyes, as fire *Q7–15*.   1080. with] *Q1*; in *Q4,5,7–16*.   1081. nor] *Q1*;
or *Q7–11,13–16*.

1078. *ensuing*] following, and so,
future.
  1079. *trim*] in good condition.
  1083. *fair*] beauty. Pooler quotes
from Greene's *Menaphon* (*Plays and
Poems*, ed. Churton Collins, vol. II,
p. 257):
    No frost their faire, no wind doth
      wast their power,
    But by her breath her beauties doo
      renew.

1084. *hiss you*] Compare *Rom.*, I. i.
117:
    He swung about his head, and cut
      the winds,
    Who, nothing hurt withal, hiss'd
      him in scorn.
  1085. *sharp air*] cold air.
  1088. *gaudy*] bright. Compare *2H6*,
IV. i. 1.
  1089. *being gone*] the bonnet being
gone.

And straight, in pity of his tender years,
They both would strive who first should dry his tears.

"To see his face the lion walk'd along,
Behind some hedge, because he would not fear him.
To recreate himself, when he hath sung,   1095
The tiger would be tame and gently hear him.
    If he had spoke, the wolf would leave his prey,
    And never fright the silly lamb that day.

"When he beheld his shadow in the brook,
The fishes spread on it their golden gills;   1100
When he was by, the birds such pleasure took
That some would sing, some other in their bills
    Would bring him mulberries and ripe red cherries:
    He fed them with his sight, they him with berries.

But this foul, grim, and urchin-snouted boar,   1105
Whose downward eye still looketh for a grave,
Ne'er saw the beauteous livery that he wore;
Witness the entertainment that he gave.
    If he did see his face, why then I know
    He thought to kiss him, and hath kill'd him so.   1110

'Tis true, 'tis true, thus was Adonis slain:
He ran upon the boar with his sharp spear,
Who did not whet his teeth at him again,
But by a kiss thought to persuade him there;

1095. sung] *Q14;* song *Q1–13.*   1099. his] *Q1;* the *Q5.*   the] *Q1;* a *Q9–11.*
13–16.   1113. did] *Q1;* would *Q2–16.*

1094. *fear*] frighten. Compare *3H6*,
v. ii. 2:
    For Warwick was a bug that fear'd
    us all.
    1105. *urchin-snouted*] snouted like a
hedgehog, i.e. looking down on the
ground.
    1107. *livery*] dress, outward appear-
ance. The word suggests bright colour.
    1108. *entertainment*] reception.
    1110.] This conceit goes back to
Theocritus, *Id.,* xxx. 26–31, which is
among the *Sixe Idillia* translated by
E. D. in 1588; but the fancy had
already been reproduced in several

16th-cent. poems, such as Minturno's
epigram *De Adoni ab apro interempto,*
and Tarchagnota's *L'Adone* (1550).
No Elizabethan poet reading up the
myth could fail to come across some
version of this bauble. A. T. Hatto
argues that Shakespeare has added
associations from medieval poetry,
including *Troilus and Criseyde*, v. 177–8.
In his view the boar has erotic significance, as an accepted symbol of
prepotent virility (see ' "Venus and
Adonis"—and the Boar', *Modern Language Review*, vol. XLI, pp. 353–61).
    1114. *to persuade him there*] This may

And nuzzling in his flank, the loving swine 1115
Sheath'd unaware the tusk in his soft groin.

"Had I been tooth'd like him, I must confess,
With kissing him I should have kill'd him first.
But he is dead, and never did he bless
My youth with his; the more am I accurst." 1120
With this she falleth in the place she stood,
And stains her face with his congealed blood.

She looks upon his lips, and they are pale;
She takes him by the hand, and that is cold.
She whispers in his ears a heavy tale, 1125
As if they heard the woeful words she told.
She lifts the coffer-lids that close his eyes,
Where lo, two lamps burnt out in darkness lies.

Two glasses where herself herself beheld
A thousand times, and now no more reflect; 1130
Their virtue lost, wherein they late excell'd,
And every beauty robb'd of his effect.
"Wonder of time," quoth she, "this is my spite,
That thou being dead, the day should yet be light.

"Since thou art dead, lo here I prophesy, 1135
Sorrow on love hereafter shall attend:
It shall be waited on with jealousy,
Find sweet beginning, but unsavoury end;
Ne'er settled equally, but high or low,
That all love's pleasure shall not match his woe. 1140

"It shall be fickle, false and full of fraud;
Bud, and be blasted, in a breathing while;

1116. the] *Q1*; his *Q2–16*.   1120. am I] *Q1*; I am *Q4–16*.   1125. ears] *Q1*; eare, *Q5–16*.   1126. they] *Q1*; he *Q6–16*.   1134. thou] *Q1*; you *Q5–16*.   1136. on] *Q1*; in *Q5*.   1139. but] *Q1*; too *Q6–16*.   1142. Bud, and] *Q1*; And shall *Q5–16*.

mean 'to persuade him to stay there', or 'to be reconciled to him there'.

1115. *nuzzling*] pushing with the nose, or nestling into.

1115–16.] Feuillerat compares Ovid, *Metam.*, x. 715 f.:

Trux aper insequitur totosque sub inguine dentes

Abdidit et fulva moribundum stravit harena.

1127. *coffer-lids*] lids to treasure-chests. Compare *Tw. N.*, i. v. 268.

1133. *spite*] grief. Compare *Err.*, iv. ii. 8.

1142. *in a breathing while*] in one breath. Compare *R3*, i. iii. 60:

The bottom poison, and the top o'erstraw'd
With sweets that shall the truest sight beguile;
  The strongest body shall it make most weak,   1145
  Strike the wise dumb, and teach the fool to speak.

"It shall be sparing, and too full of riot,
  Teaching decrepit age to tread the measures;
The staring ruffian shall it keep in quiet,
  Pluck down the rich, enrich the poor with treasures;   1150
  It shall be raging mad, and silly mild,
  Make the young old, the old become a child.

"It shall suspect where is no cause of fear,
  It shall not fear where it should most mistrust;
It shall be merciful, and too severe,   1155
  And most deceiving when it seems most just;
  Perverse it shall be, where it shows most toward;
  Put fear to valour, courage to the coward.

"It shall be cause of war and dire events,
  And set dissension 'twixt the son and sire;   1160
Subject and servile to all discontents,
  As dry combustious matter is to fire.
  Sith in his prime death doth my love destroy,
  They that love best, their loves shall not enjoy."

By this the boy that by her side lay kill'd   1165
Was melted like a vapour from her sight,
And in his blood that on the ground lay spill'd,
A purple flower sprung up, checker'd with white,

1143. o'erstraw'd] ore-strawd *Q1;* ore-straw *Q5.*   1144. truest] *Q1;* sharpest
Q5–16.   1157. shows] *Q1;* seems *Q7–16.*   1162. combustious] *Q1;* com-
bustions *Q3,4.*   1164. loves] *Q1;* love *Q5–16.*   1168. purple] *Q1;* purpld *Q4.*
purpul'd *Q5.*

Cannot be quiet scarce a breathing-
  while.
  1143. *o'erstraw'd*] strewn. Compare
Herbert, *Easter,* l. 19:
    I got me flowers to straw thy
      way.
  1147.] It shall be both niggardly and
prodigal.
  1148. *tread the measures*] dance.
  1149. *staring*] truculent. Compare
Pope, *Essay on Criticism,* ll. 586–7:

And stares, tremendous, with a
  threat'ning eye,
Like some fierce tyrant in old
  tapestry.
  1157. *toward*] docile, tractable.
Compare *Shr.,* v. ii. 183:
  'Tis a good hearing when children
    are toward.
  1168. *A purple flower*] The species remains vague, but Shakespeare no doubt
meant to follow *Metam.,* x. 731–9,

Resembling well his pale cheeks and the blood
Which in round drops upon their whiteness stood.   1170

She bows her head, the new-sprung flower to smell,
Comparing it to her Adonis' breath,
And says within her bosom it shall dwell,
Since he himself is reft from her by death.
 She crops the stalk, and in the breach appears   1175
 Green-dropping sap, which she compares to tears.

"Poor flower," quoth she, "this was thy father's guise,—
Sweet issue of a more sweet-smelling sire,—
For every little grief to wet his eyes;
To grow unto himself was his desire,   1180
 And so 'tis thine; but know, it is as good
 To wither in my breast as in his blood.

"Here was thy father's bed, here in my breast;
Thou art the next of blood, and 'tis thy right.
Lo in this hollow cradle take thy rest;   1185
My throbbing heart shall rock thee day and night:
 There shall not be one minute in an hour
 Wherein I will not kiss my sweet love's flower."

Thus weary of the world, away she hies,
And yokes her silver doves, by whose swift aid   1190
Their mistress mounted through the empty skies,
In her light chariot quickly is convey'd,
 Holding their course to Paphos, where their queen
 Means to immure herself and not be seen.

FINIS

1183. in] *Q1*; is *Q4–16*. 1185. Lo] *Q1*; Low *Q5,6*. 1187. in] *Q1*; of *Q7–16*.

where the anemone springs from Adonis' blood. Compare *MND.*, II. i. 166–7.
 1175. *crops the stalk*] breaks the
flower off by the stalk.
 breach] the break in the stalk.
 1177. *guise*] habit.
 1180.] See l. 166.
 1189–94.] Nothing in *Venus and
Adonis* is better than this last stanza.
The poem has been given its beauty by
its speed, by sudden fancies and dart-

ing digressions which have kept it in
constant movement; and by changes
of perspective and sudden wider-
opening views such as ll. 811–16. All
these effects are combined in these last
six lines, and Venus vanishes with a
flutter in clear skies. Compare *Tp.*,
IV. i. 92–4: I met her Deity
 Cutting the clouds towards Paphos,
  and her son
 Dove-drawn with her.

LUCRECE

To the Right Honourable
Henry Wriothesley, Earl of Southampton,
and Baron of Titchfield.

The love I dedicate to your Lordship is without end; whereof this pamphlet without beginning is but a superfluous moiety. The warrant I have of your Honourable disposition, not the worth of my untutored lines, makes it assured of acceptance. What I have done is yours, what I have to do is yours, being part in all I have devoted yours. Were my worth greater, my duty would show greater; meantime, as it is, it is bound to your Lordship, to whom I wish long life still lengthened with all happiness.

Your Lordship's in all duty,
William Shakespeare.

THE ARGUMENT

Lucius Tarquinius (for his excessive pride surnamed Superbus), after he had caused his own father-in-law Servius Tullius to be cruelly murdered, and, contrary to the Roman laws and customs, not requiring or staying for the people's suffrages, had possessed himself of the kingdom, went, accompanied with his sons and other noblemen of Rome, to besiege Ardea. During which siege, the principal men of the army meeting one evening at the tent of Sextus Tarquinius, the King's son, in their discourses after supper everyone commended the virtues of his own wife; among whom Collatinus extolled the incomparable chastity of his wife Lucretia. In that pleasant humour they all posted to Rome, and, intending by their secret and sudden arrival to make trial of that which everyone had before avouched, only Collatinus finds his wife, though it were late in the night, spinning amongst her maids; the other ladies were all found dancing and revelling, or in several disports. Whereupon the noblemen yielded Collatinus the victory, and his wife the fame. At that time Sextus Tarquinius, being inflamed with Lucrece' beauty, yet smothering his passions for the present, departed with the rest back to the camp; from whence he shortly after privily withdrew himself, and was, according to his estate, royally entertained and lodged by Lucrece at Collatium. The same night he treacherously stealeth into her chamber, violently ravished her, and early in the morning speedeth away. Lucrece, in this lamentable plight, hastily despatcheth messengers, one to Rome for her father, another to the camp for Collatine. They

THE ARGUMENT] Baldwin (*op. cit.,* pp. 108–12) shows that Shakespeare, in writing the Argument, had before him an annotated edition of Ovid's *Fasti* and a text of Livy's *Historia*; he may also have used Cooper's *Thesaurus* 'the standard and only full dictionary of his day in England', and Painter's translation of Livy. The result is a passage of English prose modelled on Latin, and completely different from any of Shakespeare's dramatic prose. Bullough refers to the 'apparent dis- crepancy between the Argument and the first three stanzas, which say nothing of the test by which Collatine proved his wife's virtue, but suggest that he boasted of her chastity a second time, on the night before Tarquin stole away from Ardea' (*op. cit.,* p. 180). He suggests that 'the poem was written without regard to the first journey and test,' (hence 'without beginning', in the Dedication), 'and the Argument was written later with the full story in mind'.

came, the one accompanied with Junius Brutus, the other with Publius Valerius; and finding Lucrece attired in mourning habit, demanded the cause of her sorrow. She, first taking an oath of them for her revenge, revealed the actor, and whole manner of his dealing, and withal suddenly stabbed herself. Which done, with one consent they all vowed to root out the whole hated family of the Tarquins and, bearing the dead body to Rome, Brutus acquainted the people with the doer and manner of the vile deed, with a bitter invective against the tyranny of the King. Wherewith the people were so moved, that with one consent and a general acclamation the Tarquins were all exiled, and the state government changed from kings to consuls.

LUCRECE

From the besieged Ardea all in post,
Borne by the trustless wings of false desire,
Lust-breathed Tarquin leaves the Roman host
And to Collatium bears the lightless fire,
Which in pale embers hid, lurks to aspire,   5
   And girdle with embracing flames the waist
   Of Collatine's fair love, Lucrece the chaste.

Haply that name of "chaste" unhapp'ly set
This bateless edge on his keen appetite,
When Collatine unwisely did not let   10
To praise the clear unmatched red and white
Which triumph'd in that sky of his delight;
   Where mortal stars as bright as heaven's beauties,
   With pure aspects did him peculiar duties.

8. unhapp'ly] unhap'ly *Q1*.   13. stars] *Q1;* star *Q6–9*.

1. *Ardea*] The accent is on the first syllable. Ardea, 'the capital of the Rutuli', was twenty-four miles south of Rome (Verity).

all in post] in great haste. To ride or travel post was to change horses at inns or other halts, hence to travel as swiftly as possible.

2. *trustless*] treacherous. Compare Sonnet cxxix, where lust is
  Savage, extreme, rude, cruel, not to trust.

3. *Lust-breathed*] inspired, invigorated by lust.

4. *lightless*] smouldering, dark, hidden.

5. *Which in pale embers hid, lurks*] While this is good in itself, and a gloss upon 'lightless' in the previous line, it also shows how the stanza encourages prolixity.

aspire] rise, mount up. Compare *Wiv.*, v. v. 101:

  whose flames aspire
As thoughts do blow them higher and higher.

7. *Lucrece*] The name occurs thirty-four times in the poem, and is usually accented on the first syllable. Here and in l. 512, the accent may be shifted to the second.

8.] Modern spelling conceals the play upon 'hap'ly' (happily) and 'unhap'ly' (unhappily).

9. *bateless*] not to be blunted. In *Ham.*, iv. vii. 139, a foil without a button is called 'unbated'.

appetite] lust. In Elizabethan usage, sexual desire often has an 'edge'; this is a source of much word-play.

10. *let*] forbear. Compare l. 328.

12. *that sky of his delight*] Lucrece's face.

13. *mortal stars*] eyes.

14. *aspects*] glances, looks. The sense is coloured by the original astrological

67

For he the night before, in Tarquin's tent   15
Unlock'd the treasure of his happy state:
What priceless wealth the heavens had him lent,
In the possession of his beauteous mate;
Reck'ning his fortune at such high proud rate
    That kings might be espoused to more fame,   20
    But king nor peer to such a peerless dame.

O happiness enjoy'd but of a few,
And if possess'd, as soon decay'd and done
As is the morning's silver melting dew
Against the golden splendour of the sun!   25
An expir'd date cancell'd ere well begun!
    Honour and beauty in the owner's arms,
    Are weakly fortress'd from a world of harms.

Beauty itself doth of itself persuade
The eyes of men without an orator;   30
What needeth then apologies be made,
To set forth that which is so singular?

17. heavens] *Q1*; heaven *Q4*.   19. such high proud] *Q1*; so high a *Q6–9*.
21. peer] *Q1*; prince *Q2–9*.   24. is] *Q1*; in *Q4*; if *Q6–9*.   morning's]
mornings *Q1* (*all copies except Malone 34 and Yale, which have* morning).   silver
melting] *Q1*; silver melted *Q4*.   26. An . . . well] *Q1*; A date expir'd: and
canceld ere *Q6–9*.   31. apologies] Apologies *Q1* (*all copies except Malone 34 and
Yale, which have* Appologie).

meaning. An 'aspect' was the relative positions of the planets as seen from the earth at any given time. Compare *Troil.*, I. iii. 92.

peculiar] The Latin sense of 'private' or 'particular' is preserved.

15. *the night before*] 'Only Ovid gives such a sense of haste, and he is not quite so definite as Shakespeare' (Porter). The striving for speed in the succession of events is an interesting feature of these poems, clearly related to Shakespeare's practice in drama.

19. *high proud*] The intensifying use of 'high' appears also in *All's W.*, v. iii. 36, 'high-repented blames' and *Tw. N.*, I. i. 15.

21.] For similar jingles or puns see ll. 43–4 and l. 342.

22. *of*] by. See *Ven.*, l. 718.

23. *done*] consumed. See *Ven.*, l. 749.

26. *expir'd*] The accent is on the first syllable. Such recessions of accent were common in Elizabethan and 17th-cent. verse, and perhaps in speech. See also ll. 87, 230, 780, 828, 1805.

date] The meaning here would seem to be 'lease' or 'bond'. Compare Sonnet xviii:
    And summer's lease hath all too
        short a date.
For the recurrence of 'date' and 'cancelled' see ll. 934–5 and l. 1729.

29–42.] The psychology of Iachimo's challenge to Posthumus in *Cym.*, I. iv is akin to Tarquin's reaction here.

31. *apologies*] Perhaps 'eulogies', though Pooler considers that 'defence' is enough.

32. *singular*] rare.

Or why is Collatine the publisher
  Of that rich jewel he should keep unknown
  From thievish ears, because it is his own ?   35

Perchance his boast of Lucrece' sov'reignty
Suggested this proud issue of a king;
For by our ears our hearts oft tainted be.
Perchance that envy of so rich a thing,
Braving compare, disdainfully did sting   40
  His high-pitch'd thoughts, that meaner men should vaunt
  That golden hap which their superiors want.

But some untimely thought did instigate
His all-too-timeless speed, if none of those;
His honour, his affairs, his friends, his state,   45
Neglected all, with swift intent he goes
To quench the coal which in his liver glows.
  O rash false heat, wrapp'd in repentant cold,
  Thy hasty spring still blasts and ne'er grows old !

When at Collatium this false lord arrived,   50
Well was he welcom'd by the Roman dame,
Within whose face beauty and virtue strived

41. high-pitch'd] high pitcht *Q2*; high picht *Q1*.   47. his] *Q1*; the
Q4.   glows] *Q1*; growes *Q4,8,9*.   48. repentant] *Q1*; repentance *Q3,4*.
50. Collatium] Colatium *Q1* (*Malone 34, Yale; all other copies of Q1 have
Colatia*).   arrived] arriued *Q1* (*all copies except Malone 34 and Yale, which have
ariued*).

33. *publisher*] one who reveals or
makes public. Compare *Gent.*, III. i.
34:
  For love of you, not hate unto my
    friend,
  Hath made me publisher of this
    pretence.
37. *Suggested*] prompted, tempted.
Compare *Gent.*, III. i. 34:
  Knowing that tender youth is soon
    suggested,
  I nightly lodge her in an upper
    tower.
See also *Mac.*, I. iii. 134, *Pilgr.*, II. 2,
and *Ven.*, l. 651 n.
  issue] child.
  40. *Braving compare*] challenging
comparison. See *Ven.*, l. 8.

disdainfully] with disdain, or indignation.
  42. *hap*] luck, fortune.
  43–4. *untimely . . . timeless*] The word-
play is characteristic.
  44. *all-too-timeless*] too speedy.
  47. *liver*] The liver was supposed to
be the seat of sexual desire. See *Tp.*, IV.
i. 56, *Wiv.*, II. i. 121, and *Ado*, IV. i.
233.
  49.] Malone compares *R3*, III. i. 94:
  Short summers lightly have a
    forward spring.
  blasts] is blasted.
  52–70.] One could scarcely find a
better example of the poetic procedure
of *Lucrece*. Pooler comments: 'The
general sense is obvious. Seeing

Which of them both should underprop her fame.
When virtue bragg'd, beauty would blush for shame;
    When beauty boasted blushes, in despite   55
    Virtue would stain that o'er with silver white.

But beauty in that white entituled
From Venus' doves, doth challenge that fair field;
Then virtue claims from beauty beauty's red,
Which virtue gave the golden age to gild   60
Their silver cheeks, and call'd it then their shield;
    Teaching them thus to use it in the fight,
    When shame assail'd, the red should fence the white.

56. o'er] ore *Q1–4;* or'e *Q5;* o're *Q6–9.*

Lucrece, one would hesitate to say whether her face expressed more completely the perfection of beauty or the perfection of virtue. . . Nature's own red and white are identified or confounded with a blush and its fading. The transition to gold and silver may be natural and was certainly common, and these in turn suggest the or and argent of heraldry, so that for a moment we have a glimpse of Lucrece's face as a blazoned shield for which beauty and virtue are rival claimants. The imagery suffers from the intrusion of the idea of a shield used for defence, and finally changes (in l. 71) to the lilies and roses, *lilia mixta rosis,* of convention.' M. C. Bradbrook perhaps takes from this passage the idea of 'moral heraldry' which she applies both to *Lucrece* and to *Titus Andronicus* (*op. cit.,* pp. 104–16). She refers to *Astrophel and Stella,* Sonnet xiii, for a similar description of the lady's face as a shield. But 'moral heraldry' seems to mean only a certain staring or brilliant artificiality of treatment, and here in contexts which fail of their effect. The phrase may describe some of our impressions; but Miss Bradbrook uses it to persuade us that Shakespeare has in mind a special poetic convention or method, and that we should consequently try to judge his effects by some special standard, though she admits of

Titus that 'It is quite possible that Shakespeare himself did not know exactly what he meant by this play' (*op. cit.,* p. 110).

53. *underprop*] support.

56. *o'er*] It was suggested by Malone that the true reading is *or,* as opposed to the argent of 'silver white'. But to 'stain over' would be for virtue to spread her own colour over beauty; and, complex as Shakespeare's fusions of imagery are, Malone's reading would seem to over-complicate the development of the various conceits. Steevens pointed out the parallel between this passage and *Mac.,* ii. iii. 118:

His silver skin laced with his
    golden blood.

57. *entituled*] having a title or claim.

58.] Beauty's claim is meant to derive 'from Venus' doves', always described as white. See *Pilgr.,* ix. 3.

59–63.] Virtue makes a counter-claim to the possession of beauty's colour, red, because it is also the colour of shame, virtue's defence.

58. *field*] 'Field is here equivocally used. The war of lilies and roses requires a *field* of battle; the *heraldry* in the preceding stanza demands another field, i.e. the ground or surface of a shield or escutcheon armorial' (Steevens).

63. *fence*] shut in, defend.

This heraldry in Lucrece' face was seen,
Argu'd by beauty's red and virtue's white;   65
Of either's colour was the other queen,
Proving from world's minority their right.
Yet their ambition makes them still to fight;
   The sov'reignty of either being so great,
   That oft they interchange each other's seat.   70

This silent war of lilies and of roses,
Which Tarquin view'd in her fair face's field,
In their pure ranks his traitor eye encloses;
Where, lest between them both it should be kill'd,
The coward captive vanquished doth yield   75
   To those two armies, that would let him go
   Rather than triumph in so false a foe.

Now thinks he that her husband's shallow tongue,—
The niggard prodigal that prais'd her so,—
In that high task hath done her beauty wrong,   80
Which far exceeds his barren skill to show.
Therefore that praise which Collatine doth owe
   Enchanted Tarquin answers with surmise,
   In silent wonder of still-gazing eyes.

73. eye] *Q1;* eyes *Q4.*   82. that] *Q1;* the *Q4.*

65. *Argu'd*] expressed. Compare *3H6*, III. ii. 84.

66.] The sense is that both beauty and virtue had a right to both colours, as each had claimed in the preceding stanza.

67. *from world's minority*] referring back to 'the golden age', and to 'Venus' doves'. The notion of a chivalric contest is vaguely borne out by the legal term 'minority'.

68–70.] Despite the undoubted right both beauty and virtue have to both red and white, their aspirations drive them to war; for each has so much power ('sovereignty') that it is often able to usurp that of the other.

69. *sov'reignty*] Wyndham finds here a distinct heraldic meaning: 'the dignity attaching to certain dispositions of heraldic bearings'.

71. *silent war*] There is a rapid and intricate development of metaphor, from warring colours to an army, or two armies, which take captive the observer's eye. Compare *Shr.*, IV. v. 30:

   Such war of red and white within
     her cheeks.

See also *Ven.*, l. 346.

82–3.] The debt of praise which Collatine left unpaid is paid by Tarquin in the form of admiration.

answers] pays. Compare *Err.*, IV. i. 82:

   you shall buy this sport as dear
   As all the metal in your shop shall
     answer.

Also *1H4*, I. iii. 185:

   who studies day and night
   To answer all the debt he owes to
     you.

surmise] conjecture, imagination. See *2H4*, I. iii. 23, and l. 1579 below.

This earthly saint adored by this devil,   85
Little suspecteth the false worshipper;
For unstain'd thoughts do seldom dream on evil,
Birds never lim'd no secret bushes fear:
So guiltless she securely gives good cheer
    And reverend welcome to her princely guest,   90
    Whose inward ill no outward harm express'd.

For that he colour'd with his high estate,
Hiding base sin in pleats of majesty,
That nothing in him seem'd inordinate,
Save sometime too much wonder of his eye,   95
Which having all, all could not satisfy;
    But poorly rich, so wanteth in his store
    That cloy'd with much, he pineth still for more.

But she that never cop'd with stranger eyes,
Could pick no meaning from their parling looks,   100
Nor read the subtle shining secrecies
Writ in the glassy margents of such books;
She touch'd no unknown baits, nor fear'd no hooks:
    Nor could she moralize his wanton sight,
    More than his eyes were open'd to the light.   105

87. unstain'd thoughts] *Q1;* thoughts unstain'd *Q6–9.*   105. open'd] *Q1;* open *Q4.*

88. *lim'd*] caught by bird-lime. Compare *3H6*, v. vi. 13:
> The bird that hath been limed in a bush
> With trembling wings misdoubteth every bush.

89. *securely*] with a sense of security, unsuspectingly.

90. *reverend*] reverent.

92. *that*] his 'inward ill'.

colour'd] cloaked, gave a fair appearance.

estate] rank.

93. *pleats*] folds. Compare *Lr.*, I. i. 283:
> Time shall unfold what plaited
> (Ff: plighted) cunning hides.

94. *That*] so that.

97. *store*] wealth, plenty.

99. *cop'd with*] dealt with. See *Ven.*, l. 888, and *Ham.*, III. ii. 60.

stranger] for 'strangers''.

100. *pick*] extract.

parling] speaking. Pooler notes, 'It implies a desire to come to terms', and cites *LLL.*, v. ii. 122, *Shr.*, I. i. 177, and *John*, II. i. 205.

102. *glassy margents*] margins. 'Glassy' gives the clear gleam or glint in the corner of an eye, but also suggests a quality of frailty or transience, as in *Meas.*, II. ii. 119–20:
> Most ignorant of what he's most assur'd,
> His glassy essence.

The metaphor of the marginal comment occurs also in *Rom.*, I. iii. 85 f.:
> And what obscur'd in this fair volume lies
> Find written in the margent of his eyes.

104. *moralize*] interpret, draw a conclusion from.

105. *More than*] more than that.

He stories to her ears her husband's fame,
Won in the fields of fruitful Italy;
And decks with praises Collatine's high name,
Made glorious by his manly chivalry
With bruised arms and wreaths of victory.   110
    Her joy with heav'd-up hand she doth express,
    And wordless so greets heaven for his success.

Far from the purpose of his coming thither,
He makes excuses for his being there;
No cloudy show of stormy blust'ring weather   115
Doth yet in his fair welkin once appear,
Till sable night, mother of dread and fear,
    Upon the world dim darkness doth display,
    And in her vaulty prison stows the day.

For then is Tarquin brought unto his bed,   120
Intending weariness with heavy sprite;
For after supper long he questioned
With modest Lucrece, and wore out the night.
Now leaden slumber with life's strength doth fight,

113. his] *Q1*; this *Q5*.   117. mother] *Q1*; sad source *Q6–9*.   119. stows] *Q1*;
shuts *Q6–9*.   124. life's] lifes *Q3,4*; lives *Q1*.

106. *stories*] See *Ven.*, l. 1013, and
Cym., I. iv. 34.
    110. *bruised arms*] battered armour.
Compare *R3*, I. i. 5–6:

    Now are our brows bound with
        victorious wreaths;
    Our bruised arms hung up for
        monuments.

See also *H5*, v. Prol. 18, and *Ant.*, IV.
xiii. 42.
    111. *heav'd-up*] raised. 'Heave' con-
tinued to be used in the old sense of
'lift' in alliterative phrases referring to
hand and head. Compare Herrick,
*Noble Numbers (Another Grace for a
Child)*. See *Ven.*, l. 351.
    116. *welkin*] sky. See also *LLL.*, IV. ii.
5, and *Tw. N.*, III. i. 65.
    117–19.] Malone compares a pass-
age from Daniel's *Complaint of Rosa-
mond* (see *Works*, ed. Grosart, vol. I,
p. 96):

    Com'd was the Night (mother of
        sleepe and feare)
    Who with her sable-mantle friendly
        covers
    The sweet-stolne sport of joyfull
        meeting Lovers.

See also *Ven.*, l. 456.
    118. *display*] spread.
    119. *stows*] puts away, puts under
cover. Compare *Tp.*, I. ii. 230, and
Oth., I. ii. 62.
    121. *Intending*] pretending, giving as
a motive. Compare *R3*, III. v. 8, and
Shr., IV. i. 206:

        amid this hurly I intend
    That all is done in reverent care of
        her.

    122. *questioned*] held conversation
with. Compare *Mer. V.*, IV. i. 70, and
AYL., III. iv. 39.
    123. *wore out*] passed. See *Ven.*, l. 841
n.

And every one to rest themselves betake,   125
Save thieves and cares and troubled minds that wake.

As one of which doth Tarquin lie revolving
The sundry dangers of his will's obtaining,
Yet ever to obtain his will resolving,
Though weak-built hopes persuade him to abstaining.   130
Despair to gain doth traffic oft for gaining,
    And when great treasure is the meed proposed,
    Though death be adjunct, there's no death supposed.

Those that much covet are with gain so fond
That what they have not, that which they possess   135
They scatter and unloose it from their bond;
And so by hoping more they have but less,
Or gaining more, the profit of excess
    Is but to surfeit, and such griefs sustain,
    That they prove bankrout in this poor rich gain.   140

125, 126. themselves betake, . . . wake.] *Q1* (*all copies except Malone 34 and Yale, which have* himselfe betakes, . . . wakes).   135. That what] *Q1;* That oft *Q6–9.*   not, that . . . possess] *Q1;* not that . . . possesse *Q4;* not that . . . possesse, *Q6–9.*

127. *revolving*] turning over in his mind.

130. *weak-built hopes*] the fact that his hopes are ungrounded.

131. *traffic*] trade.

132. *the meed proposed*] the reward held out, or kept in mind.

133. *adjunct*] joined, attendant. Compare *John*, III. iii. 57:

    Though that my death were adjunct
       of my act,
    By heaven, I would do it.

134–40.] 'Gildon long since noted that the first of these four stanzas (134–40) is woven upon a *sententia*, a sentence as Tarquin is later to call it, from Publilius Syrus, "Tam avaro deest quod habet, quam quod non habet", which probably hails from Shakespere's earliest school days. The whole is a perfect illustration of Erasmian *ratiocinatio* as Shakespere had learned in grammar school' (Baldwin, *op. cit.*, p. 117).

134. *fond*] foolish, infatuated.

135–6.] Pooler's is the neatest of suggested emendations; by placing the comma between 'have' and 'not', he says, 'the rhythm is perhaps improved and a more natural order of thought secured—"That what they have (not that which they possess) They scatter," etc. The money is theirs, but they cannot strictly be called its possessors, for it is not in their possession, being scattered and unloosed'. This explanation refers only to the speculative use of money indicated by 'bond'. But the notion of 'having' and yet not 'possessing' could also refer to the state of mind of those who are never contented with what they have, and cannot enjoy it. Some editors—Knight, Gollancz, and Wyndham—have thought no change necessary.

138. *the profit of excess*] what they gain from having more than enough.

The aim of all is but to nurse the life
With honour, wealth and ease, in waning age;
And in this aim there is such thwarting strife
That one for all or all for one we gage:
As life for honour in fell battle's rage,   145
  Honour for wealth; and oft that wealth doth cost
  The death of all, and all together lost.

So that in vent'ring ill we leave to be
The things we are, for that which we expect;
And this ambitious foul infirmity,   150
In having much, torments us with defect
Of that we have: so then we do neglect
  The thing we have, and all for want of wit,
  Make something nothing by augmenting it.

Such hazard now must doting Tarquin make,   155
Pawning his honour to obtain his lust;
And for himself himself he must forsake.
Then where is truth if there be no self-trust?
When shall he think to find a stranger just,
  When he himself himself confounds, betrays   160
  To sland'rous tongues and wretched hateful days?

Now stole upon the time the dead of night,

162. upon] vppon *Q1* (*all copies except British Museum C.21.c.45, which has* uppon).

144. *gage*] pledge, in the sense of 'wager' or 'venture'.

145. *As*] for example.

148. *vent'ring ill*] Pooler explains: 'by making a bad bargain, such as an unlucky investment or unsuccessful voyage', and quotes *2H4*, Epilogue, 12: 'If like an ill venture it comes unluckily home, I break'.

leave] cease. See l. 1089, and *Ven.*, ll. 422 and 715.

150. *this ambitious foul infirmity*] this foul infirmity, ambition.

151. *defect*] deficiency or insufficiency.

156. *Pawning*] endangering, risking the loss of.

160. *himself himself*] Compare *Ven.*, l. 161, and *R3*, iv. iv. 376 and 399 and v. iii. 182.

confounds] destroys. See also ll. 250 290, 1202, 1489.

164. *comfortable*] comforting; often used of the sun, as in *Lr.*, ii. ii. 172:

  Approach, thou beacon to this
   under globe,
  That by thy comfortable beams
   I may
  Peruse this letter.

See *Ven.*, l. 529 n., and compare *Tim.*, v. i. 134.

162–8.] The passage from *Mac.*, ii. i. 49–56, first cited here by Malone, is an interesting illustration of the difference between Shakespeare's earlier and later treatment of what is essentially the same poetic material:

   Now o'er the one half-world
  Nature seems dead, and wicked
   dreams abuse

When heavy sleep had clos'd up mortal eyes.
No comfortable star did lend his light,
No noise but owls' and wolves' death-boding cries;   165
Now serves the season that they may surprise
    The silly lambs: pure thoughts are dead and still,
    While lust and murder wakes to stain and kill.

And now this lustful lord leap'd from his bed,
Throwing his mantle rudely o'er his arm;   170
Is madly toss'd between desire and dread:
Th'one sweetly flatters, th' other feareth harm.
But honest fear, bewitch'd with lust's foul charm,
    Doth too too oft betake him to retire,
    Beaten away by brain-sick rude desire.   175

His falchion on a flint he softly smiteth,
That from the cold stone sparks of fire do fly;
Whereat a waxen torch forthwith he lighteth,
Which must be lodestar to his lustful eye:
And to the flame thus speaks advisedly: 180
  "As from this cold flint I enforc'd this fire,
    So Lucrece must I force to my desire."

Here pale with fear he doth premeditate
The dangers of his loathsome enterprise;
And in his inward mind he doth debate   185
What following sorrow may on this arise.
When looking scornfully, he doth despise
    His naked armour of still slaughter'd lust,
    And justly thus controls his thoughts unjust:

163. eyes] *Q1*; eye *Q6–9*.   177. do] *Q1*; doth *Q6–9*.   185. his] *Q1*; *omitted Q3*.

The curtain'd sleep: witchcraft
  celebrates
Pale Hecate's offerings: and
  wither'd murder,
Alarum'd by his sentinel, the wolf,
Whose howl's his watch, thus with
  his stealthy pace,
With Tarquin's ravishing strides,
  towards his design
Moves like a ghost.
167. *silly*] simple. See l. 1812, and
Ven., l. 1098.
  173. *honest*] honourable, virtuous.
  174. *retire*] The word can be used as

a substantive, as in *LLL.*, II. i. 234,
John, II. i. 326, and *1H4*, II. iii. 54. But
here a verb would seem more natural.
  175. *brain-sick*] mad.
  176. *falchion*] a curved sword.
  softly] silently.
  179. *lodestar*] guiding star.
  180. *advisedly*] deliberately, thought-
fully; here, having made up his mind.
See ll. 1527, 1816, and *Ven.*, l. 457.
  181.] Compare *Cæs.*, IV. iii. 11 f.
  188.] This mysterious line has inspired much and various comment.
'Naked' undoubtedly carries in part

"Fair torch, burn out thy light, and lend it not   190
   To darken her whose light excelleth thine;
   And die, unhallow'd thoughts, before you blot
   With your uncleanness that which is divine;
   Offer pure incense to so pure a shrine.
      Let fair humanity abhor the deed   195
      That spots and stains love's modest snow-white weed.

"O shame to knighthood and to shining arms!   *knowam*
   O foul dishonour to my household's grave!   *transgression*
   O impious act including all foul harms!
   A martial man to be soft fancy's slave!   200
   True valour still a true respect should have.
      Then my digression is so vile, so base,
      That it will live engraven in my face.

"Yea, though I die the scandal will survive
   And be an eye-sore in my golden coat;   205
   Some loathsome dash the herald will contrive,

205. an] *Q1;* my *Q4.*

the sense of 'unarmed', and therefore makes a startling companion for 'armour'. 'Still slaughter'd' can only mean 'repeatedly slaughtered'; but this sense scarcely carries its own explanation. The only full statement of the logical meaning is by Kittredge, who says: 'His only armor in this enterprise is lust . . . which is no real armor, for it is always slain (perishes, comes to naught) when it is satisfied. The fulfilment of such desire kills the desire'. It must be added that the power of the line comes not only from this compressed and paradoxical conceit, but from all the images suggested by a naked and lustful body, which also carries a weapon, or is 'armoured' or in itself resembles armour, and which is moreover in some way destroyed or ruined ('slaughtered') by its own desire, or perhaps even by repression of its desire.

196. *weed*] clothing. 'Love's modest snow-white weed' is chastity.

198. *my household's grave*] the tomb of my family. Wyndham points to the heraldic images in the next stanza, and says: 'The escutcheons of ancestors were displayed on the mortuary chapels of noble families. . . The epithet "household" is twice applied by Shakespeare to armorial bearings [*2H6,* v. i. 201, *R2,* iii. i. 24].'

200. *martial man*] soldier.

soft fancy's slave] love's slave. 'Fancy' was used especially of frivolous or fickle love, as in *Mer. V.,* iii. ii. 63.

201. *a true respect*] a careful regard for what is good. No doubt the line can also be taken to mean 'True valour should always *receive* true respect', but the predominant sense is surely that it should *give* it.

202. *Then*] and then, further.

digression] deviation (from right). Compare *R2,* v. iii. 66:

   And thy abundant goodness shall excuse
   This deadly blot in thy digressing son.

205. *eye-sore*] an ugly mark

coat] coat of arms.

206. *loathsome dash*] a stroke or mark

To cipher me how fondly I did dote:
That my posterity sham'd with the note,
   Shall curse my bones, and hold it for no sin
    To wish that I their father had not been.   210

"What win I if I gain the thing I seek?
A dream, a breath, a froth of fleeting joy.
Who buys a minute's mirth to wail a week,
Or sells eternity to get a toy?
For one sweet grape who will the vine destroy?   215
   Or what fond beggar, but to touch the crown,
   Would with the sceptre straight be strucken down?

"If Collatinus dream of my intent,
   Will he not wake, and in a desp'rate rage
Post hither, this vile purpose to prevent?—   220
This siege that hath engirt his marriage,
This blur to youth, this sorrow to the sage,
   This dying virtue, this surviving shame,
   Whose crime will bear an ever-during blame.

"O what excuse can my invention make   225
   When thou shalt charge me with so black a deed?
   Will not my tongue be mute, my frail joints shake,

217. strucken] *Q7–9;* stroken *Q1–6.*

indicating disgrace. Wyndham quotes from Guillim's *Display of Heraldrie*, 1610, and says the passage 'deals explicitly with "abatements", which are "accidentall marke[s] annexed to Coate-Armour, denoting some ungentleman-like, dishonourable, or disloiall demeanour, qualities, or staine in the Bearer, whereby the dignity of the Coate-Armour is greatly abased".' According to R. H. Case, 'The heralds devised nine "Abatements of Honour", which, however, do not appear to have come into use. For the offence in question, the abatement was '*an escutcheon reversed, sanguine, occupying the middle point of the escutcheon of arms*".'

207. *cipher me*] figure or symbolize concerning me. See also l. 1396.

208. *note*] mark, sign. Compare *LLL.,* iv. iii. 125, v. ii. 75, and *R2,* i. i. 43.

209. *hold it for no sin*] think it justifiable.

210. *been*] The pronunciation represented by this rhyme was common in the 16th and 17th cents. and has been retained in American English.

212. *dream*] See Sonnet cxxix, l. 12: Before, a joy proposed; behind, a dream.

froth] something insubstantial or valueless.

220. *Post*] hasten. See l. 1 n.

221. *engirt*] encompassed. See l. 1173, and *Ven.,* l. 364.

222. *blur*] blot.

224. *ever-during*] everlasting.

226. *thou*] The rhetoric of the passage does not require a definite reference for 'thou'.

Mine eyes forgo their light, my false heart bleed?
The guilt being great, the fear doth still exceed;
    And extreme fear can neither fight nor fly,   230
    But coward-like with trembling terror die.

"Had Collatinus kill'd my son or sire,
Or lain in ambush to betray my life;
Or were he not my dear friend, this desire
Might have excuse to work upon his wife,   235
As in revenge or quittal of such strife:
    But as he is my kinsman, my dear friend,
    The shame and fault finds no excuse nor end.

"Shameful it is,—ay, if the fact be known.
Hateful it is,—there is no hate in loving.   240
I'll beg her love,—but she is not her own.
The worst is but denial and reproving.
My will is strong past reason's weak removing:
    Who fears a sentence or an old man's saw
    Shall by a painted cloth be kept in awe."   245

Thus graceless holds he disputation
'Tween frozen conscience and hot burning will,

239. ay, if] I, if *Q1;* if once *Q6–9.*

228. *Mine eyes forgo their light*] My eyes cease to function. Vision was thought to reside in a beam of light issuing from the eye.

229. *exceed*] abound, be excessive. Compare *Ado,* III. iv. 17.

230. *extreme*] The accent is on the first syllable.

235. *work upon*] meddle with, seduce.

236. *quittal*] requital, payment.

237. *my kinsman*] Compare sentiment and situation with *Mac.,* I. vii. 13.

239–42.] The balancing of objections and answers resembles some of the Senecan rhetoric in *R3,* I. ii and IV. iii. 199–432. For the rhetoric of the retort to oneself see *R3,* V. iii. 181 f., and *Spanish Tragedy,* II. i. 19–28. See ll. 841–2.

239. *fact*] deed. See l. 349.

243. *past reason's weak removing*] beyond the feeble power of reason to move or dissuade. Compare *Shr.,* I. ii. 72:

    She moves me not, or not removes,
        at least,
    Affection's edge in me.

244. *sentence*] maxim, moral judgment. See *Ado,* II. iii. 130, and *Mer. V.,* I. ii. 11.

saw] saying. 'An old man's saw' would be a *moral* saying.

245. *a painted cloth*] Cloth or canvas painted with pictures and patterns in oil colours was commonly used for wall-hangings, as a cheap substitute for tapestry. The subjects were often Biblical or classical, and texts or proverbs were common in the designs. Hence the association in Tarquin's mind between 'saws' and 'sentences' and this form of interior decoration. For other references see *AYL.,* II. ii. 290, and *Troil.,* V. x. 46.

246–7.] The traditional devices for

And with good thoughts makes dispensation,
Urging the worser sense for vantage still;
Which in a moment doth confound and kill   250
    All pure effects, and doth so far proceed
    That what is vile shows like a virtuous deed.

Quoth he, "She took me kindly by the hand,
And gaz'd for tidings in my eager eyes,
Fearing some hard news from the warlike band   255
Where her beloved Collatinus lies.
O how her fear did make her colour rise!
    First red as roses that on lawn we lay,
    Then white as lawn, the roses took away.

"And how her hand in my hand being lock'd,   260
Forc'd it to tremble with her loyal fear!
Which strook her sad, and then it faster rock'd,
Until her husband's welfare she did hear;
Whereat she smiled with so sweet a cheer
    That had Narcissus seen her as she stood,   265
    Self-love had never drown'd him in the flood.

---

251. effects] *Qq;* affects *conj. Steevens.*   260. how] *Q1;* now *Q6–9.*

---

representing a divided mind have been
used in the preceding soliloquy (see
ll. 239–41 and n.); this comment suggests a consciousness of their medieval
ancestry. See C. S. Lewis, *Allegory of
Love,* pp. 30 and 113, and *passim.*

246. *graceless*] Tarquin is 'graceless'
because in his moral conflict he
receives no divine aid.

247. *frozen conscience*] Conscience is
called frozen, because numbed and
ineffective.

248–9.] The sense is that out of even
his good thoughts Tarquin draws a
'dispensation', i.e. a permission to act
as he desires, by twisting their sense in
a way which suits him.

for vantage] to gain a better position.
Compare *1H6,* iv. v. 28:

        You fled for vantage, every one will
            swear.

251. *effects*] For 'affects', i.e. desires,
emotions. Steevens compared *Oth.,* i.
iii. 264:

            the young affects
        In me defunct.
In defence of the text Malone quoted
Ham., iii. iv. 129:

            Do not look upon me,
        Lest with this piteous action you
            convert
        My stern effects.
Clearly Shakespeare did not always
distinguish the sense 'affects' by the
spelling. See *Ven.,* l. 605.

258–9.] See *Ven.,* l. 590.

259. *took*] being taken.

262. *Which*] her fear.

it faster rock'd] The reference seems
to have shifted from Lucrece's hand to
her heart.

264. *cheer*] countenance, expression.

265–6.] See *Ven.,* ll. 161–2 and n.
Narcissus was not drowned; but the
notion that he was appears in many
Elizabethan references (see Root in
Journal of English and Germanic Philology
(1902), iv. 454 f.).

"Why hunt I then for colour or excuses?
All orators are dumb when beauty pleadeth.
Poor wretches have remorse in poor abuses;
Love thrives not in the heart that shadows dreadeth.   270
Affection is my captain, and he leadeth;
  And when his gaudy banner is display'd,
  The coward fights, and will not be dismay'd.

"Then childish fear avaunt, debating die!
Respect and reason wait on wrinkled age!   275
My heart shall never countermand mine eye:
Sad pause and deep regard beseems the sage;
My part is youth, and beats these from the stage.
  Desire my pilot is, beauty my prize;
  Then who fears sinking where such treasure lies?"   280

As corn o'ergrown by weeds, so heedful fear
Is almost chok'd by unresisted lust.
Away he steals with open list'ning ear,
Full of foul hope and full of fond mistrust;
Both which, as servitors to the unjust,   285
  So cross him with their opposite persuasion
  That now he vows a league, and now invasion.

Within his thought her heavenly image sits,

268, 270, 271. pleadeth ... dreadeth ... leadeth] *Q1;* pleads ... dreads ... leades *Q6–9.*   269. poor] *Q1;* pure *Q4.*   272. his] *Q1;* this *Q5–9.*   274. Then] *Q1;* The *Q3.*   276. mine] *Q1;* my *Q4.*   282. chok'd] choakt *Q1;* cloakt *Q5–8.*   283. ear] eare *Qq;* care *Lintott.*

267. *colour*] pretext. See ll. 92 and 476. Compare *Wint.*, IV. iv. 566, and *Gent.*, IV. ii. 3.
  269.] 'Wretched creatures feel compunction, and usually in petty transgressions' (*scil.* 'which mine is not').
  271. *Affection*] desire.
  273. *The coward*] i.e. even the coward.
  274. *avaunt*] begone.
  275. *Respect*] consideration, regard for consequences.
    wait on] attend on, go with.
  276. *countermand*] contradict, check.
  277. *Sad*] serious.

deep regard] searching scrutiny (of right and wrong).
  278.] Malone suggested that Shakespeare had in mind 'the conflicts between the Devil and the *Vice* of the old moralities'; Steevens capped this with a reference to *Lusty Juventus.* Later scholars were able to show that there is no close parallel between this line and any extant morality play or interlude. The image as a general one would come easily enough to an actor of experience, and a particular reference would in fact spoil the line.
  286. *cross*] thwart.
  287. *league*] peace or truce.

NB Collatine puts Lucrece
for same reasons as motivate Tarquin's
rape her: wealth possessed rather than
subject known.

And in the self-same seat sits Collatine.
That eye which looks on her confounds his wits;   290
That eye which him beholds, as more divine,
Unto a view so false will not incline,
    But with a pure appeal seeks to the heart,
    Which once corrupted takes the worser part:

And therein heartens up his servile powers,   295
Who flatter'd by their leader's jocund show,
Stuff up his lust, as minutes fill up hours;
And as their captain, so their pride doth grow,
Paying more slavish tribute than they owe.
    By reprobate desire thus madly led,   300
    The Roman lord marcheth to Lucrece' bed.

The locks between her chamber and his will,
Each one by him enforc'd, retires his ward;
But as they open, they all rate his ill,
Which drives the creeping thief to some regard.   305
The threshold grates the door to have him heard;
    Night-wand'ring weasels shriek to see him there:
    They fright him, yet he still pursues his fear.

As each unwilling portal yields him way,
Through little vents and crannies of the place   310
The wind wars with his torch to make him stay,

301. marcheth] *Q1;* doth march *Q6–9.*   303. retires] *Q1;* recites *Q6–9.*
308. he still pursues his] *Q1;* still pursues him *Q4.*

290. *confounds his wits*] destroys his
reason, or perhaps merely throws his
thoughts into confusion.
    293. *seeks to*] applies to, seeks aid
of.
    295. *heartens up*] encourages, with a
play upon 'heart'.
    his servile powers] sense, bodily ener-
gies, or appetites, imagined as sub-
servient to the heart, the seat of life.
    296. *their leader's*] the heart's.
    298. *their captain*] the heart again,
thought of as swelling with exultation
or excitement.
    303. *enforc'd*] forced.
    retires his ward] draws back its ward.
A ward is one of 'the ridges projecting

from the inside plate of a lock, serving
to prevent the passage of any key the
bit of which is not provided with in-
cisions of corresponding form and
size' (O.E.D.).
    304. *rate*] scold, i.e. by creaking.
    305. *regard*] heed.
    306. *to have him heard*] in order to
make him heard.
    307. *Night-wand'ring weasels*] We
may wonder what weasels are doing in
a noble Roman mansion, but it seems
that they were kept in houses, instead
of cats, for the purpose of killing ver-
min. As for their restless habits, these
are referred to by Pliny, xxix. 4, and
Plautus, *Stichus,* III. ii (Pooler).

And blows the smoke of it into his face,
Extinguishing his conduct in this case;
　But his hot heart, which fond desire doth scorch,
　Puffs forth another wind that fires the torch.　　315

And being lighted, by the light he spies
Lucretia's glove, wherein her needle sticks;
He takes it from the rushes where it lies,
And gripping it, the needle his finger pricks,
　As who should say, "This glove to wanton tricks　320
　Is not inur'd; return again in haste;
　Thou seest our mistress' ornaments are chaste."

But all these poor forbiddings could not stay him;
He in the worst sense consters their denial.
The doors, the wind, the glove, that did delay him,　325
He takes for accidental things of trial;
　Or as those bars which stop the hourly dial,
　Who with a ling'ring stay his course doth let,
　Till every minute pays the hour his debt.

"So, so," quoth he, "these lets attend the time,　330
Like little frosts that sometime threat the spring,
To add a more rejoicing to the prime,

314. desire] *Q1; delight* Q4.　321. not] *Q1; nor* Q6,7.　inur'd] *Q1;*
iniur'd *Q5.*　331. sometime] *Q1;* somtimes *Q4.*

313. *conduct*] guide. Compare *Rom.*,
v. i. 116:
　Come, bitter conduct; come
　　unsavoury guide!
316. *being lighted*] the torch being
lighted again.
318. *rushes*] Malone explains: 'The
apartments in England being strewed
with rushes in our author's time, he has
given Lucretia's chamber the same
covering'. Compare *Cym.*, II. ii. 13.
319. *needle*] The word was pronounced 'neeld', and sometimes so spelt,
as in *Per.*, v. Gower, l. 5:
　and with her neeld composes
Nature's own shape, of bud, bird,
　branch, or berry.
320. *As who should say*] See *Ven.*, l.
280.
321. *inur'd*] accustomed.

324. *consters*] construes. 'Conster' is a
common Elizabethan form. See *Shr.*,
III. i. 30. O.E.D. cites Lyly, *Euphues*:
'She drew out her petrarke, requesting
him to conster hir a lesson.'
326. *accidental things of trial*] chance
happenings which test his resolution.
327. *those bars*] lines which mark off
the hour into minutes.
　dial] clock. See *AYL.*, II. vii. 20.
328. *Who*] which, referring to 'bars'.
　stay] delay, barrier.
　let] hinder. Compare *Ham.*, I. iv. 85;
see also l. 330 below.
330. *attend the time*] accompany this
period (of my enterprise).
332. *a more rejoicing*] a greater rejoicing.
　prime] spring.

And give the sneaped birds more cause to sing.
Pain pays the income of each precious thing:
  Huge rocks, high winds, strong pirates, shelves and sands
  The merchant fears, ere rich at home he lands."   336

Now is he come unto the chamber door
That shuts him from the heaven of his thought,
Which with a yielding latch, and with no more,
Hath barr'd him from the blessed thing he sought.   340
So from himself impiety hath wrought,
  That for his prey to pray he doth begin,
  As if the heavens should countenance his sin.

But in the midst of his unfruitful prayer,
Having solicited th' eternal power   345
That his foul thoughts might compass his fair fair,
And they would stand auspicious to the hour,
Even there he starts; quoth he, "I must deflower:
  The powers to whom I pray abhor this fact;
  How can they then assist me in the act?   350

"Then love and fortune be my gods, my guide!
My will is back'd with resolution;
Thoughts are but dreams till their effects be tried;
The blackest sin is clear'd with absolution.

---

347. auspicious] *Q1;* suspicious *Q4.*
Q6–9.   354. The blackest] *Q1;* Blacke

333. *sneaped*] nipped, checked. Compare *Wint.,* i. ii. 13, and *LLL.,* i. i. 100.

334. *income*] gathering in, harvest.

335. *shelves*] sandbanks.

341.] Impiety has so carried him out of himself.

342. *prey . . . pray*] Steevens points to one of the chief models for this sort of pun: 'A jingle not less disgusting occurs in Ovid's narration of the same event, *Fasti,* ii. 787' (see Appendix II, p. 197).

346. *his fair fair*] his virtuous beauty. There is a play on the different applications of the word, suggested by the antithesis with 'foul'.

347. *they*] The transition from 'heaven' to a plural pronoun is common in Elizabethan drama. Malone

gives examples from *R3,* i. iii. 217–19 and iv. iv. 72. Shakespeare is often careless in such things, but might have been influenced by the Lord Chamberlain's prohibition of oaths or references to specific theological concepts.

349–50.] Compare *Ham.,* iii. iii. 36 ff.

349. *fact*] deed, crime. See l. 239.

352. *back'd*] supported.

352, 4.] On the imperfect rhyme see Lewis, *English Literature in the Sixteenth Century,* p. 502.

353–7.] This jumble of unrelated maxims may correspond to Tarquin's moral confusion; but Shakespeare can force his verse with a high hand when he wants to bring something to a conclusion.

Against love's fire fear's frost hath dissolution: 355
    The eye of heaven is out, and misty night
    Covers the shame that follows sweet delight."

This said, his guilty hand pluck'd up the latch,
And with his knee the door he opens wide.
The dove sleeps fast that this night-owl will catch;   360
Thus treason works ere traitors be espied.
Who sees the lurking serpent steps aside;
    But she, sound sleeping, fearing no such thing,
    Lies at the mercy of his mortal sting.

Into the chamber wickedly he stalks,   365
And gazeth on her yet unstained bed.
The curtains being close, about he walks,
Rolling his greedy eyeballs in his head;
By their high treason is his heart misled,
    Which gives the watch-word to his hand full soon,   370
    To draw the cloud that hides the silver moon.

Look as the fair and fiery-pointed sun
Rushing from forth a cloud, bereaves our sight:
Even so, the curtain drawn, his eyes begun
To wink, being blinded with a greater light.   375
Whether it is that she reflects so bright,

368. eyeballs] *Q1*; eye-ball *Q4*.   370. full] *Q1*; too *Q6–9*.   371. the silver]
Qq; this silver *conj. Walker.*

355. *hath dissolution*] dissolves.

356. *out*] put out, or extinguished.
Compare *Mac.*, II. i. 5.

364. *mortal*] deadly.

sting] often used to mean 'lust',
or the male organ. See *AYL.*, II. vii.
66.

365. *stalks*] 'The poet meant by the
word *stalk* to convey the notion, not of
a boisterous, but quiet movement'
(Malone). Knight adds: 'The fowler
who creeps upon the bird *stalks*, and
his *stalking*-horse derives its name from
the character of the fowler's movement'.

367. *close*] drawn close.

about] round about.

371. *the cloud*] i.e. the curtains. For
'draw' see *Troil.*, III. ii. 49:
    Come draw this curtain, and let's
      see your picture.

372. *fiery-pointed*] This is vivid
enough, and need not be emended to
fire-ypointed (Steevens), or be under-
stood to mean *fire-appointed* (Rolfe).

373. *bereaves*] takes away.

375. *wink*] close. See ll. 458, 553, and
1139, and *Ven.*, ll. 90 and 121.

376. *reflects*] shines. Compare *Tit.*, I.
ii. 225–6:
    Lord Saturnine: whose virtues will,
      I hope,
    Reflect on Rome as Titan's rays on
      earth.

That dazzleth them, or else some shame supposed;
But blind they are, and keep themselves enclosed.

O had they in that darksome prison died,
Then had they seen the period of their ill!   380
Then Collatine again by Lucrece' side
In his clear bed might have reposed still.
But they must ope, this blessed league to kill;
    And holy-thoughted Lucrece to their sight
    Must sell her joy, her life, her world's delight.   385

Her lily hand her rosy cheek lies under,
Coz'ning the pillow of a lawful kiss;
Who therefore angry, seems to part in sunder,
Swelling on either side to want his bliss:
Between whose hills her head entombed is,   390
    Where like a virtuous monument she lies,
    To be admir'd of lewd unhallowed eyes.

Without the bed her other fair hand was,
On the green coverlet; whose perfect white
Show'd like an April daisy on the grass,   395
With pearly sweat resembling dew of night.
Her eyes like marigolds had sheath'd their light,
    And canopied in darkness sweetly lay,
    Till they might open to adorn the day.

Her hair like golden threads play'd with her breath: 400
O modest wantons, wanton modesty!

377. dazzleth] dazleth *Q1*; dazled *Q4*.   386. cheek] *Q1*; cheekes *Q4,6–9*.
396. pearly] pearlie *Q1*; perlie *Q1* (*Folger-Devonshire, Huntington*).   400. play'd]
Q1; omitted *Q4*.

377. *supposed*] suggested or imagined.
    379. *darksome prison*] Compare *Ven.*,
l. 1038.
    380. *period*] end.
    382. *clear*] unstained.
    383. *this blessed league*] the union be-
tween Lucrece and Collatine.
    387. *Coz'ning*] cheating.
    388. *therefore angry*] 'The conceit
. . . would have been tolerable in
Hero and Leander but is here repel-
lent' (C. S. Lewis, *op. cit.*, p. 499).
    391. *monument*] an effigy on a tomb.
Compare *Cym.*, II. ii. 32:
    O sleep, thou ape of death, lie dull
        upon her!
    And be her sense but as a monument
    Thus in a chapel lying.
    397. *like marigolds*] Compare the
'winking Mary-buds' of *Cym.*, II. iii. 26,
and *Wint.*, IV. iv. 105:
    The marigold that goes to bed wi'
        the sun.

Showing life's triumph in the map of death,
And death's dim look in life's mortality.
Each in her sleep themselves so beautify,
　　As if between them twain there were no strife,　405
　　But that life liv'd in death and death in life.

Her breasts like ivory globes circled with blue,
A pair of maiden worlds unconquered;
Save of their lord, no bearing yoke they knew,
And him by oath they truly honoured.　410
These worlds in Tarquin new ambition bred;
　　Who like a foul usurper went about,
　　From this fair throne to heave the owner out.

What could he see but mightily he noted?
What did he note but strongly he desired?　415
What he beheld, on that he firmly doted,
And in his will his wilful eye he tired.
With more than admiration he admired
　　Her azure veins, her alablaster skin,
　　Her coral lips, her snow-white dimpled chin.　420

As the grim lion fawneth o'er his prey,
Sharp hunger by the conquest satisfied;
So o'er this sleeping soul doth Tarquin stay,

402. Showing] *Q1;* Showring *Q6–9.*

402.] The breathing indicated by the movement of her hair reveals that Lucrece is alive, not dead.
　map] picture or diagram. 'Map' is a frequent image for 'face'; see l. 1712.
　404. *Each*] both life and death.
　407.] The imagery recalls a passage from *Hero and Leander,* ii. 271–8:
　　And every limb did as a soldier stout
　　Defend the fort, and keep the foeman out.
　　For though the rising ivory mount he scal'd,
　　Which is with azure circling lines empal'd,
　　Much like a globe (a globe may I term this,
　　By which Love sails to regions full of bliss),

Yet there with Sisyphus he toil'd in vain,
Till gentle parley did the truce obtain.
　408. *maiden worlds*] Shakespeare makes it clear in the next lines that 'maiden' means 'chaste', not 'virginal'. Malone cites Ovid, *Fasti,* ii. 803–4 (see Appendix II, p. 198).
　413. *heave*] throw. Compare *First Part of the Contention,* v. i. 22:
　　And heave proud Somerset from out the court.
　414. *noted*] observed.
　417.] In his lust he wearied his lustful eye. See l. 486 n.
　421. *fawneth*] shows pleasure, grows mild.
　422. *Sharp hunger*] Compare *Ven.,* l. 55.

His rage of lust by gazing qualified,—
Slak'd not suppress'd, for standing by her side,   425
   His eye which late this mutiny restrains,
   Unto a greater uproar tempts his veins.

And they like straggling slaves for pillage fighting,
Obdurate vassals fell exploits effecting,
In bloody death and ravishment delighting,   430
Nor children's tears nor mothers' groans respecting,
Swell in their pride, the onset still expecting.
   Anon his beating heart, alarum striking,
   Gives the hot charge, and bids them do their liking.

His drumming heart cheers up his burning eye,   435
His eye commends the leading to his hand;
His hand, as proud of such a dignity,
Smoking with pride, march'd on to make his stand
On her bare breast, the heart of all her land;
   Whose ranks of blue veins, as his hand did scale,   440
   Left their round turrets destitute and pale.

They must'ring to the quiet cabinet
Where their dear governess and lady lies,

439. breast] *Q1*; breasts *Q6–9*.

424. *qualified*] tempered, softened.
Compare *Gent.*, ii. vii. 21–2:
   I do not seek to quench your love's
      hot fire
   But qualify the fire's extreme
      rage.
425. *Slak'd*] reduced in strength.
428–45.] 'A sustained conceit taken
from the assault of a fortress. It is resumed 464–483' (Wyndham). There
is nothing original about this fancy in
this situation. But we must note how
effectively, with what nervous intensity, Shakespeare uses his crowded
details to animate the verse, to convey
the disorder and excitement and half-
frightened determination of the ravisher.
428. *straggling*] unmarshalled in
military order. The word is contemp-
tuous. See *R3*, v. iii. 327, and *Tim.*, v.
i. 7.
429. *Obdurate*] See *Ven.*, l. 199.

428–34.] Shakespeare can seldom
have used double rhymes more effectively.
435. *cheers up*] encourages, as a
leader shouting to his men in attack.
436. *commends*] entrusts, commits.
Compare *LLL.*, iii. i. 169:
   And to her white hand see thou do
      commend
   This seal'd up counsel.
437. *as proud*] as if proud.
438. *Smoking*] Compare *Ven.*, l. 555.
The heat and intention of the hand are
vividly conveyed.
442. *must'ring*] rallying.
   the quiet cabinet] the heart. The
notion is of a small and retired dwelling, as in *Ven.*, l. 854. But the metaphor
shifts, for 'their dear governess and
lady' turns out to be Lucrece, and she
cannot be thought of as lying in her
own heart.
443. *governess*] ruler.

Do tell her she is dreadfully beset,
And fright her with confusion of their cries.   445
She much amaz'd, breaks ope her lock'd-up eyes,
    Who peeping forth this tumult to behold,
    Are by his flaming torch dimm'd and controll'd.

Imagine her as one in dead of night
From forth dull sleep by dreadful fancy waking,   450
That thinks she hath beheld some ghastly sprite,
Whose grim aspect sets every joint a-shaking:
What terror 'tis! but she in worser taking,
    From sleep disturbed, heedfully doth view
    The sight which makes supposed terror true.   455

Wrapp'd and confounded in a thousand fears,
Like to a new-kill'd bird she trembling lies.
She dares not look, yet winking there appears
Quick-shifting antics, ugly in her eyes.
Such shadows are the weak brain's forgeries;   460
    Who, angry that the eyes fly from their lights,
    In darkness daunts them with more dreadful sights.

His hand that yet remains upon her breast,—
Rude ram, to batter such an ivory wall!—
May feel her heart, poor citizen! distress'd,   465
Wounding itself to death, rise up and fall,—
Beating her bulk, that his hand shakes withal:
    This moves in him more rage and lesser pity,
    To make the breach and enter this sweet city.

450. dreadful] *Q1;* deadfull *Q4.*   453. 'tis] *Q1;* ist *Q4.*   454. disturbed] *Q1;*
disturb'd *Q6,8.*   455. true] trew *Q1-5;* rew *Q6-9.*   462. daunts] *Q1;*
daunt *Q4.*   469. the] *Q1;* his *Q4.*

444. *beset*] assailed.
448. *controll'd*] overpowered; here,
dazzled.
453. *in worser taking*] in greater agitation. Compare *Wiv.,* iii. iii. 190:
'What a taking was he in when your
husband asked who was in the basket!'
The double comparative in 'worser'
was common. See *1H6,* v. iii. 36.
454. *heedfully*] warily.
456. *Wrapp'd*] enveloped.
458. *winking*] See l. 375.
459. *antics*] grotesque figures. The

word was used for certain kinds of
dances or masquers. See *LLL.,* v. i. 119.
460. *shadows*] images, shapes.
464. *ram*] battering ram.
467. *bulk*] body. See *R3,* i. iv. 40, and
Ham., ii. i. 95. Pooler cites Golding,
viii. 998:
    Her skin was starched and so sheere
        a man might well espye
    The very bowels in her bulk how
        every one did lye.
469. *make the breach*] break through
the walls or defences.

First like a trumpet doth his tongue begin   470
To sound a parley to his heartless foe,
Who o'er the white sheet peers her whiter chin,
The reason of this rash alarm to know;
Which he by dumb demeanour seeks to show:
    But she with vehement prayers urgeth still   475
    Under what colour he commits this ill.

Thus he replies: "The colour in thy face,
That even for anger makes the lily pale
And the red rose blush at her own disgrace,
Shall plead for me and tell my loving tale.   480
Under that colour am I come to scale
    Thy never-conquer'd fort: the fault is thine,
    For those thine eyes betray thee unto mine.

"Thus I forestall thee, if thou mean to chide:
Thy beauty hath ensnar'd thee to this night,   485
Where thou with patience must my will abide,
My will that marks thee for my earth's delight;
Which I to conquer sought with all my might:
    But as reproof and reason beat it dead,
    By thy bright beauty was it newly bred.   490

"I see what crosses my attempt will bring,
I know what thorns the growing rose defends;

472. Who] *Q1*; When *Q4*.   487. marks] *Q1*; makes *Q4*.   490. was it]
Q1; it was *Q3–9*.   491. attempt] *Q1*; attempts *Q6–9*.   492. what] *Q1*;
that *Q4*.

471. *sound a parley*] summon the
defenders to discuss terms.

  heartless] cowardly. See l. 1392.
Compare *Rom.*, I. ii. 73:

    What, art thou drawn among these
      heartless hinds?

472. *peers*] lets peep out. This transitive use is rare.

473. *rash alarm*] sudden summons or
attack.

474. *by dumb demeanour*] This dumb-
show is hardly consistent with the
'parley' of l. 471.

475. *prayers*] The word must be
given two syllables, as in Daniel,
Delia, XI (quoted by Pooler):

  Tears, vowes, and prayers winne
    the hardest hart.

  urgeth] insists, beseeches.

476. *colour*] pretext. See ll. 267, 481.
The play on the word in the next line is
paralleled in *2H4*, v. v. 91.

478–9.] Compare Sonnet xcix.

481. *Under that colour*] Yet another
pun, since the phrase here is turned to
mean 'under that flag'.

485. *ensnar'd thee to this night*] This
probably means: 'led you into being
thus caught by me tonight'.

486. *will*] desire, lust.

488. *Which*] i.e. my will.

489–90.] See l. 188 n.

I think the honey guarded with a sting:
All this beforehand counsel comprehends.
But will is deaf, and hears no heedful friends;   495
　　Only he hath an eye to gaze on beauty,
　　And dotes on what he looks, 'gainst law or duty.

"I have debated even in my soul,
　　What wrong, what shame, what sorrow I shall breed;
But nothing can affection's course control,   500
Or stop the headlong fury of his speed.
I know repentant tears ensue the deed,
　　Reproach, disdain and deadly enmity;
　　Yet strive I to embrace mine infamy."

This said, he shakes aloft his Roman blade,   505
Which like a falcon tow'ring in the skies,
Coucheth the fowl below with his wings' shade,
Whose crooked beak threats, if he mount he dies:
So under his insulting falchion lies
　　Harmless Lucretia, marking what he tells   510
　　With trembling fear, as fowl hear falcons' bells.

"Lucrece," quoth he, "this night I must enjoy thee.
If thou deny, then force must work my way:
For in thy bed I purpose to destroy thee;
That done, some worthless slave of thine I'll slay,   515
To kill thine honour with thy life's decay;
　　And in thy dead arms do I mean to place him,
　　Swearing I slew him, seeing thee embrace him.

"So thy surviving husband shall remain
　　The scornful mark of every open eye;   520
　　Thy kinsmen hang their heads at this disdain,

493.] 'I am aware that the honey is guarded with a sting' (Malone).

494. *counsel*] advice, deliberate thought, with perhaps a legal significance here.

495. *heedful*] discreet, wary.

496. *Only he hath*] he hath only.

497. *on what he looks*] on what he looks on. See Abbott, § 394.

500. *affection's*] desire's. See l. 271.

502. *ensue*] pursue.

506. *tow'ring*] flying high to fall on its prey. See *Mac.*, II. iv. 12.

507. *Coucheth*] makes cower or lie close. Compare *Tim.*, II. ii. 181:
　　one cloud of winter showers,
　　These flies are couch'd.

508. *crooked*] curved.

511. *as . . . bells*] Steevens cites *3H6*, I. i. 47: nor he that loves him best . . . Dares stir a wing if Warwick shake his bells.

Thy issue blurr'd with nameless bastardy.
And thou, the author of their obloquy,
    Shalt have thy trespass cited up in rhymes
    And sung by children in succeeding times.   525

"But if thou yield, I rest thy secret friend;
The fault unknown is as a thought unacted.
A little harm done to a great good end
For lawful policy remains enacted.
The poisonous simple sometime is compacted   530
    In a pure compound; being so applied,
    His venom in effect is purified.

"Then for thy husband and thy children's sake,
Tender my suit; bequeath not to their lot
The shame that from them no device can take,   535
The blemish that will never be forgot,
Worse than a slavish wipe or birth-hour's blot:
    For marks descried in men's nativity
    Are nature's faults, not their own infamy."

Here with a cockatrice' dead-killing eye   540

524. Shalt] *Q1;* Shall *Q4,6–9.*   530. sometime] *Q1;* sometimes *Q4,7–9.*
531. a pure compound] *Q1;* purest compounds *Q6–9.*

522. *blurr'd*] blotted, defamed.
nameless] as having no known father.
'The poet calls bastardy *nameless*, because an illegitimate child has no name
by inheritance, being considered by
the law as *nullius filius*' (Malone).

524. *cited up*] called to mind. Compare *R3,* I. iv. 13–16:

    we look'd toward England
    And cited up a thousand heavy
        times,
    During the wars of York and
        Lancaster,
    That had befall'n us.

526.] Compare *Oth.,* III. iii. 202–3
and 341–51.

529. *enacted*] ordained by legislative
authority. The sense is that the 'little
harm' 'becomes a law of society,
accepted as being justified by reasons
of state'.

530. *simple*] 'A medicine or medica-

ment composed or concocted of only
one constituent, *esp.* of one herb or
plant' (O.E.D.).
compacted] compounded.

534. *Tender*] regard. Compare *Ham.,*
I. iii. 107.

537. *slavish wipe*] 'the brand with
which slaves were marked' (Malone).
birth-hour's blot] Malone says: 'It
appears that in Shakespeare's time the
arms of bastards were distinguished by
some kind of blot'; but he considers
that the meaning here is 'those cor-
poral blemishes with which children
are sometimes born'. Wyndham believes that the heraldic mark of illegi-
timacy is meant, and supports his
belief with a reference to Guillim's
Display of Heraldrie, ineffectively.

540. *cockatrice*] a mythical serpent,
more often called a basilisk. Topsel's
History of Serpents (1608) says of its

He rouseth up himself, and makes a pause;
While she, the picture of pure piety,
Like a white hind under the gripe's sharp claws,
Pleads in a wilderness where are no laws,
   To the rough beast that knows no gentle right,   545
   Nor aught obeys but his foul appetite.

But when a black-fac'd cloud the world doth threat,
In his dim mist th' aspiring mountains hiding
From earth's dark womb some gentle gust doth get,
Which blow these pitchy vapours from their biding,   550
Hind'ring their present fall by this dividing:
   So his unhallowed haste her words delays,
   And moody Pluto winks while Orpheus plays.

Yet, foul night-waking cat, he doth but dally,
While in his hold-fast foot the weak mouse panteth.   555
Her sad behaviour feeds his vulture folly,
A swallowing gulf that even in plenty wanteth.

543. a] *Q1;* as *Q4.*   under] *Q1;* beneath *Q6–9.*   548. mountains] *Q1;*
mountaine *Q6–9.*   552. unhallowed] *Q1;* unhollowed *Q4.*

deadly effect on man: 'with his sight he killeth him, because the beams of the Cockatrices eyes do corrupt the visible spirit of a man, which visible spirit corrupted, all the other spirits coming from the brain and life of the heart, are thereby corrupted, and so the man dyeth' (Pooler). Shakespeare refers to the cockatrice in *Tw. N.,* III. iv. 215, *R3,* IV. i. 55, and *Rom.,* III. ii. 47.

542–3.] Dryden's use of a 'milk-white hind' as a symbol of the true Church (see *Hind and Panther,* l. 1) may derive from these lines.

543. *gripe*] vulture or eagle. Pooler comments: 'That vultures were called gripes is clear from the complaint of Turner (1544), *De Historia Avium,* Cambridge ed. p. 178, that the vulture is wrongly called gryps, "quum gryps sit 'a griffin', animal ut creditur volatile & quadrupes"; but vultures do not prey on living animals, and Shakespeare may here refer to the eagle. The bird of Prometheus was an eagle and

is often called "gripe".' He quotes Sidney, *Astrophel and Stella,* 1591, xiv:
   Uppon whose breast, a fiercer gripe
     doth tyre,
   Than did on him, who first stole
     downe the fyre.

551. *present*] immediate.

552. *delays*] delay. See Abbott, § 333.

553. *winks*] closes his eyes. See l. 375.

554. *dally*] play. Compare *Oth.,* III. iii. 170–1, which is basically a cat-and-mouse image.

555. *hold-fast*] that holds fast. Compare Tennyson, *Becket,* II. ii. See also Tilley, B588, 'Brag is a good dog but Holdfast is a better', and for the same usage *H5,* II. ii. 53.

556. *sad*] serious. There is an antithesis with 'folly'.

vulture folly] devouring, lustful madness.

557. *wanteth*] feels want, craves more.

His ear her prayers admits, but his heart granteth
  No penetrable entrance to her plaining:
  Tears harden lust, though marble wear with raining.   560

Her pity-pleading eyes are sadly fixed
In the remorseless wrinkles of his face.
Her modest eloquence with sighs is mixed,
Which to her oratory adds more grace.
She puts the period often from his place,   565
  And 'midst the sentence so her accent breaks
  That twice she doth begin ere once she speaks.

She conjures him by high almighty Jove,
By knighthood, gentry, and sweet friendship's oath,
By her untimely tears, her husband's love,   570
By holy human law and common troth,
By heaven and earth, and all the power of both,
  That to his borrowed bed he make retire,
  And stoop to honour, not to foul desire.

Quoth she, "Reward not hospitality   575
With such black payment as thou hast pretended.

560. wear] *Q1;* weares *Q6–9.*

559. *penetrable*] capable of being penetrated. The word is associated with pity or sympathy, as in *Ham.,* III. iv. 36:

And let me wring your heart; for so I shall,
If it be made of penetrable stuff.

562. *remorseless*] pitiless. Compare *2H6,* III. i. 213:

And as the butcher takes away the calf...
Even so remorseless have they borne him hence.

wrinkles] frown. Compare *R2,* II. i. 170:   sour my patient cheek
Or bend one wrinkle on my sovereign's face.

565. *period*] full-stop. Steevens compares *MND.,* v. i. 97–8:

Make periods in the midst of sentences,
Throttle their practis'd accents in their fears...

White comments: 'An extreme example of the multitude of cold conceits with which these poems are deformed. The meaning is simply that Lucrece, in her agitation, does not punctuate her sentences rightly'.

566. *accent*] speech.

569. *gentry*] good birth and breeding; sometimes a synonym for 'courtesy', as in *Ham.,* II. ii. 22.

571. *troth*] good faith, honesty.

573. *make retire*] withdraw. 'Retire' is here a substantive, as in *LLL.,* II. i. 234:

All his behaviours did make their retire
To the court of his eye.

See also *H5,* IV. iii. 85–7, and l. 174 above.

574. *stoop to*] submit to.

576. *pretended*] proposed. The word has its Latin sense of 'held out, offered'.

Mud not the fountain that gave drink to thee,
Mar not the thing that cannot be amended.
End thy ill aim before thy shoot be ended;
   He is no woodman that doth bend his bow   580
   To strike a poor unseasonable doe.

"My husband is thy friend; for his sake spare me.
Thyself art mighty; for thine own sake leave me.
Myself a weakling; do not then ensnare me.
Thou look'st not like deceit; do not deceive me.   585
My sighs like whirlwinds labour hence to heave thee;
   If ever man were mov'd with woman's moans,
   Be moved with my tears, my sighs, my groans.

"All which together, like a troubled ocean,
   Beat at thy rocky and wrack-threat'ning heart,   590
To soften it with their continual motion;
For stones dissolv'd to water do convert.
   O if no harder than a stone thou art,
      Melt at my tears and be compassionate!
      Soft pity enters at an iron gate.   595

"In Tarquin's likeness I did entertain thee:
Hast thou put on his shape to do him shame?
To all the host of heaven I complain me,
Thou wrong'st his honour, wound'st his princely name;
Thou art not what thou seem'st, and if the same,   600

583. thine] *Q1;* thy *Q4.*

577.] A 17th-cent. proverb, 'Never cast dirt into that fountain of which thou hast sometimes drunk', which is given in the O.D.E.P., p. 311, and by Tilley, p. 157. See also *Tit.,* v. ii. 171.

579. *shoot*] act of shooting. Pooler quotes *Toxophilus* (ed. Arber, p. 146), and compares *LLL.,* iv. i. 10, and *2H4,* iii. ii. 49. Malone thought that a play on 'suit' was intended, and this is certainly possible, despite the indignant denials of some scholars.

580. *woodman*] sportsman, hunter. Compare *Cym.,* iii. vi. 28:

  You, Polydore, have proved best woodman and

Are master of the feast.

581. *unseasonable*] not in season for hunting.

doe] Compare *Tit.,* ii. i. 93, 117.

586. *heave*] throw. See l. 413.

592. *convert*] change. Compare *R2,* v. i. 66:

  The love of wicked men converts to fear;
  That fear to hate.

For the imagery of water beating on stone see ll. 560, 959 and n., and *Ven.,* l. 200.

597.] The idea is that an evil spirit has assumed Tarquin's form to carry out the crime.

Thou seem'st not what thou art, a god, a king:
For kings like gods should govern everything.

"How will thy shame be seeded in thine age,
    When thus thy vices bud before thy spring?
    If in thy hope thou dar'st do such outrage,   605
    What dar'st thou not when once thou art a king?
    O be remember'd, no outrageous thing
        From vassal actors can be wip'd away:
        Then kings' misdeeds cannot be hid in clay.

"This deed will make thee only lov'd for fear;   610
    But happy monarchs still are fear'd for love.
    With foul offenders thou perforce must bear,
    When they in thee the like offences prove.
    If but for fear of this, thy will remove,
        For princes are the glass, the school, the book,   615
        Where subjects' eyes do learn, do read, do look.

"And wilt thou be the school where lust shall learn?
    Must he in thee read lectures of such shame?
    Wilt thou be glass wherein it shall discern
    Authority for sin, warrant for blame?   620
    To privilege dishonour in thy name,
        Thou back'st reproach against long-living laud,
        And mak'st fair reputation but a bawd.

603. seeded] *Q1*; feeded *Q6,7*.   606. dar'st] *Q1*; darest *Q4*.   once] *Q1*;
omitted *Q4*.   610. will] *Q1*; shall *Q6–9*.   thee] *Q1*; the *Q4*.   613. like]
Q1; light *Q4*.   616. subjects'] *Q1*; subject *Q4*.   619. Wilt] *Q1*; Will *Q4*.

601. *a god, a king*] For the political
theory here see New Arden *R2*, p.
xlviii n. and v. iii. 134 n.

602. *govern*] control, subdue.

603. *seeded*] fruited, matured.

605. *in thy hope*] as being heir to the
throne.

607. *be remember'd*] remember. Compare *Shr.*, iv. iii. 96:

Marry, and did; but if you be
    remember'd,

I did not bid you mar it to the time.

608. *vassal actors*] those who do the
deed, even if subjects.

609.] 'The memory of the ill actions
of kings will remain even after their
death' (Malone).

612–13.] For a similar argument see
Meas., ii. i. 8 ff.

614. *thy will remove*] See l. 243 n.

615–16.] Malone compares *2H4*,
ii. iii. 31:

He was the mark and glass, copy
    and book,

That fashioned others.

618. *lectures*] lessons.

of such shame] Compare *Ant.*, iii. x.
22.

622. *back'st*] supportest. O.E.D.
quotes Greene, *Orlando Furioso* (*Plays
& Poems*, ed. Churton Collins, vol. i,
p. 244):

He backt the Prince of Cuba for my
    foe.

"Hast thou command? by him that gave it thee,
 From a pure heart command thy rebel will.   625
 Draw not thy sword to guard iniquity,
 For it was lent thee all that brood to kill.
 Thy princely office how canst thou fulfil,
  When pattern'd by thy fault, foul sin may say
  He learn'd to sin, and thou didst teach the way? 630

"Think but how vile a spectacle it were,
 To view thy present trespass in another.
 Men's faults do seldom to themselves appear;
 Their own transgressions partially they smother.
 This guilt would seem death-worthy in thy brother. 635
  O how are they wrapp'd in with infamies,
  That from their own misdeeds askance their eyes!

"To thee, to thee, my heav'd-up hands appeal,
 Not to seducing lust, thy rash relier.
 I sue for exil'd majesty's repeal: 640
 Let him return, and flatt'ring thoughts retire;
 His true respect will prison false desire,
  And wipe the dim mist from thy doting eyne,
  That thou shalt see thy state, and pity mine."

---

628. Thy] *Q1*; The *Q4*. 630. to] *Q1*; no *Q4*. 632. in] *Q1*; to *Q4*. 639.
seducing] *Q1*; reducing *Q4*. relier] *Q1*; reply *Q6–9*. 643. eyne] eien *Q1–5*;
eies *Q6–9*.

Compare *1H4*, II. iv. 151:
 Call you that backing of your
  friends?
laud] praise.
624. *him that gave it thee*] God.
629. *pattern'd by thy fault*] shown a
precedent by thy fault. See *Wint.*, III. ii.
37:
   which is more
 Than history can pattern.
634. *partially*] with partiality (sc. to
themselves). Compare *Oth.*, II. iii.
218:
 If partially affined or leagued in
  office,
 Thou dost deliver more or less
  than truth,
 Thou art no soldier.
637. *askance*] turn aside. See Abbott,
p. 5, and *Ven.*, l. 342.

638 f.] For the appeal from a man in
a mood or a passion to the same man in
his true mind see the two anecdotes
of Philip of Macedon given by Elyot,
Book of the Governour.
638. *heav'd-up*] lifted. See l. 111.
639. *thy rash relier*] This has been explained as 'lust which confides too
rashly in thy present disposition and
does not foresee its necessary change'
(Schmidt). Shakespeare probably intended it as 'lust, which you rashly
rely on'.
640. *repeal*] recall from exile. Compare *R2*, IV. i. 86–7:
  These differences shall all rest
   under gage
  Till Norfolk be repeal'd.
642. *His true respect*] his true respect-
fulness; see l. 201.

"Have done," quoth he, "my uncontrolled tide   645
Turns not, but swells the higher by this let.
Small lights are soon blown out, huge fires abide,
And with the wind in greater fury fret;
The petty streams that pay a daily debt
    To their salt sovereign, with their fresh falls' haste   650
    Add to his flow, but alter not his taste."

"Thou art," quoth she, "a sea, a sovereign king,
And lo there falls into thy boundless flood
Black lust, dishonour, shame, misgoverning,
Who seek to stain the ocean of thy blood.   655
If all these petty ills shall change thy good,
    Thy sea within a puddle's womb is hearsed,
    And not the puddle in thy sea dispersed.

"So shall these slaves be king, and thou their slave:
Thou nobly base, they basely dignified;   660
Thou their fair life, and they thy fouler grave;
Thou loathed in their shame, they in thy pride.
The lesser thing should not the greater hide:
    The cedar stoops not to the base shrub's foot,
    But low shrubs wither at the cedar's root.   665

"So let thy thoughts, low vassals to thy state"—
"No more," quoth he, "by heaven I will not hear thee.
Yield to my love: if not, enforced hate
Instead of love's coy touch, shall rudely tear thee.
That done, despitefully I mean to bear thee   670
    Unto the base bed of some rascal groom,
    To be thy partner in this shameful doom."

This said, he sets his foot upon the light,
For light and lust are deadly enemies:

649. petty] *Q1;* pretty *Q6–9.*   651. to his] *Q1;* to the *Q4;* to this *Q5–9.*
655. seek] *Q1;* seekes *Q4.*   657. puddle's] *Q1;* puddle *Q4,6–9.*   658.
puddle] *Q1;* puddles *Q4.*   671. some] *Q1;* the *Q4.*

645–6.] Compare *Oth.,* III. iii. 456 ff.   657. *hearsed*] enclosed as in a bier or
646. *let*] See l. 328.   tomb.
647.] Compare *3H6,* IV. viii. 7 f.;   669. *coy*] gentle, respectful.
and *Ven.,* l. 388.   670. *despitefully*] shamefully, cruelly.
648. *fret*] rage.   671. *rascal*] mean, worthless.
653. *falls*] runs as a river (continuing   *groom*] serving-man.
the metaphor in ll. 649–51).   674.] See *Ven.,* l. 773.

Shame folded up in blind concealing night,   675
When most unseen, then most doth tyrannize.
The wolf hath seiz'd his prey, the poor lamb cries,
    Till with her own white fleece her voice controll'd
    Entombs her outcry in her lips' sweet fold.

For with the nightly linen that she wears   680
He pens her piteous clamours in her head,
Cooling his hot face in the chastest tears
That ever modest eyes with sorrow shed.
O that prone lust should stain so pure a bed!
    The spots whereof could weeping purify,   685
    Her tears should drop on them perpetually.

But she hath lost a dearer thing than life,
And he hath won what he would lose again.
This forced league doth force a further strife;
This momentary joy breeds months of pain;   690
This hot desire converts to cold disdain.
    Pure chastity is rifled of her store,
    And lust the thief, far poorer than before.

Look as the full-fed hound or gorged hawk,
Unapt for tender smell or speedy flight,   695

680. nightly] *Q1;* mighty *Q6,7.*   684. prone] *Q1–3,5;* proud *Q4;* fowle *Q6–9.*

677.] Malone pointed out the resemblance to *Fasti,* II. 800 (see
Appendix II, p. 198). But the conceit
of Lucrece's nightclothes as the lamb's
fleece is Shakespeare's own.

678. *controll'd*] See l. 448.

680. *nightly linen*] Commentators are
reluctant to envisage a night-dress.
White says: 'Not a night-gown, but a
linen cloth worn around the head and
shoulders, and called in later times a
night-rail'. Wyndham points out that
'night-rail' seems to have the same
meaning as 'night-gown', but that in
any case 'Night-gowns were not worn
in bed in Shakespeare's day, and the
word, when he uses it, stands for a
dressing-gown'. He suggests that
'nightly linen' means linen sheets; but
Porter remarks that Lucrece 'could
scarcely be said to wear' these. Any

attempt to establish details must recog-
nize that Shakespeare has not render-
ed the scene very clearly: in ll. 680–1
Tarquin smothers Lucrece's cries by
wrapping her linen round her head;
yet in the next two lines her tears are
able to wet his face. Dr H. F. Brooks
suggests that this last difficulty dis-
appears if we suppose that Tarquin
binds the linen round the lower part
of Lucrece's head, gagging her without
covering her eyes.

681. *pens*] shuts up.

684. *prone*] headstrong, impulsive
(Malone, Schmidt). But the meaning of
'prostrate, face downwards' enters in.

691. *converts*] See l. 592 n.

693–714.] M. C. Bradbrook notes
the connection with Sonnet cxxix (*op.
cit.,* p. 116).

695. *tender smell*] delicate or weak

Make slow pursuit, or altogether balk
The prey wherein by nature they delight:
So surfeit-taking Tarquin fares this night.
   His taste delicious, in digestion souring,
   Devours his will that liv'd by foul devouring.   700

O deeper sin than bottomless conceit
Can comprehend in still imagination!
Drunken desire must vomit his receipt,
Ere he can see his own abomination.
While lust is in his pride no exclamation   705
   Can curb his heat or rein his rash desire,
   Till, like a jade, self-will himself doth tire.

And then with lank and lean discolour'd cheek,
With heavy eye, knit brow, and strengthless pace,
Feeble desire, all recreant, poor and meek,   710
Like to a bankrout beggar wails his case.
The flesh being proud, desire doth fight with grace;
   For there it revels, and when that decays,
   The guilty rebel for remission prays.

So fares it with this faultful lord of Rome,   715
Who this accomplishment so hotly chased;
For now against himself he sounds this doom,

---

704. own] *Q1; omitted Q4.*

smell, i.e. a scent which the hound would need keen appetite and nose to follow.

696. *balk*] miss, omit. Pooler compares *Tw. N.*, III. ii. 26: 'This was looked for at your hand, and this was balk'd: the double gilt of this opportunity you let time wash off.'

700. *will*] appetite, lust.

701. *bottomless conceit*] infinite thought or imagination.

703. *receipt*] what it has received, as in *Cor.*, I. i. 116:

  it [the belly] tauntingly replied
To the discontented members, the
  mutinous parts,
That envied his receipt.

705. *exclamation*] reproof, outcry. Compare *John*, II. i. 558:

Yet in some measure satisfy her so

That we shall stop her exclamation.

707. *like a jade*] like a poor or unwilling horse. See *Ven.*, l. 391 n. 'Self-will', after behaving as a horse with mettle, will tire itself out and become spiritless. Compare *H8*, I. i. 133:
             anger is like
A full-hot horse, who being allow'd
  his way,
Self-mettle tires him.

710. *recreant*] Literally, 'confessing oneself to be overcome or vanquished': hence, false or cowardly.

713. *that*] the pride of the flesh.

714. *remission*] forgiveness.

715. *faultful*] sinful, culpable.

716. *accomplishment*] action, consummation. Compare *H5*, I. Prol. 30.

717. *sounds this doom*] proclaims this judgment (as with a trumpet).

That through the length of times he stands disgraced.
Besides, his soul's fair temple is defaced,
    To whose weak ruins muster troops of cares,   720
    To ask the spotted princess how she fares.

She says her subjects with foul insurrection
Have batter'd down her consecrated wall,
And by their mortal fault brought in subjection
Her immortality, and made her thrall   725
To living death and pain perpetual:
    Which in her prescience she controlled still,
    But her foresight could not forestall their will.

Ev'n in this thought through the dark night he stealeth,
A captive victor that hath lost in gain,   730
Bearing away the wound that nothing healeth,
The scar that will despite of cure remain;
Leaving his spoil perplex'd in greater pain:
    She bears the load of lust he left behind,
    And he the burden of a guilty mind.   735

He like a thievish dog creeps sadly thence,
She like a wearied lamb lies panting there;
He scowls, and hates himself for his offence,
She desperate, with her nails her flesh doth tear.
He faintly flies, sweating with guilty fear;   740
    She stays, exclaiming on the direful night,
    He runs, and chides his vanish'd loath'd delight.

He thence departs a heavy convertite,

729. Ev'n] *Q1–3;* Even *Q4–9.*   738. scowls] *Q1;* schowles *Q2.*

719. *his soul's fair temple*] Compare l. 1172.

721. *the spotted princess*] the soul, as being defiled.

722. *her subjects*] the senses or passions.

724. *mortal*] deadly.

727. *Which*] i.e. her subjects. The soul had always in theory or knowledge ('prescience') governed her subject passions or senses, but her foresight could not in fact restrain them when roused.

730.] See l. 688. Both lines have

been compared to *Fasti,* II. 811 f. (see Appendix II, p. 198).

731. *the wound that nothing healeth*] guilt or dishonour.

733. *his spoil*] his victim.

740. *faintly*] cowardly.

741. *exclaiming on*] crying out against. See *Ven.,* l. 930 n.

743. *heavy convertite*] sad penitent. See *AYL.,* v. iv. 190, and *John,* v. i. 19:
    It was my breath that blew this tempest up
    Upon your stubborn usage of the Pope;

She there remains a hopeless castaway;
He in his speed looks for the morning light,   745
She prays she never may behold the day:
"For day," quoth she, "night's 'scapes doth open lay,
    And my true eyes have never practis'd how
    To cloak offences with a cunning brow.

"They think not but that every eye can see   750
The same disgrace which they themselves behold;
And therefore would they still in darkness be,
To have their unseen sin remain untold.
For they their guilt with weeping will unfold,
    And grave like water that doth eat in steel,   755
    Upon my cheeks, what helpless shame I feel."

Here she exclaims against repose and rest,
And bids her eyes hereafter still be blind.
She wakes her heart by beating on her breast,
And bids it leap from thence, where it may find   760
Some purer chest, to close so pure a mind.
    Frantic with grief, thus breathes she forth her spite
    Against the unseen secrecy of night:

"O comfort-killing night, image of hell,
Dim register and notary of shame,   765
Black stage for tragedies and murders fell,
Vast sin-concealing Chaos, nurse of blame!

---

747. night's 'scapes] nights scapes *Q1–5;* night scapes *Q6,7.*   752. be] *Q1;* lie
Q6–9.

But since you are a gentle conver-
    tite,
My tongue shall hush again the
    storm of war.

744. *castaway*] lost soul, reprobate.
This theological sense was common in
the 16th cent. See the *Homilies* II,
Passion II, 419 (1563).

747. *'scapes*] transgressions, esca-
pades. Compare l. 806, and *2H6,* IV.
i. I.

755. *water that doth eat in steel*] *Aqua
fortis* is meant.

757. *exclaims against*] See l. 741.

761. *chest*] There is a play on the two
senses, 'breast' and 'case'.

close] enclose.

762. *spite*] See *Ven.,* l. 1133 n.

764–70.] With this denunciation of
night Bush compares Prince Arthur's
apostrophe in *F.Q.,* III. iv. 55–8.
Behind them both lies the medieval
tradition seen in *Troilus and Criseyde,*
III. 1429–42 and 1450–70.

765. *notary*] recorder. See l. 494, and
Ven., l. 516.

766.] Malone first remarked the
reference to Elizabethan stage practice: 'In our author's time, I believe,
the stage was hung with black when
tragedies were performed.' See *1H6,*
I. i. I.

Blind muffled bawd, dark harbour for defame,
   Grim cave of death, whisp'ring conspirator
   With close-tongued treason and the ravisher!   770

"O hateful, vaporous and foggy night,
   Since thou art guilty of my cureless crime,
   Muster thy mists to meet the eastern light,
   Make war against proportion'd course of time:
   Or if thou wilt permit the sun to climb   775
      His wonted height, yet ere he go to bed,
      Knit poisonous clouds about his golden head.

"With rotten damps ravish the morning air;
   Let their exhal'd unwholesome breaths make sick
   The life of purity, the supreme fair,   780
   Ere he arrive his weary noontide prick.
   And let thy musty vapours march so thick,
      That in their smoky ranks his smother'd light
      May set at noon and make perpetual night.

"Were Tarquin night, as he is but night's child,   785
   The silver-shining queen he would distain;
   Her twinkling handmaids too, by him defil'd,
   Through night's black bosom should not peep again.
   So should I have co-partners in my pain;

778. rotten] *Q1*; rotting *Q4*.   782. vapours] *Q1*; vapour *Q4*.   783. ranks] *Q1*; rackes *Q4*.   786. distain] *Q1*; disdaine *Q6-9*.

768. *harbour*] refuge, shelter.
defame] infamy. See also ll. 817, 1033.
770. *close-tongued*] speaking secretly.
774. *proportion'd*] regular, regulated. See *Troil.*, I. iii. 87.
778. *ravish*] seize or spoil.
780.] the sun.
supreme] ruler, king. See *Ven.*, l. 996; for the recession of accent see *John*, III. i. 155.
781. *arrive*] arrive at. See also *Cæs.*, I. ii. 110.
noontide prick] the point of noon, so-called from the mark on the sun-dial. The expression is made much of in *Rom.*, II. iv. 119, and is also used in *3H6*, I. iv. 34:

Now Phaeton hath tumbled from his car,
And made an evening at the noon-tide prick.
With 'weary' compare *Ven.*, l. 177.
782. *musty*] Malone's adoption of 'misty' (from *Q3-9*) destroys the force of these lines. See Sisson, *New Readings*, I, p. 209.
784.] Compare *R3*, I. iv. 77, and *Lr.*, III. v. 92.
785. *night's child*] as being a 'child of darkness', i.e. wicked.
786. *distain*] defile. See *R3*, v. iii. 322.
787. *handmaids*] Malone quotes the reference to the stars as 'Diana's waiting-women' in *Troil.*, v. ii. 92.

And fellowship in woe doth woe assuage,   790
As palmers' chat makes short their pilgrimage.

"Where now I have no one to blush with me,
To cross their arms and hang their heads with mine,
To mask their brows and hide their infamy;
But I alone, alone must sit and pine,   795
Seasoning the earth with showers of silver brine,
    Mingling my talk with tears, my grief with groans,
    Poor wasting monuments of lasting moans.

"O night, thou furnace of foul reeking smoke,
Let not the jealous day behold that face   800
Which underneath thy black all-hiding cloak
Immodestly lies martyr'd with disgrace!
Keep still possession of thy gloomy place,
    That all the faults which in thy reign are made
    May likewise be sepulchred in thy shade.   805

"Make me not object to the tell-tale day:
The light will show character'd in my brow
The story of sweet chastity's decay,
The impious breach of holy wedlock vow;

791. palmers' chat makes] Palmers chat makes *Q1*; palmers that make *Q4*;
palmers that makers *Q6*.   their] *Q1*; the *Q4*.   807. will] *Q1*; shal *Q5–9*.
my] *Q1*; thy *Q5*.   808. story] *Q1*; stories *Q4*.   809. breach] *Q1*; breath *Q4*.
wedlock] wedlocke *Q1*; wedlocks *Q3,5–9*; weldocks *Q4*.

790.] The Latin 'Solamen miseris
socios habuisse doloris' was constantly
quoted or echoed in medieval and
16th-cent. literature. See *Troilus and
Criseyde*, I. cii, and also *Rom.*, III. ii. 116,
and *Lr.*, III. vi. 114.

791. *palmers' chat*] conversation
among pilgrims. Those who had made
the pilgrimage to the Holy Land in
the Middle Ages wore a palm-leaf, as
those who went to Santiago wore a
cockle-shell.

792. *Where now*] whereas. See *R2*,
III. ii. 185, and Abbott, § 134.

793. *cross their arms*] 'Folded arms
were a recognized sign of melancholy'
(Herford). See l. 1662.

794. *mask their brows*] To pull one's
hat down over one's face was an-

other sign of grief. See *Mac.*, IV. iii.
208.

795.] See *Compl.*, l. 18.

796. *brine*] Compare *3H6*, III. i. 41.

797–8.] For tears as monuments see
also *2H6*, III. ii. 342.

800. *jealous*] watchful.

805. *sepulchred*] The accent is on the
second syllable, as in *Gent.*, IV. ii. 118
See also *R2*, I. iii. 196.

806. *object*] something exposed to
sight. See l. 747 and n.

807. *character'd*] inscribed. The
accent may be on the second syllable
here, as in *Ham.*, I. iii. 59.

808. *decay*] downfall. See l. 516.
Compare *F.Q.*, I. vi. 48:

    In hope to bring her to her last
        decay.

Yea, the illiterate that know not how   810
   To cipher what is writ in learned books,
   Will quote my loathsome trespass in my looks.

"The nurse to still her child will tell my story,
   And fright her crying babe with Tarquin's name.
   The orator to deck his oratory   815
   Will couple my reproach to Tarquin's shame.
   Feast-finding minstrels tuning my defame,
      Will tie the hearers to attend each line,
      How Tarquin wronged me, I Collatine.

"Let my good name, that senseless reputation,   820
   For Collatine's dear love be kept unspotted.
   If that be made a theme for disputation,
   The branches of another root are rotted,
   And undeserv'd reproach to him allotted
      That is as clear from this attaint of mine   825
      As I ere this was pure to Collatine.

"O unseen shame, invisible disgrace!
   O unfelt sore, crest-wounding private scar!
   Reproach is stamp'd in Collatinus' face,
   And Tarquin's eye may read the mot afar,   830
   How he in peace is wounded, not in war:

821. be] *Q1;* he *Q5.*

811. *cipher*] read, spell out.
812. *quote*] note, mark. Compare *Ham.,* II. i. 112, *Tit.,* IV. i. 50, *LLL.,* v. ii. 796, and *Rom.,* I. iv. 31 : what care I
What curious eye may quote
   deformities?
813–14.] Compare *1H6,* II. iii. 17.
817. *Feast-finding minstrels*] minstrels who seek out feasts (where they may entertain the company and be rewarded).
818. *tie*] hold.
820. *that senseless reputation*] It is impossible to decide whether this means 'that reputation which is based on hearsay, not knowledge'; or 'that unfelt, impalpable reputation'; or 'that reputation for being "senseless", i.e. free from sensuality'.
825. *attaint*] disgrace: but this mean-

ing has become confused with that of physical 'infection' (see *Ven.,* l. 741). Lucrece uses the word again in l. 1072. The earlier legal or social sense appears in *Err.,* III. ii. 16:
What simple thief brags of his own
   attaint?
828. *crest-wounding*] striking at family or personal honour, represented heraldically by a crest. But there is also an allusion to the horned head, the emblem of cuckoldry. There is an oxymoron between 'crest-wounding' and 'private', as there is between 'unfelt' and 'sore'.
830. *mot*] motto, device. O.E.D. quotes an example from Marston, *Antonio and Mellida,* v: 'I did send for you to draw me a devise, an Imprezza, by Sinecdoche a Mott'.

Alas how many bear such shameful blows,
Which not themselves, but he that gives them knows!

"If, Collatine, thine honour lay in me,
　From me by strong assault it is bereft:　　　　　835
　My honey lost, and I a drone-like bee,
　Have no perfection of my summer left,
　But robb'd and ransack'd by injurious theft;
　　In thy weak hive a wand'ring wasp hath crept,
　　And suck'd the honey which thy chaste bee kept.　840

"Yet am I guilty of thy honour's wrack;
　Yet for thy honour did I entertain him:
　Coming from thee I could not put him back,
　For it had been dishonour to disdain him.
　Besides, of weariness he did complain him,　　845
　　And talk'd of virtue: O unlook'd-for evil,
　　When virtue is profan'd in such a devil!

"Why should the worm intrude the maiden bud,
　Or hateful cuckoos hatch in sparrows' nests?
　Or toads infect fair founts with venom mud,　　850
　Or tyrant folly lurk in gentle breasts?
　Or kings be breakers of their own behests?
　　But no perfection is so absolute
　　That some impurity doth not pollute.

"The aged man that coffers up his gold　　　　855
　Is plagu'd with cramps and gouts and painful fits,
　And scarce hath eyes his treasure to behold;
　But like still-pining Tantalus he sits,

---

835. *bereft*] taken away.

836. *drone-like bee*] Drones do not gather honey. Lucrece compares herself to a bee that is *like* a drone because its honey has been stolen. Pooler quotes Topsel, *Fourfooted Beasts*, p. 919.

841–2.] These two lines represent a debate like that in ll. 239–42. Lucrece first accuses, then excuses, herself. In such passages Shakespeare's training in dramatic verse is evident; the method came from Seneca.

848. *intrude*] enter forcibly.

850.] Compare *Oth.*, IV. ii. 60–3, and *3H6*, II. ii. 138.

851. *folly*] sensuality. See l. 556.

852. *behests*] commands, i.e. laws.

853. *absolute*] complete. Compare *Oth.*, II. i. 193, *1H4*, IV. iii. 50, *H5*, III. vii. 27, and elsewhere.

858. *still-pining*] forever hungry.

Tantalus] See *Ven.*, l. 599 n. Baldwin investigates Shakespeare's authority for thus connecting Tantalus with maxims on avarice (*op. cit.*, pp. 133–6).

And useless barns the harvest of his wits,
   Having no other pleasure of his gain   860
   But torment that it cannot cure his pain.

"So then he hath it when he cannot use it,
   And leaves it to be master'd by his young,
   Who in their pride do presently abuse it;
   Their father was too weak, and they too strong,   865
   To hold their cursed-blessed fortune long:
     The sweets we wish for turn to loathed sours
     Even in the moment that we call them ours.

"Unruly blasts wait on the tender spring;
   Unwholesome weeds take root with precious flowers;   870
   The adder hisses where the sweet birds sing;
   What virtue breeds iniquity devours.
   We have no good that we can say is ours,
     But ill-annexed opportunity
     Or kills his life, or else his quality.   875

"O opportunity, thy guilt is great!
   'Tis thou that execut'st the traitor's treason;
   Thou sets the wolf where he the lamb may get;
   Whoever plots the sin, thou poinst the season.
   'Tis thou that spurn'st at right, at law, at reason;   880
     And in thy shady cell where none may spy him,
     Sits sin to seize the souls that wander by him.

"Thou mak'st the vestal violate her oath;
   Thou blow'st the fire when temperance is thaw'd;

859. barns] barnes *Q1–5;* bannes *Q6–9.*   871. hisses] *Q1;* hisseth *Q3–9.*
879. poinst] *Q1;* points *Q5–9.*   881, 882. him . . . him] *Q1;* her . . . her
Q6–9.

859. *barns*] garners, stores in a barn.
862–3.] Compare *Meas.,* iii. i. 36–8:
   when thou art old and rich
Thou has neither heat, affection,
   limb, nor beauty
To make thy riches pleasant.
master'd] taken control of.
864. *presently*] immediately.
868. *call them ours*] Compare *Oth.,*
ii. iii. 273, and l. 873.
874. *ill-annexed*] disastrously added.

opportunity] occasion, chance, or
circumstance. Compare the Bastard's
tirade on Commodity in *John,* ii. i.
574 ff.
875. *quality*] nature or temper. See
ll. 1313 and 1702.
879. *poinst*] appointest. See *Shr.,* iii.
i. 19, and iii. ii. 1. 'Points', as in Q5,
would be in accord with the usage described in Abbott, § 340. See *Pilgr.,*
x. 9 n.

Thou smother'st honesty, thou murder'st troth,   885
Thou foul abettor, thou notorious bawd!
Thou plantest scandal, and displacest laud:
   Thou ravisher, thou traitor, thou false thief!
   Thy honey turns to gall, thy joy to grief.

"Thy secret pleasure turns to open shame,   890
Thy private feasting to a public fast,
Thy smoothing titles to a ragged name,
Thy sugar'd tongue to bitter wormwood taste;
Thy violent vanities can never last.
   How comes it then, vile opportunity,   895
   Being so bad, such numbers seek for thee?

"When wilt thou be the humble suppliant's friend,
And bring him where his suit may be obtained?
When wilt thou sort an hour great strifes to end,
Or free that soul which wretchedness hath chained?   900
Give physic to the sick, ease to the pained?
   The poor, lame, blind, halt, creep, cry out for thee;
   But they ne'er meet with opportunity.

"The patient dies while the physician sleeps;
The orphan pines while the oppressor feeds;   905
Justice is feasting while the widow weeps;
Advice is sporting while infection breeds.
Thou grant'st no time for charitable deeds;
   Wrath, envy, treason, rape, and murder's rages,
   Thy heinous hours wait on them as their pages.   910

---

892. smoothing] *Q1;* smothering *Q6–9.*   893. to] *Q1;* to a *Q4.*   899. strifes]
Q1; strife *Q4.*   903. meet] *Q1;* met *Q3–9.*   909. murder's] murthers *Q1–5;*
murther *Q6–9.*

---

892. *smoothing*] flattering. Compare
R3, I. iii. 48, and *Tit.,* v. ii. 140:
  Yield to his humour, smooth and
    speak him fair.
  ragged] tattered, i.e. torn in public
estimation.
  894.] Compare *Rom.,* II. vi. 9:
  These violent delights have violent
    ends.
  899. *sort*] fit, adapt. Compare *R3,* II.
ii. 148, and *1H6,* II. iii. 27:
  I'll sort some other time to visit you.

  902.] Compare the use of this
rhetorical figure in *Ham.,* III. i.
151.
  905. *pines*] starves.
  907. *Advice*] medical advice or attention. There is no need to see here a
critical reference to the spread of
the plague in Elizabethan London
(Steevens and Knight); the authorities were by no means heedless of the
danger.
  910. *heinous*] hateful.

"When truth and virtue have to do with thee,
A thousand crosses keep them from thy aid;
They buy thy help, but sin ne'er gives a fee:
He gratis comes, and thou art well appaid,
As well to hear as grant what he hath said.   915
    My Collatine would else have come to me
    When Tarquin did, but he was stay'd by thee.

"Guilty thou art of murder and of theft,
Guilty of perjury and subornation,
Guilty of treason, forgery and shift,   920
Guilty of incest, that abomination:
An accessory by thine inclination
    To all sins past and all that are to come
    From the creation to the general doom.

"Mis-shapen time, copesmate of ugly night,   925
Swift subtle post, carrier of grisly care,
Eater of youth, false slave to false delight,
Base watch of woes, sin's pack-horse, virtue's snare!
Thou nursest all, and murder'st all that are:
    O hear me then, injurious shifting time!   930
    Be guilty of my death, since of my crime.

"Why hath thy servant opportunity
Betray'd the hours thou gav'st me to repose,
Cancell'd my fortunes and enchained me
To endless date of never-ending woes?   935

922. An] *Q1;* And *Q4.*

914. *gratis*] without a fee.
well appaid] fully satisfied.
919. *subornation*] bribing someone to commit a crime, particularly to bear false witness.
920. *shift*] trickery. Compare *Wiv.,* I. iii. 37: 'I must cony-catch; I must shift'.
924. *general doom*] the Last Judgment. Compare *R3,* III. i. 78.
925–94.] This descant on time was noted as characteristic by Paul Elmer More in *Shelburne Essays,* 2nd series (1905), pp. 28 f.: 'No single motive or theme recurs more persistently through the whole course of Shake-

speare's works than this consciousness of the servile depredations of time'. See *Ven.,* ll. 127–32, and compare J. W. Lever, *op. cit.,* p. 201 and pp. 248 f.
925. *copesmate*] companion, familiar friend.
926. *post*] post-rider. See l. 1 n.
928. *watch of woes*] watchman numbering woes like the passing hours.
930. *shifting*] not only moving, but cheating. See l. 920 n.
934–5.] A contract with fortune has been 'cancelled', and replaced by a bond binding Lucrece to sorrow, with no 'date' of expiry. See l. 1729 n.

Time's office is to fine the hate of foes,
  To eat up errors by opinion bred,
  Not spend the dowry of a lawful bed.

"Time's glory is to calm contending kings,
  To unmask falsehood and bring truth to light,   940
  To stamp the seal of time in aged things,
  To wake the morn and sentinel the night,
  To wrong the wronger till he render right,
    To ruinate proud buildings with thy hours,
    And smear with dust their glitt'ring golden tow'rs; 945

"To fill with worm-holes stately monuments,
  To feed oblivion with decay of things,
  To blot old books and alter their contents,
  To pluck the quills from ancient ravens' wings,
  To dry the old oak's sap and cherish springs,   950
    To spoil antiquities of hammer'd steel,
    And turn the giddy round of fortune's wheel;

937. errors] errours *Q1,2;* errour *Q3–9.*   939. to] *Q1;* too *Q5.*

936. *fine*] Malone glossed the word as 'refine'; Steevens interpreted it as 'bring to an end'. The latter sense has been generally accepted, Pooler giving instances of the corresponding noun from the *Wife of Bath's Prologue,* Caxton, *Recuyell of the Historyes of Troy, Ham.,* v. i. 115, and *All's W.,* IV. iv. 35:
    Still the fine's the crown,
  Whate'er the course, the end is the
    renown.
937. *opinion*] what is believed without real knowledge or certainty. Shakespeare means *common* opinion.
942. *sentinel*] stand watch, divide into watches.
943. *wrong the wronger*] According to Malone to '*punish* by the *compunctious visitings of conscience* the person who has done an injury to another'. But why should not Time, as an instrument of Providence, bring actual misfortune to a wrongdoer, as a punishment and an inducement to remorse?
    render right] make reparation for wrongs done.

944. *ruinate*] reduce to ruins. Compare Sonnet x, l. 7, and *3H6,* v. i. 83.
948.] Compare Chaucer on change in language, *Troilus and Criseyde,* II. 22 f.
949. *ancient ravens' wings*] Ravens were supposed to live three times as long as human beings. See *Phoen.,* l. 17 n.
950. *cherish springs*] Seizing on an apparent illogicality, 18th-cent. editors proposed various emendations: Warburton suggested 'tarish' for 'cherish' because the subject is 'the decays and not the repairs of time'; Johnson followed him to the point of proffering 'perish'. But Shakespeare is about to pass to the decays *and* the repairs of time, as he does in the next stanza, and this line introduces the new theme. 'Springs' may mean young oaks, or saplings of any kind, a meaning illustrated by Pooler from Turbervile's *Book of Hunting.* See *Ven.,* l. 656 n.

"To show the beldam daughters of her daughter,
To make the child a man, the man a child,
To slay the tiger that doth live by slaughter,   955
To tame the unicorn and lion wild,
To mock the subtle in themselves beguil'd,
    To cheer the ploughman with increaseful crops,
    And waste huge stones with little water-drops.

"Why work'st thou mischief in thy pilgrimage,   960
Unless thou could'st return to make amends?
One poor retiring minute in an age
Would purchase thee a thousand thousand friends,
Lending him wit that to bad debtors lends:
    O this dread night, would'st thou one hour come back,   965
    I could prevent this storm and shun thy wrack!

"Thou ceaseless lackey to eternity,
With some mischance cross Tarquin in his flight;
Devise extremes beyond extremity,

954. the child] *Q1;* a child *Q4.*   966. shun thy] *Q1;* shun this *Q6,7;* shunt his *Q8,9.*

953. *beldam*] old woman. See l. 1458.

956. *tame the unicorn*] Shakespeare seems to have fallen into some inaccuracy. Pooler quotes from Topsel, *Fourfooted Beasts*, to show that in this case 'time has an unfavourable influence': 'It [the unicorn] is a beast of an untamable nature. . . Except they be taken before they be two years old they will never be tamed, . . . when they are old, they differ nothing at all from the most barbarous bloudy and ravenous beasts.'

957.] Time mocks those who overinterpret the significance of events, by revealing that things were simpler than they thought.

958. *increaseful*] multiplying, fruitful.

959.] Shakespeare found this commonplace a useful piece of poetic equipment; see ll. 560, 592, and *Ven.,* l. 200. Pooler quotes Ovid, *Ars Amatoria,* l. 476.

959. *little water-drops*] Compare *Dr Faustus,* l. 1472.

962. *retiring*] As Malone remarks, this must mean 'returning'; but the search for other examples has produced little but a passage from *A Warning for Faire Women,* discovered by R. H. Case and quoted by Pooler:

This Mistress Drury must be made
    the mean
Whate'er it cost, to compass my
    desire.
And I hope well she doth so soon
    retire.

(Simpson's *School of Shakespeare,* II, pp. 246–7).

964.] giving wisdom through experience to one who has lost the money he lent.

967–94.] Lucrece's curses on Tarquin contain many parallels with the curses on Richard III and their results (see *R3,* I. ii. 112, I. iii. 223 f., and v. iii. 118 f.).

968. *cross*] afflict, frustrate. See *Ven.,* l. 734.

969. *extremes beyond extremity*] inconceivable freaks or monstrosities.

To make him curse this cursed crimeful night.   970
Let ghastly shadows his lewd eyes affright,
    And the dire thought of his committed evil
    Shape every bush a hideous shapeless devil.

"Disturb his hours of rest with restless trances,
Afflict him in his bed with bedrid groans;   975
Let there bechance him pitiful mischances,
To make him moan, but pity not his moans.
Stone him with harden'd hearts harder than stones,
    And let mild women to him lose their mildness,
    Wilder to him than tigers in their wildness.   980

"Let him have time to tear his curled hair,
Let him have time against himself to rave,
Let him have time of time's help to despair,
Let him have time to live a loathed slave,
Let him have time a beggar's orts to crave,   985
    And time to see one that by alms doth live
    Disdain to him disdained scraps to give.

"Let him have time to see his friends his foes,
And merry fools to mock at him resort;
Let him have time to mark how slow time goes   990
In time of sorrow, and how swift and short
His time of folly and his time of sport:
    And ever let his unrecalling crime
    Have time to wail th'abusing of his time.

---

975. bedrid] bedred *Qq*.   978. stones] *Q1*; stone *Q3–7*.   979. their] *Q1*; his
Q4.   993. crime] *Q1*; time *Q5–9*.

973.] Compare *MND.*, v. i. 22, and *3H6*, v. vi. 12.

975. *bedrid*] bedridden. The epithet is transferred from the groaner to the groans. See *LLL.*, I. i. 139.

981. *curled hair*] Shakespeare visualized Tarquin as a 16th-cent. Italian nobleman: Iachimo, himself an anachronism, refers to him in *Cym.*, II. ii. 12, as '*our* Tarquin'. The curled hair here indicates a life of luxury and youthful frivolity. Compare *Oth.*, I. ii. 68:

    The wealthy curled darlings of our
      nation.

985. *orts*] scraps of food. See *Cæs.*, IV. i. 37, *Tim.*, IV. iii. 400, and *Troil.*, v. ii. 158:

    The fractions of her faith, orts of
      her love,

    The fragments, scraps, the bits and
      greasy relics

    Of her o'er-eaten faith.

989–90.] Mockery and slow-moving time appear again in *Oth.*, IV. ii. 55–6.

993. *unrecalling*] irrevocable. Pooler cites the parallel of 'unrecuring' for 'incurable' in *Tit.*, III. i. 90.

"O time, thou tutor both to good and bad,   995
Teach me to curse him that thou taught'st this ill!
At his own shadow let the thief run mad,
Himself, himself seek every hour to kill:
Such wretched hands such wretched blood should spill,
    For who so base would such an office have   1000
    As sland'rous deathsman to so base a slave?

"The baser is he, coming from a king,
To shame his hope with deeds degenerate;
The mightier man the mightier is the thing
That makes him honour'd or begets him hate,   1005
For greatest scandal waits on greatest state.
    The moon being clouded presently is miss'd,
    But little stars may hide them when they list.

"The crow may bathe his coal-black wings in mire,
And unperceiv'd fly with the filth away;   1010
But if the like the snow-white swan desire,
The stain upon his silver down will stay.
Poor grooms are sightless night, kings glorious day;
    Gnats are unnoted wheresoe'er they fly,
    But eagles gaz'd upon with every eye.   1015

"Out idle words, servants to shallow fools,
Unprofitable sounds, weak arbitrators!

996. taught'st] *Q1*; taughts *Q5–8*.   1006. greatest state] *Q1*; greater state *Q4*.
1016. Out] *Q1*; Our *Q5–9*.

998. *Himself, himself*] See l. 160 n.
1001. *sland'rous*] ill-reputed.
deathsman] executioner; compare
3H6, v. v. 67. The profession of hang-
man or headsman was held in low
esteem; see *Meas.*, IV. i. 29 *et seq.*
1002–3.] The possible or actual
degeneracy of men of noble descent
was much debated in the 16th cent.
and earlier, in discussions on the
nature of true nobility. Dr Harold F.
Brooks points out the topic in Med-
wall's *Fulgens and Lucres* (based on a
Renaissance dialogue translated by
Tiptoft), Rastell's *Gentleness and Nobility*, Elyot's *The Book of the Governour*,
Bk II, ch. iv; Elyot echoes Juvenal VIII,
on the subject of breeding. The ques-

tion is related to that of true courtesy,
and is treated by Spenser in his own
way in *F.Q.*, Bk VI.
1003. *hope*] position as heir. See l.
605 n.
1007. *presently*] at once.
1013. *grooms*] servants, subjects,
labourers.
sightless] invisible. See *Mac.*, I. v. 50
and I. vii. 23.
1014–15.] Compare *Tit.*, IV. iv. 81–
6, and *Ant.*, II. ii. 185.
1017. *arbitrators*] arbiters. An arbiter
is one chosen by opposite parties in a
dispute to arrange or decide between
their claims; hence 'arbitrator' as one
who brings about a final issue. Compare *1H6*, II. v. 28 and *Troil.*, IV. v. 224:

Busy yourselves in skill-contending schools,
Debate where leisure serves with dull debaters;
To trembling clients be you mediators: 1020
　　For me, I force not argument a straw,
　　Since that my case is past the help of law.

"In vain I rail at opportunity,
　At time, at Tarquin, at uncheerful night;
In vain I cavil with mine infamy,   1025
In vain I spurn at my confirm'd despite;
This helpless smoke of words doth me no right:
　　The remedy indeed to do me good
　　Is to let forth my foul defiled blood.

"Poor hand, why quiver'st thou at this decree?   1030
Honour thyself to rid me of this shame:
For if I die, my honour lives in thee,
But if I live, thou liv'st in my defame.
Since thou could'st not defend thy loyal dame,
　　And wast afeard to scratch her wicked foe,   1035
　　Kill both thyself and her for yielding so."

This said, from her betumbled couch she starteth,
To find some desp'rate instrument of death;
But this no slaughterhouse no tool imparteth
To make more vent for passage of her breath,   1040
Which thronging through her lips so vanisheth

1024. uncheerful] unchearfull *Q1–4;* unsearchfull *Q5–9.*   1037, 1039. starteth
... imparteth] *Q1;* starts ... imparts *Q6–9.*   1039. no slaughterhouse]
Q5,6; no slaughter house *Q1,2;* no-slaughter house *Q3,4.*

And that old common arbitrator,
　Time,
Will one day end it.

1018. *skill-contending schools*] univer-
sities, where the medieval system of
displaying skill in debate still flourished.

1020. *clients*] suitors at law.

1021. *force not argument a straw*] care
not a straw for argument. Compare
LLL., v. ii. 440:

　Your oath once broke, you force
　　not to forswear.

1025. *cavil with*] object without good
reason, quibble about.

1026. *spurn at*] kick at, reject scornfully. Compare *R3,* 1. iv. 203.

despite] shame or wrong suffered.

1027. *helpless*] unhelping. See *Ven.,*
l. 604.

smoke of words] mere talk, obscuring
things though proceeding from passion as smoke from fire.

1034. *thy loyal dame*] thy mistress who
was virtuous.

1037. *betumbled*] disordered.

1039. *this no slaughterhouse*] Rhythm
and sense would be clearer if we read
'no-slaughterhouse'.

imparteth] provides.

As smoke from Ætna, that in air consumes,
Or that which from discharged cannon fumes.

"In vain," quoth she, "I live, and seek in vain
  Some happy mean to end a hapless life.   1045
  I fear'd by Tarquin's falchion to be slain,
  Yet for the self-same purpose seek a knife;
  But when I fear'd I was a loyal wife:
    So am I now,—O no, that cannot be!
    Of that true type hath Tarquin rifled me.   1050

"O that is gone for which I sought to live,
  And therefore now I need not fear to die!
  To clear this spot by death, at least I give
  A badge of fame to slander's livery,
  A dying life to living infamy: 1055
    Poor helpless help, the treasure stol'n away,
    To burn the guiltless casket where it lay!

"Well well, dear Collatine, thou shalt not know
  The stained taste of violated troth;
  I will not wrong thy true affection so,   1060
  To flatter thee with an infringed oath.
  This bastard graff shall never come to growth:
    He shall not boast who did thy stock pollute,
    That thou art doting father of his fruit.

"Nor shall he smile at thee in secret thought, 1065
  Nor laugh with his companions at thy state;
  But thou shalt know thy int'rest was not bought
  Basely with gold, but stol'n from forth thy gate.
  For me, I am the mistress of my fate,

1046. Tarquin's] *Q1;* Tarquin *Q4.*   falchion] Fauchion *Q1;* faunchion *Q4.*
1062. graff] graffe *Q1,2;* grasse *Q3–9.*

1045. *mean*] means.

1050. *that true type*] the stamp or
mark of faith. Compare *3H6,* I. iv.
121.

1053. *To clear this spot by death*] removing the stain of impurity by dying.

1054. *badge*] Servants of a noble
household in Elizabethan days wore
on the sleeve of their livery a badge
bearing the device, crest, or coat of
arms of their master (Malone). See
also *1H6,* IV. i. 177, *2H6,* V. i. 201–2,
and *Tit.,* I. i. 119 and II. i. 89.

1062. *graff*] a shoot, slip, or scion,
inserted ('grafted') into another stem.
See Baldwin, *op. cit.,* p. 138.

1063. *stock*] stem.

1067. *int'rest*] property, share.

1069.] Compare *Cæs.,* I. ii. 139, and
contrast *Oth.,* V. ii. 268.

And with my trespass never will dispense,   1070
Till life to death acquit my forc'd offence.

"I will not poison thee with my attaint,
　Nor fold my fault in cleanly-coin'd excuses;
　My sable ground of sin I will not paint,
　To hide the truth of this false night's abuses.   1075
　My tongue shall utter all, mine eyes like sluices,
　　As from a mountain-spring that feeds a dale,
　　Shall gush pure streams to purge my impure tale."

By this, lamenting Philomel had ended
　The well-tun'd warble of her nightly sorrow,   1080
And solemn night with slow sad gait descended
To ugly hell; when lo, the blushing morrow
Lends light to all fair eyes that light will borrow;
　　But cloudy Lucrece shames herself to see,
　　And therefore still in night would cloister'd be.   1085

Revealing day through every cranny spies,
And seems to point her out where she sits weeping;
To whom she sobbing speaks, "O eye of eyes,
Why pry'st thou through my window? leave thy peeping,
Mock with thy tickling beams eyes that are sleeping;   1090
　　Brand not my forehead with thy piercing light,
　　For day hath naught to do what's done by night."

Thus cavils she with every thing she sees.
True grief is fond and testy as a child,

1071. forc'd] forst *Q1;* forse *Q4.*   1075. false] *Q1;* falle *Q5.*   1083. will] *Q1;*
would *Q5–9.*   1085. be] *Q1; omitted Q5.*

1070. *with . . . dispense*] pardon, con-
done. See ll. 1279 and 1704.

1072. *attaint*] taint. See l. 825 n.

1073. *fold my fault*] wrap up, hide,
my fault.

cleanly-coin'd] forged, but with an
appearance of purity.

1074. *My sable ground*] black background. 'Ground' is another of the
heraldic terms common in this poem,
'the surface of a shield on which are
represented the ensigns armorial com-
posing a coat of arms' (Feuillerat).

1076. *sluices*] Compare *Ven.,* l. 956.

1079. *Philomel*] the nightingale. See
Pilg., xx. 14 n.

1084. *cloudy*] sorrowful. See *Ven.,*
l. 725.

shames] is ashamed. Compare l.
1143.

1088. *O eye of eyes*] Compare l. 356.

1090. *tickling*] stroking, lightly
touching.

1092. *to do*] to do with. See Abbott,
§ 200.

1093. *cavils*] See l. 1025 n.

1094. *fond and testy*] foolish and irrit-
able.

Who wayward once, his mood with naught agrees; 1095
Old woes, not infant sorrows, bear them mild.
Continuance tames the one; the other wild,
    Like an unpractis'd swimmer plunging still,
    With too much labour drowns for want of skill.

So she deep-drenched in a sea of care, 1100
Holds disputation with each thing she views,
And to herself all sorrow doth compare;
No object but her passion's strength renews,
And as one shifts another straight ensues.
    Sometime her grief is dumb and hath no words, 1105
    Sometime 'tis mad and too much talk affords.

The little birds that tune their morning's joy
Make her moans mad with their sweet melody,
For mirth doth search the bottom of annoy;
Sad souls are slain in merry company, 1110
Grief best is pleas'd with grief's society:
    True sorrow then is feelingly suffic'd
    When with like semblance it is sympathis'd.

'Tis double death to drown in ken of shore;
He ten times pines that pines beholding food; 1115
To see the salve doth make the wound ache more;
Great grief grieves most at that would do it good;
Deep woes roll forward like a gentle flood,
    Who being stopp'd, the bounding bank o'erflows;
    Grief dallied with, nor law nor limit knows. 1120

"You mocking birds," quoth she, "your tunes entomb
    Within your hollow swelling feather'd breasts,

1105. Sometime] *Q1;* Sometimes *Q5–9.*　　1107. morning's] *Q1;* morning
Q4.

1095. *wayward once*] once having become angry.
1096. *bear them mild*] behave mild-
ly.
1104. *straight*] straightway.
1107–9.] Malone refers to *R2,* v. v.
61.
1109. *search the bottom*] pierce to the
depth.

annoy] grief, injury. See l. 1370.
1112. *suffic'd*] satisfied.
1113.] When it receives sympathy
from similar impressions or behaviour.
1114. *in ken of shore*] within sight of
shore.
1115. *pines*] starves, hungers. See
l. 905.
1120. *dallied with*] trifled with.

And in my hearing be you mute and dumb;
My restless discord loves no stops nor rests.
A woeful hostess brooks not merry guests.   1125
    Relish your nimble notes to pleasing ears;
    Distress likes dumps, when time is kept with tears.

"Come Philomel, that sing'st of ravishment,
Make thy sad grove in my dishevel'd hair;
As the dank earth weeps at thy languishment,   1130
So I at each sad strain will strain a tear
And with deep groans the diapason bear;
    For burden-wise I'll hum on Tarquin still,
    While thou on Tereus descants better skill.

"And whiles against a thorn thou bear'st thy part   1135
To keep thy sharp woes waking, wretched I
To imitate thee well, against my heart
Will fix a sharp knife to affright mine eye,
Who if it wink shall thereon fall and die:

1123. mute and] *Q1;* ever *Q6–9.*   1126. Relish] *Q4,6;* Ralish *Q1.*   1129.
grove] *Q1;* grone *Q5.*   1134. Tereus] *Q1;* Iereus *Q5.*

1124.] There is a play on 'restless' and 'rests': the birds' song, being harmony, would be a stop or rest to discord.

1126. *Relish*] warble. According to Naylor (*Shakespeare and Music*), ' "relish" . . . [is] the name for an elaborate ornament in lute music'. Compare *Gent.,* ii. i. 21–2: 'to relish a love-song like a robin-redbreast'.

1127. *dumps*] slow, sad tunes or songs. Compare *Gent.,* iii. ii. 85:

        to their instruments
    Tune is a despairing dump.

time is kept with tears] Compare Jonson, *Cynthias Revells,* i. ii. 65.

1131. *strain*] 'A "strain" is the proper Elizabethan word for a formal phrase of a musical composition' (Naylor).

1132. *diapason*] 'an air or base sounding in exact concord' (O.E.D.).

1133. *burden-wise*] 'Burden from confusion with "bourdon" came to mean "the base, undersong, or accompaniment" ' (O.E.D.). O.E.D. further explains: 'Apparently the notion was that the base or undersong was heavier than the air. The bourdon usually continued when the singer of the air paused at the end of a stanza, and (when vocal) was usually sung to words forming a refrain, being often taken up in chorus'. Shakespeare often puns on the word; see *Gent.,* i. ii. 85, and *AYL.,* ii. ii. 261.

1134. *Tereus*] See *Pilg.,* xx. 14 n.

descants] To descant is 'to play or sing an air in harmony with a fixed theme' (O.E.D.). See Abbott, § 340, for other examples of verbs ending in *t* in which 'the second person singular often becomes *-ts* for euphony'.

better skill] The sense is 'with better skill'; but Shakespeare must be using 'descant' transitively, with 'better skill' as object.

1135. *against a thorn*] See *Pilgr.,* xx. 10–24.

1139. *Who if it wink*] 'Who' probably refers to 'heart' in l. 1137.

wink] See l. 375.

These means as frets upon an instrument   1140
Shall tune our heart-strings to true languishment.

"And for, poor bird, thou sing'st not in the day,
As shaming any eye should thee behold,
Some dark deep desert seated from the way,
That knows not parching heat nor freezing cold,   1145
Will we find out; and there we will unfold
    To creatures stern, sad tunes to change their kinds:
    Since men prove beasts, let beasts bear gentle minds."

As the poor frighted deer that stands at gaze,
Wildly determining which way to fly,   1150
Or one encompass'd with a winding maze,
That cannot tread the way out readily;
So with herself is she in mutiny,
    To live or die which of the twain were better,
    When life is sham'd and death reproach's debtor.   1155

"To kill myself," quoth she, "alack what were it,
But with my body my poor soul's pollution?
They that lose half with greater patience bear it
Than they whose whole is swallowed in confusion.
That mother tries a merciless conclusion,   1160

1141. tune] *Q1*; give *Q4*.   1145. not] *Q1*; nor *Q6–9*.

1140. *frets*] 'In musical instruments like the guitar, formerly a ring of gut . . . now a bar or ridge of wood, metal, etc. . . . placed on the fingerboard to regulate the fingering' (O.E.D.).

1142. *And for*] and because.

1143. *shaming*] being ashamed. See l. 1084.

1144. *from the way*] out of the way. See *John*, IV. i. 86, and *Tit.*, IV. iii. 533.

1147. *kinds*] natures.

1148.] Compare *Cæs.*, III. ii. 104–5.

1149. *stands at gaze*] This was a hunting term used of a deer 'in the attitude of gazing, esp. in wonder, expectancy, bewilderment' (O.E.D.).

1150. *determining*] deciding.

1155.] The last few words of this line have been interpreted variously by Malone, Pooler, and others. Brown's explanation is adequate: 'As the first part of the line gives the motive for suicide, the last part gives the reason for *not* taking her own life: namely, that her death would be debtor to reproach. That is, she fears her death might become an occasion of reproach.'

1157. *with my body*] with my body's pollution. 'Suicide would add to the ruin of her body, the ruin of her soul. It is not a Roman thought' (Pooler). It is indeed a Christian thought; but Shakespeare's whole procedure precludes historical accuracy, and we would rather have his Elizabethan interpretations of Roman character and thought than reconstructions by more scholarly minds.

1160. *tries a . . . conclusion*] tries an experiment. Compare *Ham.*, III. iv. 195:

Who having two sweet babes, when death takes one,
Will slay the other and be nurse to none.

"My body or my soul, which was the dearer,
When the one pure, the other made divine?
Whose love of either to myself was nearer,   1165
When both were kept for heaven and Collatine?
Ay me, the bark pill'd from the lofty pine,
  His leaves will wither and his sap decay;
  So must my soul, her bark being pill'd away.

"Her house is sack'd, her quiet interrupted,   1170
Her mansion batter'd by the enemy,
Her sacred temple spotted, spoil'd, corrupted,
Grossly engirt with daring infamy.
Then let it not be call'd impiety,
  If in this blemish'd fort I make some hole,   1175
  Through which I may convey this troubled soul.

"Yet die I will not, till my Collatine
Have heard the cause of my untimely death,
That he may vow in that sad hour of mine
Revenge on him that made me stop my breath.   1180
My stained blood to Tarquin I'll bequeath,
  Which by him tainted shall for him be spent,
  And as his due writ in my testament.

"My honour I'll bequeath unto the knife
That wounds my body so dishonoured.   1185
'Tis honour to deprive dishonour'd life;
  The one will live, the other being dead.

1182. by him] *Q1* (*all copies except Malone 34, Malone 886, and Sion, which have* for him).

like the famous ape,
To try conclusions, in the basket creep,
And break your own neck down.
1164.] The body being pure made the soul worthy of Heaven.
1167. *pill'd*] peeled. Compare *Mer.*, I. iii. 79.
1170–3.] See ll. 722–8.
1173. *engirt*] See l. 221, and *Ven.*, l. 364.

1180. *stop my breath*] Compare *Oth.*, v. ii. 202.
1181–206.] This 'testament' follows a well-worn medieval poetic formula, still capable of renovation by the Elizabethans. Compare *Troilus and Criseyde*, Book v, and Donne, *The Will*. The most elaborate examples by a great poet are Villon's *Testaments*.
1186. *deprive*] take away.

So of shame's ashes shall my fame be bred,
    For in my death I murder shameful scorn:
    My shame so dead, mine honour is new born.   1190

"Dear lord of that dear jewel I have lost,
    What legacy shall I bequeath to thee?
    My resolution, love, shall be thy boast,
    By whose example thou reveng'd mayst be.
    How Tarquin must be us'd, read it in me: 1195
        Myself thy friend will kill myself thy foe,
        And for my sake serve thou false Tarquin so.

"This brief abridgement of my will I make:
    My soul and body to the skies and ground;
    My resolution, husband, do thou take;   1200
    Mine honour be the knife's that makes my wound;
    My shame be his that did my fame confound;
        And all my fame that lives disbursed be
        To those that live and think no shame of me.

"Thou Collatine, shalt oversee this will;   1205
    How was I overseen that thou shalt see it!
    My blood shall wash the slander of mine ill;
    My life's foul deed my life's fair end shall free it.
    Faint not, faint heart, but stoutly say 'So be it';
        Yield to my hand, my hand shall conquer thee: 1210
        Thou dead, both die, and both shall victors be."

This plot of death when sadly she had laid,
    And wip'd the brinish pearl from her bright eyes,

1190. mine] *Q1*; my *Q4–9*.   1200. thou] *Q1*; you *Q4–9*.   1201. makes] *Q1*;
make *Q6–7*.   1205. Thou] *Q1*; Then *Q5–9*.   shalt] *Q1*; shall *Q6–9*.

1196. *Myself . . . myself*] See l. 998
n.
    1199.] Pooler quotes Shakespeare's
own will (Chambers, II. 170): 'I Commend my Soule into the handes of
god. . . And my bodye to the Earth'.
    1202. *confound*] overthrow, destroy.
    1203. *disbursed*] paid out.
    1205. *oversee*] be executor of.
Malone says that 'overseers' had no
legal standing: '*Overseers* were frequently added in Wills from the
superabundant caution of our ancestors; but our law acknowledges no
such persons, nor are they (as contra-
distinguished from executors), in-
vested with any legal rights whatever.
In some old wills the term *overseer* is
used instead of *executor*.' In his own
will Shakespeare appointed overseers
as well as executors.
    1206. *overseen*] deceived, deluded
(O.E.D.). Littledale holds that
Lucrece is alluding to witchcraft and
the Evil Eye (*Shakespeare's England*, I,
pp. 531 f.).

With untun'd tongue she hoarsely calls her maid,
Whose swift obedience to her mistress hies;   1215
For fleet-wing'd duty with thought's feathers flies.
   Poor Lucrece' cheeks unto her maid seem so
   As winter meads when sun doth melt their snow.

Her mistress she doth give demure good-morrow,
With soft slow tongue, true mark of modesty,   1220
And sorts a sad look to her lady's sorrow,
For why her face wore sorrow's livery;
   But durst not ask of her audaciously
   Why her two suns were cloud-eclipsed so,
   Nor why her fair cheeks over-wash'd with woe.   1225

But as the earth doth weep, the sun being set,
Each flower moisten'd like a melting eye,
Even so the maid with swelling drops 'gan wet
Her circled eyne, enforc'd by sympathy
Of those fair suns set in her mistress' sky,   1230
   Who in a salt-way'd ocean quench their light;
   Which makes the maid weep like the dewy night.

A pretty while these pretty creatures stand,
Like ivory conduits coral cisterns filling.
One justly weeps, the other takes in hand   1235
No cause, but company, of her drops' spilling;
   Their gentle sex to weep are often willing,
   Grieving themselves to guess at others' smarts,
   And then they drown their eyes or break their hearts.

---

214. calls] cals *Q1;* calds *Q2;* cald *Q3–8;* call'd *Q9.*   1220. mark] *Q1;*
arkes *Q4–9.*   1238. others'] *Q1;* other *Q6–8.*

1219. *demure*] modest, grave.

1221. *sorts*] fits. See l. 899 n. Other
examples are *2H6,* ii. iv. 68, and *Gent.,*
i. iii. 63.

1222. *For why*] because. See *Pilgr.,*
x. 8, 10.

1229. *circled*] rounded.

1234. *conduits*] 'Structure for the dis-
tribution of water, which is made to
spout from it, often in the form of a
human figure' (Onions).

Compare *Rom.,* iii. v. 130:
How now! a conduit, girl? what,
  still in tears?

coral cisterns] It is not easy to see the
precise relationship between Lucrece
and her maid, the conduits and the
cisterns, or why the latter should be
'coral'. Coral, as red, is in antithesis to
ivory, as white; and Shakespeare probably had in mind the redness of eye
resulting from tears, contrasting with
the pallor of their faces.

1235–6. *takes in hand No cause*]
acknowledges no reason or motive.

but company] except companionship.

1239. *drown their eyes*] Compare Sonnet xxx, l. 5:

For men have marble, women waxen, minds,   1240
And therefore are they form'd as marble will;
The weak oppress'd, th' impression of strange kinds
Is form'd in them by force, by fraud, or skill.
Then call them not the authors of their ill,
    No more than wax shall be accounted evil,   1245
    Wherein is stamp'd the semblance of a devil.

Their smoothness, like a goodly champaign plain,
Lays open all the little worms that creep;
In men as in a rough-grown grove remain
Cave-keeping evils that obscurely sleep;   1250
Through crystal walls each little mote will peep;
    Though men can cover them with bold stern looks,
    Poor women's faces are their own faults' books.

No man inveigh against the withered flower,
But chide rough winter that the flower hath kill'd;   1255
Not that devour'd, but that which doth devour
Is worthy blame; O let it not be hild
Poor women's faults, that they are so fulfill'd
    With men's abuses! those proud lords to blame
    Make weak-made women tenants to their shame.   1260

The precedent whereof in Lucrece view,
Assail'd by night with circumstances strong
Of present death, and shame that might ensue

1243. or] *Q1*; and *Q4*.   1247. like a goodly] *Q1*; like a *Q6–8*; like unto a *Q9*.
1248. that] *Q1*; to *Q4*.   1254. inveigh] *Q1*; inveighs *Q2–9*.   against] *Q1*;
againsts *Q2*.   1255. chide] *Q1*; chides *Q4,8,9*.   1257. hild] *Q1*; held *Q6–9*.

Then can I drown an eye, unused
    to flow.
1240. *waxen, minds*] Compare *Tw.
N.*, II. ii. 31 :
    How easy is it for the proper-false
    In women's waxen hearts to set
        their forms.
1242. *strange kinds*] dispositions
other than their own.
1247. *champaign plain*] open, level
country. See *Tw. N.*, II. v. 176.
1248. *Lays open*] reveals.
1250. *Cave-keeping*] dwelling in
caves.
1251. *mote*] speck.

1254. *No man inveigh*] Let no man
inveigh.
1257. *hild*] held.
1258. *fulfill'd*] filled up. This use
of 'fulfil' is found in the Anglican
Liturgy. Compare *Troil.*, Prol. 18:
        massy staples
    And corresponsive and fulfilling
        bolts
    Sperr up the sons of Troy.
1259. *to blame*] The meaning must
be either: 'lords *of* blame' or, paren-
thetically, '(to their blame)'.
1261. *precedent*] proof or example.
See *Ven.*, l. 26.

By that her death, to do her husband wrong;
Such danger to resistance did belong,   1265
    That dying fear through all her body spread;
    And who cannot abuse a body dead?

By this, mild patience bid fair Lucrece speak
To the poor counterfeit of her complaining.
"My girl," quoth she, "on what occasion break   1270
Those tears from thee, that down thy cheeks are raining?
If thou dost weep for grief of my sustaining,
    Know, gentle wench, it small avails my mood:
    If tears could help, mine own would do me good.

"But tell me, girl, when went"—and there she stay'd, 1275
    Till after a deep groan—"Tarquin from hence?"
"Madam, ere I was up," replied the maid,
"The more to blame my sluggard negligence.
    Yet with the fault I can thus far dispense:
        Myself was stirring ere the break of day,   1280
        And ere I rose was Tarquin gone away.

"But lady, if your maid may be so bold,
    She would request to know your heaviness."
"O peace," quoth Lucrece, "if it should be told,
    The repetition cannot make it less;   1285
For more it is than I can well express,
    And that deep torture may be call'd a hell,
    When more is felt than one hath power to tell.

"Go get me hither paper, ink and pen;

1266. That] *Q1*; Thy *Q5*; The *Q6–9*.   1268. bid] *Q1*; did *Q4,9*.   1274. help, mine] *Q1*; helpe, my *Q4*.   1278. sluggard] *Q1*; sluggish *Q4*.

1266.] This may or may not mean that Lucrece fainted, as she does in Chaucer's account (ll. 1814–18; see Appendix II, p. 191). Shakespeare does not make it appear that she did so in ll. 677–83; and since the present lines are not conclusive, it is better to take them to mean simply that she was unnerved by fear.

1267. *abuse*] ill-use.

1269. *counterfeit*] image or picture. Compare *Mer. V.*, III. ii. 115:

What find I here? Fair Portia's counterfeit!

1272. *of my sustaining*] that I sustain.

1273. *my mood*] my grief. 'Mood' can be used with various implications—anger, passionate grief, pride or courage.

1273–4.] Compare *R2*, III. iv. 21–3.

1279. *dispense*] See ll. 1070 and 1704.

1283. *heaviness*] grief.

1285. *repetition*] recital.

1289–95.] Like some of the pre-

Yet save that labour, for I have them here.   1290
—What should I say?—One of my husband's men
Bid thou be ready by and by to bear
A letter to my lord, my love, my dear:
  Bid him with speed prepare to carry it;
  The cause craves haste, and it will soon be writ."   1295

Her maid is gone, and she prepares to write,
First hovering o'er the paper with her quill;
Conceit and grief an eager combat fight,
What wit sets down is blotted straight with will:
This is too curious-good, this blunt and ill.   1300
  Much like a press of people at a door,
  Throng her inventions, which shall go before.

At last she thus begins: "Thou worthy lord
Of that unworthy wife that greeteth thee,
Health to thy person! next, vouchsafe t'afford—   1305
If ever, love, thy Lucrece thou wilt see—
Some present speed to come and visit me.
  So I commend me, from our house in grief;
  My woes are tedious, though my words are brief."

Here folds she up the tenure of her woe,   1310
Her certain sorrow writ uncertainly.
By this short schedule Collatine may know

1299. straight] *Q1*; still *Q3–9*.   1308. grief] *Q1*; briefe *Q5*.   1310. tenure] *Q1*;
tenor *Q6–9*.   1312. schedule] *Q8*; Cedule *Q1–3*; shedule *Q4*; sedule *Q5–7*.

ceding dialogue, this shows how busi-
nesslike Shakespeare can be when he
ceases to strive after effect.

1292. *by and by*] straightway. Compare *Pilgr.*, xx. 14.

1298. *Conceit*] thought.

1299. *will*] emotion.

1300. *curious-good*] too well-express-
ed: 'smelling of the lamp'.

1301.] Cf. Arden *John*, v. vii. 19–20 n.

1302. *which shall go before*] striving
which shall enter first.

1308.] Malone comments: 'Shakespeare has here closely followed the
practice of his own times. Thus Anne
Bullen, concluding her pathetick
letter to her savage murderer: "From

my doleful prison in the Tower, this 6th of
May".' Baldwin calls the letter 'a
familiar epistle of the variety Terentia
was taught to write Cicero in 16th century grammar school' (*op.cit.*, p. 140).

1310. *tenure*] transcript, statement;
'In law a transcript or copy which
implies that . . . the instrument must
have been set out correctly, even
though the pleader need not have set
out more than the substance or pur-
port of the instrument. This technical
term exactly illustrates the nature of
Lucrece' letter and of the circumstances under which it was sent'
(Wyndham).

1312. *schedule*] summary.

Her grief, but not her grief's true quality;
She dares not thereof make discovery,
    Lest he should hold it her own gross abuse,   1315
    Ere she with blood had stain'd her stain'd excuse.

Besides, the life and feeling of her passion
She hoards, to spend when he is by to hear her,
When sighs and groans and tears may grace the fashion
Of her disgrace, the better so to clear her   1320
From that suspicion which the world might bear her:
    To shun this blot, she would not blot the letter
    With words, till action might become them better.

To see sad sights moves more than hear them told,
For then the eye interprets to the ear   1325
The heavy motion that it doth behold,
When every part a part of woe doth bear.
'Tis but a part of sorrow that we hear:
    Deep sounds make lesser noise than shallow fords,
    And sorrow ebbs, being blown with wind of words.   1330

Her letter now is seal'd, and on it writ
"At Ardea to my lord with more than haste."
The post attends, and she delivers it,
Charging the sour-fac'd groom to hie as fast
As lagging fowls before the northern blast;   1335
    Speed more than speed but dull and slow she deems:
    Extremity still urgeth such extremes.

1335. blast] *Q1* (*all copies except Malone 34, Malone 886, and Sion, which have* blasts).

1316. *her stain'd excuse*] the account
she will give of her 'stain'.

1319. *the fashion*] the shaping forth or
appearance.

1324. *hear them told*] to hear them
told. The practice and observation of
the Elizabethan dramatist are evident
in this remark.

1326. *motion*] action. 'Our author
seems to have been thinking of the
Dumb-shows, which were exhibited on
the stage in his time. Motion, in
old language, signifies a *puppet-show*;
and the person who spoke for the
puppets was called an *interpreter*'
(Malone).

1329. *sounds*] 'A *sound*, in naval language, is such a part of the sea as may
be *sounded*' (Steevens). The line con-
flates 'Still waters run deep' and
'Shallow streams make most din'; see
O.D.E.P., pp. 386, 403 f.

1332. *with more than haste*] The
phrase is one of Shakespeare's ana-
chronisms (Steevens). It reflects the
old custom of inscribing urgent letters
'with post post haste'.

1333. *The post*] the carrier.

1334. *sour-fac'd*] This suggests un-
willingness, but may mean no more
than a long face assumed out of
respect.

The homely villain cur'sies to her low,
And blushing on her with a steadfast eye,
Receives the scroll without or yea or no,					1340
And forth with bashful innocence doth hie;
But they whose guilt within their bosoms lie,
    Imagine every eye beholds their blame,
    For Lucrece thought he blush'd to see her shame:

When, silly groom! God wot, it was defect					1345
Of spirit, life and bold audacity;
Such harmless creatures have a true respect
To talk in deeds, while others saucily
Promise more speed, but do it leisurely.
    Even so this pattern of the worn-out age					1350
    Pawn'd honest looks, but us'd no words to gage.

His kindled duty kindled her mistrust,
That two red fires in both their faces blazed;
She thought he blush'd, as knowing Tarquin's lust,
And blushing with him, wistly on him gazed.					1355
Her earnest eye did make him more amazed;
    The more she saw the blood his cheeks replenish,
    The more she thought he spied in her some blemish.

1338. cur'sies] cursies *Qq*.   1341. forth with] *Q1;* forthwith *Q3,5–7,9*.   hie]
Q1; lie *Q5–7;* flie *Q8,9*.   1345. silly] *Q4–9;* seelie *Q1–3*.   1350. this . . . the]
*Q1 (all copies except British Museum C.21.c.45, Folger-Devonshire, Huntington,
Rosenbach, which have* the . . . this*).*   1353. their] *Q1;* there *Q4.*

1338. *villain*] servant; from *villein*, a
peasant or country labourer. Compare
Err., I. ii. 19.
    cur'sies] bows. Compare *Tw. N.*, II.
v. 67: 'Toby approaches: courtesies
there to me'.
    1339. *blushing on her*] looking on her
with a blush.
    1345. *silly*] simple. 'Silly groom' is
of course an interjection, conveying
that the fault or 'defect' was in the
servant's nature.
    1348. *To talk in deeds*] to act and not
to talk. Malone quotes *Troil.*, IV. v. 98:
    Speaking in deeds and deedless in
        his tongue.
    saucily] presumptuously.
    1350. *pattern*] example, model. See
AYL., IV. i. 100.
    worn-out] past. Compare *R2*, IV. i.

258, and Sonnet lxviii, l. 1:
    Thus is his cheek the map of days
        outworn.
For the sentiment see also *AYL.*, II
iii. 57:
    O good old man, how well in thee
        appears
    The constant service of the antique
        world.
    1351. *Pawn'd honest looks*] gave only
honest looks as pledge of obedience.
    gage] pledge.
    1355. *wistly*] earnestly, significantly.
See *Ven.*, l. 343, *Pilgr.*, VI. 10, and *R2*,
v. iv. 7:
    And speaking it, he wistly look'd
        on me;
    As who should say, 'I would thou
        wert the man'.
    1357–8.] Note the imperfect rhyme.

But long she thinks till he return again,
And yet the duteous vassal scarce is gone;   1360
The weary time she cannot entertain,
For now 'tis stale to sigh, to weep and groan:
So woe hath wearied woe, moan tired moan,
    That she her plaints a little while doth stay,
    Pausing for means to mourn some newer way.   1365

At last she calls to mind where hangs a piece
Of skilful painting, made for Priam's Troy,
Before the which is drawn the power of Greece,
For Helen's rape the city to destroy,
Threat'ning cloud-kissing Ilion with annoy;   1370
    Which the conceited painter drew so proud,
    As heaven, it seem'd, to kiss the turrets bow'd.

A thousand lamentable objects there,
In scorn of nature, art gave lifeless life:

1361. weary] *Q1;* very *Q4.*   1374. lifeless] livelesse *Qq.*

1359. *long she thinks*] she thinks time passes slowly. 'To think long', for 'to grow weary with waiting' is obsolete except in dialect (O.E.D.).

1361. *entertain*] pass away.

1366-7. *a piece Of skilful painting*] Nowhere does Shakespeare speak of this as a tapestry; it may have figured in his imagination as a painted cloth, but there is no indication of this. Rollins gives nearly four pages of compressed annotation by commentators who have tried to uphold some conjecture of their own by wresting Shakespeare's description to fit it. Most of these arguments depend on the assumption that Shakespeare could not have written his description without having seen a picture or tapestry which would supply him with every detail he mentions. This remarkable supposition is used to 'prove' that *Lucrece* could not have been written before Shakespeare came to London, or that he must have visited the Low Countries or Italy. In fact the passage is very literary, both in conception and execution. It was probably suggested by the first book of the *Aeneid* (ll. 455-93), 'where Dido's temple-painting of Troy is described through the tearful eyes of Aeneas' (Marschall, *Anglia*, LIV. 83-96); and it evokes a picture that would be impossible in reality and whose supposed mastery indicates a somewhat naive taste in the writer. Virgilian and Ovidian parallels are discussed by Baldwin, *op. cit.*, pp. 143-6, and summarized by Bullough, *op. cit.*, p. 181. See also l. 1497 n.

1368. *drawn*] drawn up. Pooler compares *John*, IV. ii. 118:

    Where is my mother's care
That such an army could be drawn
    in France,
And she not hear of it.

1370. *cloud-kissing Ilion*] Malone notes similar phrases in *Ham.*, III. iv. 59, and *Per.*, I. iv. 24. The archetype was doubtless Marlowe's: 'the topless towers of Ilium'.

annoy] injury. Compare *2H6*, III. i. 67, and *Cæs.*, I. iii. 22.

1371. *conceited*] ingenious. See l. 701.

1372. *As*] that. Compare l. 1420, and *Phoen.*, l. 25; see Abbott, § 109.

Many a dry drop seem'd a weeping tear,   1375
Shed for the slaughter'd husband by the wife;
The red blood reek'd to show the painter's strife,
    And dying eyes gleam'd forth their ashy lights,
    Like dying coals burnt out in tedious nights.

There might you see the labouring pioner   1380
Begrim'd with sweat and smeared all with dust;
And from the towers of Troy there would appear
The very eyes of men through loop-holes thrust,
Gazing upon the Greeks with little lust:
    Such sweet observance in this work was had,   1385
    That one might see those far-off eyes look sad.

In great commanders grace and majesty
You might behold, triumphing in their faces,
In youth, quick bearing and dexterity;
And here and there the painter interlaces   1390
Pale cowards marching on with trembling paces,
    Which heartless peasants did so well resemble,
    That one would swear he saw them quake and tremble.

In Ajax and Ulysses, O what art
Of physiognomy might one behold!   1395
The face of either cipher'd either's heart;
Their face their manners most expressly told.
In Ajax' eyes blunt rage and rigour roll'd,
    But the mild glance that sly Ulysses lent
    Show'd deep regard and smiling government.   1400

1375. dry] *Q1;* dire *Q5–9.*   1383. thrust] *Q1;* thurst *Q5.*   1386. might] *Q1;*
night *Q4.*   1399. sly] slie *Q1;* she *Q4.*

1377. *the painter's strife*] the painter's
striving to compete with Nature. The
word 'strife' occurs in several such
passages in Shakespeare; see *Ven.,* l. 11,
and *Tim.,* i. i. 37:   I will say of it,
    It tutors nature: artificial strife
    Lives in these touches, livelier than
        life.
1380. *pioner*] pioneer, soldier who
works in digging trenches, laying
mines, building defences, etc.
1384. *lust*] liking, pleasure.
1385. *sweet observance*] delightful
accuracy.

1390. *interlaces*] weaves into his
design.
1392. *heartless*] cowardly. See l. 471.
peasants] men of base birth, therefore of little or no value in war. Compare *Ham.,* ii. ii. 584:
    O! what a rogue and peasant slave
        am I.
1396. *cipher'd*] spelt out. See l. 207.
1398–407.] According to Bullough,
'the descriptions of Ajax and Ulysses
... and Nestor ... come from Ovid's
Metamorphoses, xiii' (*op. cit.,* p. 181).
1400. *deep regard and smiling govern-*

There pleading might you see grave Nestor stand,
As 'twere encouraging the Greeks to fight,
Making such sober action with his hand
That it beguil'd attention, charm'd the sight;
In speech it seem'd his beard all silver white   1405
    Wagg'd up and down, and from his lips did fly
    Thin winding breath which purl'd up to the sky.

About him were a press of gaping faces,
Which seem'd to swallow up his sound advice,
All jointly list'ning, but with several graces,   1410
As if some mermaid did their ears entice,—
Some high, some low, the painter was so nice:
    The scalps of many almost hid behind,
    To jump up higher seem'd, to mock the mind.

Here one man's hand lean'd on another's head,   1415
His nose being shadowed by his neighbour's ear;
Here one being throng'd bears back, all boll'n and red;
Another smother'd seems to pelt and swear:
And in their rage such signs of rage they bear

---

ment] deep thought for all implications of any matter, and a serene self-control. 'Government' may mean rather that Ulysses was a skilful ruler.

1401. *pleading*] orating.

1403.] Compare *Ham.*, III. ii. 5–6.

1406. *Wagg'd up and down*] 'Wag' was 'formerly used in contexts where it would now sound ridiculous, e.g. of pines in a wind [*Mer. V.*, IV. i. 76]; and of the eyelids [*Ham.*, V. i. 290]' (Pooler). But it is precisely Shakespeare's use of such colloquialisms which gives his poetry its animation; he seems here to display a conscious mastery of the rough, almost satiric word exploited by Marlowe in such lines as:

    We saw Cassandra sprawling in
        the streets

            (*The Tragedie of Dido*, l. 569).
See T. S. Eliot, *The Blank Verse of Marlowe* (*The Sacred Wood*, pp. 93–4). The whole of Marlowe's description of the fall of Troy in *The Tragedie of Dido* should be compared with the present passage.

1407. *purl'd*] curled. Malone quotes Drayton, *Mortimeriados* (1596), ll. 2364–6:

    Whose streame an easie breath
        doth seeme to blowe;
    Which on the sparkling gravell
        runns in purles,
    As though the waves had been of
        silver curles.

1411. *mermaid*] See *Ven.*, l. 429 n.

1412. *nice*] meticulous.

1417. *throng'd*] pressed by a crowd. *bears back*] pushes back against those pushing him.

boll'n] swollen. Compare Golding, VIII. 1003:

    Her leannesse made her joynts
        bolne big, and knee-pannes for
        to swell.

1418. *smother'd*] half-stifled.

pelt] scold, be angry. O.E.D. quotes Milton, *True Religion*: 'if they who differ in matters not essential to belief, . . . shall stand jarring and pelting at one another, they will soon be routed and subdued.'

As but for loss of Nestor's golden words,   1420
It seem'd they would debate with angry swords.

For much imaginary work was there,—
Conceit deceitful, so compact, so kind,
That for Achilles' image stood his spear
Gripp'd in an armed hand; himself behind   1425
Was left unseen, save to the eye of mind:
    A hand, a foot, a face, a leg, a head
    Stood for the whole to be imagined.

And from the walls of strong besieged Troy,
When their brave hope, bold Hector, march'd to field, 1430
Stood many Trojan mothers sharing joy
To see their youthful sons bright weapons wield;
And to their hope they such odd action yield
    That through their light joy seemed to appear,
    Like bright things stain'd, a kind of heavy fear.   1435

And from the strond of Dardan where they fought,
To Simois' reedy banks the red blood ran,
Whose waves to imitate the battle sought

1430. their] *Q1;* there *Q4.*   1431. Trojan] Troian *Q1,3–8;* Troyan *Q2.*

1420. *but for loss of*] but that they would lose.

1421. *debate*] fight. Pooler cites *F.Q.,* III. ix. 14 and VI. iv. 30:

> Ne any dares with him for it debate.

1422. *imaginary work*] work of the imagination. Compare *H5,* I, Prol. 18:

> And let us, ciphers to this great accompt,
> On your imaginary forces work.

1423. *Conceit*] conception, imagination. See l. 1298.

compact] composed, well put together. See *Ven.,* l. 149 n.

kind] natural.

1424. *his spear*] Compare *2H6,* v. i. 100. Achilles' spear was more famous in the Middle Ages than his shield, as described by Homer.

1429–32.] Though most of Shakespeare's details come from the *Aeneid,* Book II, this is found in North's Plutarch, 1579 (Life of Brutus, ch. 23)

(Sarrazin, *Archiv für das Studium der neueren Sprachen,* CII. 422 f.). It is interesting that there also it occurs in the description of a picture, which represents Hector's farewell to Andromache.

1430. *their brave hope*] Compare *3H6,* II. i. 51.

1433.] They give such unfitting gestures or attitudes to the expression of their hope.

1434. *light*] happy.

1435. *heavy*] sad.

1436. *the strond of Dardan*] 'Dardania was a name of Troas, the country of which Troy was the chief city. The district was bounded by the sea, though Troy itself was an inland city on the river Simois' (Lee). 'Strond' is an obsolete form of 'strand'.

1437. *Simois*] 'A river which flows from Mount Ida, and joins the river Scamander in the plain of Troy' (Feuillerat).

With swelling ridges, and their ranks began
To break upon the galled shore, and than   1440
   Retire again, till meeting greater ranks
   They join, and shoot their foam at Simois' banks.

To this well-painted piece is Lucrece come,
To find a face where all distress is stell'd.
Many she sees where cares have carved some,   1445
But none where all distress and dolour dwell'd,
Till she despairing Hecuba beheld,
   Staring on Priam's wounds with her old eyes,
   Which bleeding under Pyrrhus' proud foot lies.

In her the painter had anatomiz'd   1450
Time's ruin, beauty's wrack, and grim care's reign;
Her cheeks with chops and wrinkles were disguis'd:
Of what she was no semblance did remain.
Her blue blood chang'd to black in every vein,
   Wanting the spring that those shrunk pipes had fed, 1455
   Show'd life imprison'd in a body dead.

On this sad shadow Lucrece spends her eyes,
And shapes her sorrow to the beldam's woes,
Who nothing wants to answer her but cries
And bitter words to ban her cruel foes;   1460

1440. *galled*] fretted, worn away.
Compare *H5*, III. i. 12:
  As fearfully as doth a galled rock
  O'erhang and jutty his confounded
    base,
  Swill'd with the wild and wasteful
    ocean.
  than] then.
1444. *stell'd*] The context indicates
that 'stell'd' means 'portrayed', rather
than the 'fixed' put forward by one
group of commentators (including
Dyce, Onions, and Kittredge). In
Sonnet xxiv we have 'steel'd' used
in the same way and rhyming with
'held':
  Mine eye hath play'd the painter
    and hath steel'd
  Thy beauty's form in table of my
    heart.

1445. *carved*] This is a synonym for
'engraved', as in the previous line.
1447. *despairing Hecuba*] Shakespeare
uses Hecuba as the type of extreme
sorrow in *Ham.*, II. ii.
1449. *under Pyrrhus' proud foot*] Bush
observes that this detail, not in Virgil,
is found in Marlowe, *The Tragedie of
Dido*, l. 537 (*op. cit.*, p. 151 n.).
1450. *anatomiz'd*] laid bare, dis-
sected.
1452. *chops*] cracks in the skin. Compare Sonnet lxii, l. 10:
  Beated and chopt with tanned
    antiquity.
1457. *shadow*] picture. See l. 460.
  spends] employs, uses up.
1458. *beldam's*] old woman's. See
l. 953.
1460. *ban*] curse. See *Ven.*, l. 326.

The painter was no god to lend her those,
    And therefore Lucrece swears he did her wrong,
    To give her so much grief, and not a tongue.

"Poor instrument," quoth she, "without a sound,
    I'll tune thy woes with my lamenting tongue,   1465
    And drop sweet balm in Priam's painted wound,
    And rail on Pyrrhus that hath done him wrong,
    And with my tears quench Troy that burns so long,
        And with my knife scratch out the angry eyes
        Of all the Greeks that are thine enemies.   1470

"Show me the strumpet that began this stir,
    That with my nails her beauty I may tear!
    Thy heat of lust, fond Paris, did incur
    This load of wrath that burning Troy doth bear;
    Thy eye kindled the fire that burneth here,   1475
        And here in Troy, for trespass of thine eye,
        The sire, the son, the dame and daughter die.

"Why should the private pleasure of some one
    Become the public plague of many moe?
    Let sin alone committed, light alone   1480
    Upon his head that hath transgressed so;
    Let guiltless souls be freed from guilty woe:
        For one's offence why should so many fall,
        To plague a private sin in general?

"Lo here weeps Hecuba, here Priam dies,   1485
    Here manly Hector faints, here Troilus swounds;
    Here friend by friend in bloody channel lies,
    And friend to friend gives unadvised wounds;

1461. *to lend her those*] who might have lent her those.

1465. *tune*] sing. See l. 1107.

1471. *stir*] action; here, war. See *Ven.*, l. 283.

1472.] Compare *2H6*, I. iii. 144, and *MND.*, III. ii. 298.

1479. *moe*] more in number.

1484.] To make the punishment of an individual a plague for the whole public.

in general] throughout the community as a whole. Compare *Troil.*, IV. v. 19.

1486. *swounds*] swoons. See *Cæs.*, I. ii. 253, and *Ham.*, V. ii. 319.

1487. *channel*] gutter. O.E.D. quotes Lyly, *Euphues*, 38:
    'Dronken sottes wallowing . . . in
        every channel'.

1488. *unadvised*] unintentional. 'It should be remembered that Troy was sacked in the night' (Malone). Compare *Ham.*, II. ii. 491.

And one man's lust these many lives confounds;
  Had doting Priam check'd his son's desire,   1490
  Troy had been bright with fame and not with fire."

Here feelingly she weeps Troy's painted woes,
For sorrow, like a heavy hanging bell
Once set on ringing, with his own weight goes;
Then little strength rings out the doleful knell.   1495
So Lucrece set a-work, sad tales doth tell
  To pencill'd pensiveness and colour'd sorrow:
  She lends them words, and she their looks doth borrow.

She throws her eyes about the painting round,
And who she finds forlorn, she doth lament.   1500
At last she sees a wretched image bound,
That piteous looks to Phrygian shepherds lent;
His face though full of cares, yet show'd content.
  Onward to Troy with the blunt swains he goes,
  So mild that patience seem'd to scorn his woes.   1505

In him the painter labour'd with his skill
To hide deceit and give the harmless show
An humble gait, calm looks, eyes wailing still,
A brow unbent that seem'd to welcome woe,
Cheeks neither red nor pale, but mingled so   1510

1498. lends] *Q1;* sends *Q4.*   1499. painting round] *Q1;* painted round *Q3–9*
1504. the] *Q1;* these *Q6–9.*   1507. deceit] *Q1–3;* conceipt *Q4.*

1489. *confounds*] destroys. See l.
1202.
  1494. *on ringing*] a-ringing. See
Abbott, § 180.
  1496. *a-work*] to work. See Abbott,
§ 24.
  1497. *pencill'd*] painted. Compare
Tim., I. i. 159: 'Painting is welcome
... these pencill'd figures are Even such
as they give out.' A 'pencil' meant
an artist's paint-brush until the early
19th cent. See *John,* III. i. 237:
  they were besmear'd and
    overstain'd
  With slaughter's pencil.
The jingle with 'pensiveness' is truly
Ovidian.

  1499. *about the painting round*] all
round the painting.
  1501–68.] The account of Sinon
provides evidence that Shakespeare's
source was Virgil, and that he read the
Aeneid, Book II (see ll. 13–267), in the
original, and not in Phaer's translation
of 1558–73 (R. K. Root, *Classical
Mythology in Shakespeare,* p. 107).
  1502.] that made the Phrygian shepherds look compassionate.
  1504. *blunt*] rough, simple.
  1505. *patience*] his patience.
  1507. *the harmless show*] the harmless
appearance, i.e. the picture.
  1509. *unbent*] not frowning, submissive.

That blushing red no guilty instance gave,
Nor ashy pale the fear that false hearts have.

But like a constant and confirmed devil,
He entertain'd a show so seeming just,
And therein so ensconc'd his secret evil,   1515
That jealousy itself could not mistrust
False creeping craft and perjury should thrust
    Into so bright a day such black-fac'd storms,
    Or blot with hell-born sin such saint-like forms.

The well-skill'd workman this mild image drew   1520
For perjur'd Sinon, whose enchanting story
The credulous old Priam after slew;
Whose words like wildfire burnt the shining glory
Of rich-built Ilion, that the skies were sorry,
    And little stars shot from their fixed places,   1525
    When their glass fell, wherein they view'd their faces.

This picture she advisedly perus'd,

1515. his] *Q1;* this *Q4–9.*   1519. hell-born] *Q1;* hell-borne *Q2–9.*   1524.
were] *Q1;* was *Q4.*

1511. *no guilty instance*] no proof or
evidence of guilt. Compare *2H4*, III. i.
103:
    I have received
A certain instance that Glendower
    is dead.
1514. *entertain'd*] sustained. See *Mer.
V.,* I. i. 90, and *R2*, II. ii. 4:
    And entertain a cheerful
        disposition.
1515. *ensconc'd*] hid, tucked away.
1516. *jealousy*] suspicion. See *Ven.,*
l. 649, *Cym.,* IV. iii. 22, and *Tw. N.,* III.
iii. 8:
    But jealousy what might befall
        your travel,
    Being skilless in these parts.
1521. *Sinon*] Compare *3H6*, III. ii.
190.
    enchanting] bewitching by spells or
charms. See *Tit.,* IV. iv. 89:
    I will enchant the old Andronicus
    With words more sweet, and yet
        more dangerous
    Than baits to fish.

1523. *wildfire*] Pooler quotes
Smyth's *Sailor's Word-Book*: 'A pyro-
technical preparation burning with
great fierceness, whether under water
or not; it is analogous to the ancient
Greek fire, and is composed mainly of
sulphur, naphtha, and pitch.'
    1525–6.] Malone remarks: 'Why
Troy, however beautiful or magnificent, should be called the mirrour in
which the fixed stars beheld themselves, I do not see. The image is very
quaint and far-fetched.' In Shakespeare's imagination Troy is associated
with Marlowe's 'topless towers' (see
ll. 1370–2). This image is maintained
in the present hyperbole. The Elizabethan conception of an hierarchical
universe, in which human society
mirrored the order of the heavenly
bodies, also helps us to see how Shakespeare arrived at his conceit.
    1525. *stars shot . . . places*] Compare
MND., II. i. 154.
    1527. *advisedly*] See l. 180 n.

And chid the painter for his wondrous skill,
Saying some shape in Sinon's was abus'd:
So fair a form lodg'd not a mind so ill.   1530
And still on him she gaz'd, and gazing still,
    Such signs of truth in his plain face she spied,
    That she concludes the picture was belied.

"It cannot be," quoth she, "that so much guile,"—
She would have said,—"can lurk in such a look."   1535
But Tarquin's shape came in her mind the while,
And from her tongue "can lurk" from "cannot" took:
"It cannot be" she in that sense forsook,
    And turn'd it thus: "It cannot be, I find,
    But such a face should bear a wicked mind.   1540

"For even as subtle Sinon here is painted,
So sober sad, so weary and so mild,—
As if with grief or travail he had fainted,—
To me came Tarquin armed to beguild
With outward honesty, but yet defil'd   1545
    With inward vice. As Priam him did cherish,
    So did I Tarquin,—so my Troy did perish.

"Look, look how list'ning Priam wets his eyes,

1528. chid] *Q1*; chide *Q6*.   1529. Sinon's] Sinons *Q1–3*; Sinon *Q4*.   1547. I]
Q1; omitted *Q2*.

1529. *some shape in Sinon's was
abus'd*] some other person's form had
been represented falsely as Sinon's.

1532. *plain*] honest. See *Cæs.*, III. ii.
222.

1533. *was belied*] was proved false.

1539. *And turn'd it*] and twisted the
sense of it.

1544.] The last three words seem
to demand emendation. The present
reading is that of Malone, who explains it thus: '*To me came Tarquin
with the same armour of hypocrisy that Sinon
wore. . . To* must, I think, have been a
misprint for *so. Beguil'd* is for *beguiling.*
Our author frequently confounds the
active and passive participle.' He
illustrates the latter confusion with
'delighted' for 'delighting' in *Oth.*,
I. iii. 290:

If virtue no delighted beauty
    lack.
'Beguil'd' has also been glossed as
'craftily disguised' (Lee). There remains something unsatisfactory about
all suggested emendations, including
that of Malone, and one cannot help
suspecting that Shakespeare wrote the
text as it is printed, and that 'beguild'
is simply a colloquial variant of
'beguile'. Pooler thus writes: 'I once
thought "beguild" might be a corrupt
form of "beguile"; an excrescent "t"
or "d" is common, e.g. *twind* and
twinde for twine (Gascoigne's *Poesies*, Cambridge ed., pp. 101, 152),
shoulds for shoals (Hakluyt, reprint
1904, vol. IV, p. 212) . . . *graft* and
waft now current for graffe and
waffe.' Compare *Ven.*, l. 873.

To see those borrow'd tears that Sinon sheds!
Priam, why art thou old and yet not wise?   1550
For every tear he falls a Trojan bleeds.
His eye drops fire, no water thence proceeds:
 Those round clear pearls of his that move thy pity
 Are balls of quenchless fire to burn thy city.

"Such devils steal effects from lightless hell,   1555
For Sinon in his fire doth quake with cold;
And in that cold hot-burning fire doth dwell.
These contraries such unity do hold,
Only to flatter fools and make them bold;
 So Priam's trust false Sinon's tears doth flatter,   1560
 That he finds means to burn his Troy with water."

Here all enrag'd, such passion her assails,
That patience is quite beaten from her breast.
She tears the senseless Sinon with her nails,
Comparing him to that unhappy guest   1565
Whose deed hath made herself herself detest.
 At last she smilingly with this gives o'er:
 "Fool, fool," quoth she, "his wounds will not be sore."

Thus ebbs and flows the current of her sorrow,
And time doth weary time with her complaining.   1570
She looks for night, and then she longs for morrow,
And both she thinks too long with her remaining.
Short time seems long in sorrow's sharp sustaining:
 Though woe be heavy, yet it seldom sleeps,
 And they that watch see time how slow it creeps.   1575

1549. sheds] *Q4,6;* sheeds *Q1–3,5.* 1551. he] *Q1;* be *Q4.* Trojan] Troian
Q1,8; Troyan *Q2–7.* 1552. eye drops] *Q1;* eyes drops *Q6,7;* eyes drop *Q8,9.*
1557. that] *Q1;* the *Q4.*

1549. *borrow'd*] feigned. See *1H4*, v.
iii. 23:

 A borrow'd title hast thou bought
  too dear.

 sheds] So in Sonnet xxxiv 'sheeds'
rhymes with 'deeds'.

 1550.] Compare *Lr.*, i. iv. 261 and
i. v. 49.

 1551. *he falls*] he lets fall. See *Oth.*,
iv. i. 257, and *Ant.*, iii. ix. 69:

  Fall not a tear, I say.

 1554. *quenchless fire*] Lee pointed out

the Marlovian quality of this phrase,
found in *Dido*, ii. i. 186, *Tamburlaine*,
Part ii, iii. v. 27, and *Edward II*, v. i. 44.

 1563. *beaten from*] See l. 278.

 1565. *unhappy*] unfortunate, i.e.
bringing misfortune.

 1567. *with this gives o'er*] ceases with
these words.

 1573. *in sorrow's sharp sustaining*] in
the sharp sorrow she sustains.

 1575. *watch*] see out a fixed period of
time (or perhaps merely 'keep awake').

Which all this time hath overslipp'd her thought,
That she with painted images hath spent,
Being from the feeling of her own grief brought
By deep surmise of others' detriment,
Losing her woes in shows of discontent.   1580
    It easeth some, though none it ever cured,
    To think their dolour others have endured.

But now the mindful messenger come back
Brings home his lord and other company;
Who finds his Lucrece clad in mourning black,   1585
And round about her tear-distained eye
Blue circles stream'd, like rainbows in the sky:
    Those water-galls in her dim element
    Foretell new storms to those already spent.

Which when her sad beholding husband saw,   1590
Amazedly in her sad face he stares;
Her eyes though sod in tears, look'd red and raw,
Her lively colour kill'd with deadly cares.
He hath no power to ask her how she fares;
    Both stood like old acquaintance in a trance,   1595
    Met far from home, wond'ring each other's chance.

1583. come] *Q1;* comes *Q3–9.*   1586. tear-distained eye] *Q1;* teares
distained-eye *Q4.*   1588. element] *Q1;* elements *Q4.*   1595. Both]
Q1; But *Q6–9.*

1579. *surmise*] meditation, contemplation.

1580. *shows*] outward appearances, pictures.

1581–2.] Compare *R2,* v. v. 23.

1588. *water-galls*] minor types of rainbow. Pooler quotes from 'Smyth, *Sailor's Word-Book*: "Water-gall. A name of the *wind-gall*"; "Wind-gall. A luminous halo on the edge of a distant cloud, where there is rain, usually seen in the wind's eye, and looked upon as a sure precursor of stormy weather. Also, an atmospheric effect of prismatic colours, said likewise to indicate bad weather if seen to leeward". The meaning here is probably the broken rainbows that sailors call "dogs".' According to Porter, 'wind-galls' are 'called in America sun-dogs'.

element] Compare *Tw. N.,* III. i. 56: 'out of my welkin—I might say "element" but the word is overworn'. See l. 116 n.

1592. *sod*] sodden, boiled. Compare *Troil.,* III. i. 44: 'Sodden business! there's a stewed phrase indeed!'

1593. *lively*] living, pertaining to life. Compare *Tit.,* III. i. 105:
    Had I but seen thy picture in this
        plight
    It would have madded me: what
        shall I do
    Now I behold thy lively body
        so?

1595. *old acquaintance*] old acquaintances.

1596. *wond'ring*] wondering at, or conjecturing.
    chance] fortune, life-adventures.

At last he takes her by the bloodless hand,
And thus begins: "What uncouth ill event
Hath thee befall'n, that thou dost trembling stand?
Sweet love, what spite hath thy fair colour spent?   1600
Why art thou thus attir'd in discontent?
   Unmask, dear dear, this moody heaviness,
   And tell thy grief, that we may give redress."

Three times with sighs she gives her sorrow fire,
Ere once she can discharge one word of woe.   1605
At length address'd to answer his desire,
She modestly prepares to let them know
Her honour is ta'en prisoner by the foe;
   While Collatine and his consorted lords
   With sad attention long to hear her words.   1610

And now this pale swan in her wat'ry nest
Begins the sad dirge of her certain ending:
"Few words," quoth she, "shall fit the trespass best,
Where no excuse can give the fault amending.
In me moe woes than words are now depending;   1615
   And my laments would be drawn out too long,
   To tell them all with one poor tired tongue.

"Then be this all the task it hath to say:
Dear husband, in the interest of thy bed
A stranger came, and on that pillow lay   1620
Where thou wast wont to rest thy weary head;

1614. Where] *Q1*; Wherein *Q5,6,8*.   1615. moe] *Q1*; more *Q5,6-9*.   1616
too] *Q1*; to *Q5*.   1621. wast] *Q1*; was *Q4-7*.

1598. *uncouth*] unknown, strange.
1600. *spite*] feeling of annoyance.
1602. *dear dear*] dear one.
moody] See l. 1273 n.
1604-5.] 'The allusion here is to the manner of discharging ancient fire-arms by means of a match' (Staunton). With Lucrece's three attempts compare *Fasti*, ii. 823 (see Appendix II, p. 198).
1606. *address'd*] prepared.
1609. *consorted*] associated, leagued. Compare *R2*, v. vi. 15:
  Two of the dangerous consorted
    traitors.

1611-12.] Other references by Shakespeare to the swan that dies singing are: *Mer. V.*, iii. ii. 44-7, *Oth.*, v. ii. 247 f., *John*, v. vii. 21-4, and *Phoen.*, l. 15.
1615. *moe*] more. See l. 1479 n.
depending] pending or impending. Compare *Troil.*, ii. iii. 21.
1617. *To tell them all*] if they were all told.
1619. *interest*] possession. Malone compares this and the next line to Livy, i. 58: 'Vestigia viri alieni, Colatine, in lecto sunt tuo' (see Painter, Appendix II, p. 194).

And what wrong else may be imagined
    By foul enforcement might be done to me,
    From that, alas, thy Lucrece is not free.

"For in the dreadful dead of dark midnight,   1625
    With shining falchion in my chamber came
    A creeping creature with a flaming light,
    And softly cried 'Awake, thou Roman dame,
    And entertain my love; else lasting shame
        On thee and thine this night I will inflict,   1630
        If thou my love's desire do contradict.

" 'For some hard-favour'd groom of thine,' quoth he,
    'Unless thou yoke thy liking to my will,
    I'll murder straight, and then I'll slaughter thee,
    And swear I found you where you did fulfil   1635
    The loathsome act of lust, and so did kill
        The lechers in their deed: this act will be
        My fame, and thy perpetual infamy.'

"With this I did begin to start and cry,
    And then against my heart he set his sword,   1640
    Swearing, unless I took all patiently,
    I should not live to speak another word.
    So should my shame still rest upon record,
        And never be forgot in mighty Rome
        Th'adulterate death of Lucrece and her groom.   1645

"Mine enemy was strong, my poor self weak,
    And far the weaker with so strong a fear.
    My bloody judge forbod my tongue to speak;
    No rightful plea might plead for justice there.
    His scarlet lust came evidence to swear   1650
        That my poor beauty had purloin'd his eyes;
        And when the judge is robb'd, the prisoner dies.

1633. will] *Q1;* well *Q4.*   1640. set] *Q1;* sets *Q2–9.*   1644. Rome] *Q3;*
Roome *Q1,2.*   1648. forbod] *Q1;* forbad *Q4–9.*

1627. *A creeping creature*] See l. 365.
1629. *entertain*] receive, submit to.
1632. *hard-favour'd*] Compare *Ven.,*
l. 133.
    1633. *yoke*] submit.
    1647.] See l. 1266 n.

1648. *forbod*] forbade.
1650–2.] Lust is both judge and witness. 'Scarlet' is a dress appropriate
to lust, and also 'a conceit drawn
from a judge's scarlet robe' (Wyndham).

"O teach me how to make mine own excuse,
  Or at the least, this refuge let me find:
  Though my gross blood be stain'd with this abuse,   1655
  Immaculate and spotless is my mind;
  That was not forc'd, that never was inclin'd
    To accessory yieldings, but still pure
    Doth in her poison'd closet yet endure."

Lo here the hopeless merchant of this loss,   1660
  With head declin'd and voice damm'd up with woe,
  With sad set eyes and wretched arms across,
  From lips new-waxen pale begins to blow
  The grief away that stops his answer so;
    But wretched as he is, he strives in vain: 1665
    What he breathes out his breath drinks up again.

As through an arch the violent roaring tide
  Outruns the eye that doth behold his haste,
  Yet in the eddy boundeth in his pride
  Back to the strait that forc'd him on so fast,   1670
  In rage sent out, recall'd in rage being past:
    Even so his sighs, his sorrows make a saw,
    To push grief on and back the same grief draw.

1661. declin'd] *Q1;* inclin'd *Q2–9.*   1662. wretched] *Q1;* wreathed *conj.*
Walker, Sisson.

1655–6.] Livy says: 'ceterum corpus est tantum violatum, animus insons' (I. 58; see Appendix II, p. 194).

1657. *forc'd*] ravished.

1658. *accessory yieldings*] surrender that would imply consent, and so be 'accessory' to the crime. The accent is on the first and third syllables of 'accessory', as in Sonnet xxxv, l. 13.

1660. *merchant of this loss*] Shakespeare seems about to launch into an extended conceit in which Collatinus would be a speculator who has financed a ship for overseas trade: the ship then being wrecked, he loses his money. But the fancy is not worked out with the thoroughness found in earlier passages; the poet rightly feels that the poem ought to be drawing to a close.

1662. *wretched arms across*] See l. 793

n. 'Wreathed', suggested by Walker and Sisson, is not an improvement; it introduces a new tautology, and one less emphatic than 'wretched'.

1667–71.] Furnivall suggested that this comparison derives from Shakespeare's observation of 'the tide through old London Bridge, whose 19 massive piers and sterlings choked up nearly half the bed of the river.' The violence of the outflow and eddy, as well as the word 'tide' itself seems to make unlikely any reference to 'the movement of the Avon through the eighteenth arch of the old Clopton Bridge at Stratford' (C. F. E. Spurgeon, *Shakespeare's Imagery*, pp. 96–9).

1672–3.] 'His sighs make a saw, the tool so called, of his sorrows by pushing grief forwards and drawing it back

Which speechless woe of his poor she attendeth,
And his untimely frenzy thus awaketh: 1675
"Dear lord, thy sorrow to my sorrow lendeth
Another power; no flood by raining slaketh;
My woe too sensible thy passion maketh
    More feeling-painful. Let it then suffice
    To drown one woe, one pair of weeping eyes.   1680

"And for my sake, when I might charm thee so,
For she that was thy Lucrece, now attend me:
Be suddenly revenged on my foe,—
Thine, mine, his own. Suppose thou dost defend me
From what is past: the help that thou shalt lend me   1685
    Comes all too late, yet let the traitor die,
    For sparing justice feeds iniquity.

"But ere I name him, you fair lords," quoth she,
Speaking to those that came with Collatine,
"Shall plight your honourable faiths to me,   1690
With swift pursuit to 'venge this wrong of mine;
For 'tis a meritorious fair design
    To chase injustice with revengeful arms:
    Knights by their oaths should right poor ladies' harms."

At this request, with noble disposition   1695
Each present lord began to promise aid,

1680. one woe, one] *Q3–9; on woe, one Q1,2;* in woe one *conj. Malone.*

again; i.e. his sighs give him only
momentary relief, a repetition of ll.
1663–1666, he sighs away his grief and
drinks it up again' (Pooler).

1675. *frenzy*] distraction, here a
trance-like condition.

1678. *sensible*] sensitive. Compare
LLL., IV. iii. 337:

Love's feeling is more soft and
    sensible
Than are the tender horns of
    cockled snails.

1680. *one woe*] Q1 has *on woe.* See
Sisson, *New Readings,* I, p. 209.

1681–98.] The suggestion for this
appeal is in Livy, I. 58: 'Sed date dex-
teras fidemque haud inpune adultero
fore, . . . si vos viri estis, pestiferum hinc
abstulit gaudium' (Ewig, *Anglia,* XXII.

22). See also Baldwin, *op. cit.,* p. 148.

1681. *so*] in such things.

1682. *she*] See Abbott, § 211.

1683. *suddenly*] immediately.

1684. *his own*] Tarquin is his own
enemy, as being enemy to his own sal-
vation; the thought is Christian.

1687.] Malone compares *Rom.,* III. i.
202:

Mercy but murders, pardoning
    those that kill.

1694.] 'Here one of the laws of
chivalry is somewhat prematurely
introduced', comments Malone. But
Shakespeare would have been a fool
indeed to try to exclude medieval traditions from his poetry; they are
everywhere present in this poem. See
l. 197, and ll. 204–7.

As bound in knighthood to her imposition,
Longing to hear the hateful foe bewray'd;
But she that yet her sad task hath not said,
    The protestation stops. "O speak," quoth she: 1700
    "How may this forced stain be wip'd from me?

"What is the quality of my offence,
Being constrain'd with dreadful circumstance?
May my pure mind with the foul act dispense,
My low-declined honour to advance?   1705
May any terms acquit me from this chance?
    The poisoned fountain clears itself again,
    And why not I from this compelled stain?"

With this they all at once began to say,
Her body's stain her mind untainted clears,   1710
While with a joyless smile she turns away
The face, that map which deep impression bears
Of hard misfortune, carv'd in it with tears.
    "No, no," quoth she, "no dame hereafter living
    By my excuse shall claim excuse's giving."   1715

Here with a sigh as if her heart would break,
She throws forth Tarquin's name. "He, he," she says,
But more than "he" her poor tongue could not speak;
Till after many accents and delays,
Untimely breathings, sick and short assays,   1720

1702. my] *Q1;* mine *Q3–9.*   1703. circumstance] *Q1;* circumstances *Q6–9.*
1710. her] *Q1;* he *Q3,4,5 (Huntington);* the *Q5 (Trinity College, Cambridge), Q6–9.*
1712. which] *Q1;* with *Q4,5,9.*   1713. in it] *conj. Malone (Capell MS.);* it in
Q1–8; in *Q9.*   1718. could] *Q1;* would *Q5.*

1697. *imposition*] the task she has
imposed. Compare *Mer. V.,* i. ii. 114,
and *Troil.,* iii. ii. 86.
    1698. *bewray'd*] revealed.
    1702. *quality*] See l. 875 n.
    1704. *dispense*] See l. 1070 n.
    1706. *terms*] words, arguments.
    acquit me from this chance] declare me
not guilty of what has happened.
Compare l. 1071.
    1712. *map*] See l. 402 n. Compare
Tit., iii. ii. 12, and *2H6,* iii. i. 203:
            in thy face I see
The map of honour, truth and
    loyalty.

'There is a special allusion to the lines
in a map, somewhat as in the jesting
reference in *Tw. N.,* iii. ii. 85' (Pooler).
    1714–15.] Malone compares Livy,
i. 58: 'nec ulla deinde inpudica
Lucretiae exemplo vivet', and the
translation of these words in Painter
(see Appendix II, p. 195). This detail
is not in Ovid, though the passage
as a whole follows both Ovid and
Livy (see Baldwin, *op. cit.,* pp. 147–
9).
    1719. *accents*] spoken sounds.
    1720. *assays*] attempts.

She utters this: "He, he, fair lords, 'tis he,
That guides this hand to give this wound to me."

Even here she sheathed in her harmless breast
A harmful knife, that thence her soul unsheathed;
That blow did bail it from the deep unrest   1725
Of that polluted prison where it breathed.
Her contrite sighs unto the clouds bequeathed
    Her winged sprite, and through her wounds doth fly
    Life's lasting date from cancell'd destiny.

Stone-still, astonish'd with this deadly deed,   1730
Stood Collatine and all his lordly crew,
Till Lucrece' father that beholds her bleed,
Himself on her self-slaughter'd body threw,
And from the purple fountain Brutus drew
    The murd'rous knife, and as it left the place,   1735
    Her blood in poor revenge held it in chase.

And bubbling from her breast, it doth divide
In two slow rivers, that the crimson blood
Circles her body in on every side,
Who like a late-sack'd island vastly stood   1740
Bare and unpeopled in this fearful flood.
    Some of her blood still pure and red remain'd,
    And some look'd black, and that false Tarquin stain'd.

1721. lords] *Q1*; lord *Q5–9*.   1723. she sheathed] *Q1*; sheathed *Q5*; sheath'd
Q6–9.   1743. stain'd] *Q1*; sham'd *Q5 (Huntington)*.

1723. *harmless*] innocent. Compare
2H6, III. i. 71.

1725. *bail it*] buy its release.

1729.] The group of images and
words containing 'date' and 'cancell'd' constantly appears in Shakespeare's verse (see ll. 26 and 934–5).
Here eternal life, a lease of endless life,
escapes from the life on earth ('des-
tiny') which has been cancelled.

1730. *astonish'd*] stunned. See *Ven.*,
l. 825, and *Cæs.*, I. iii. 56.

1731. *crew*] company. Compare
F.Q., I. iv. 7:

There a noble crew
Of Lords and ladies stood on every
side.

1732–3 and 1772–5.] Lucretius and

Collatine fall on Lucretia's body in
Fasti, II. 835 f. (Ewig, *Anglia*, XXII. 25 f.
and Baldwin, *op. cit.*, p. 149; see
Appendix II, p. 201).

1736. *held it in chase*] Compare *Cæs.*,
III. ii. 181–4.

1738. *that*] so that.

1740. *Who*] which.

vastly] in desolation, like a waste.

1741. *unpeopled*] dispeopled. Compare *Ant.*, I. v. 78.

1742–50.] 'The phenomenon which
attends the coagulation of blood in the
separation of the serum from the clot is
obviously referred to in the "watery
rigol" which surrounds the "congealed
face of that black blood". Knowledge
of this separation of blood into clot and

About the mourning and congealed face
Of that black blood a watery rigol goes,   1745
Which seems to weep upon the tainted place;
And ever since, as pitying Lucrece' woes,
Corrupted blood some watery token shows,
  And blood untainted still doth red abide,
  Blushing at that which is so putrified.   1750

"Daughter, dear daughter," old Lucretius cries,
"That life was mine which thou hast here deprived;
If in the child the father's image lies,
Where shall I live now Lucrece is unlived?
Thou wast not to this end from me derived: 1755
  If children predecease progenitors,
  We are their offspring, and they none of ours.

"Poor broken glass, I often did behold
In thy sweet semblance my old age new-born;
But now that fair fresh mirror, dim and old,   1760
Shows me a bare-bon'd death by time outworn.
O from thy cheeks my image thou hast torn,
  And shiver'd all the beauty of my glass,
  That I no more can see what once I was.

"O time, cease thou thy course and last no longer,   1765
  If they surcease to be that should survive!

1755. wast] *Q1*; was *Q4,5*.   1762, 1763. thy . . . of] *Q1*; my . . . from *Q4–9*.
1765. last] *Q1*; hast *Q4–9*.   1766. they] *Q1*; thou *Q4–9*.

serum is also evident from . . . [l. 1748],
although the theory of its production
is, of course, merely poetic. . . That the
dramatist had observed the different
colours of the two kinds of blood is
evident; but that he should know the
cause of it was not to be expected. . .'
(Bucknill, *Medical Knowledge of Shakespeare*, pp. 283 f.).
  1745. *rigol*] a circle (Malone).
Steevens compares *2H4*, IV. v. 36:
        this is a sleep
  That from this golden rigol hath
    divorced
  So many English kings.
  1752. *deprived*] taken away. See
l. 1186.

1754. *unlived*] bereft of life.
  1756–71.] Compare *Rom.*, v. iii.
213–14.
  1758. *glass*] Compare Sonnet iii,
ll. 9–11:
  Thou art thy mother's glass, and
    she in thee
  Calls back the lovely April of her
    prime.
See also *Err.*, v. i. 417.
  1761. *death*] death's head or skele-
ton. Compare *John*, v. ii. 176–7:
        and in his forehead sits
        A bare-ribb'd death.
See also *LLL.*, v. ii. 616, and *Mer. V.*,
II. vii. 63.
  1763. *shiver'd*] shattered.

Shall rotten death make conquest of the stronger,
And leave the falt'ring feeble souls alive?
The old bees die, the young possess their hive;
   Then live, sweet Lucrece, live again and see   1770
     Thy father die, and not thy father thee!"

By this, starts Collatine as from a dream,
And bids Lucretius give his sorrow place;
And then in key-cold Lucrece' bleeding stream
He falls, and bathes the pale fear in his face,   1775
And counterfeits to die with her a space;
   Till manly shame bids him possess his breath,
     And live to be revenged on her death.

The deep vexation of his inward soul
Hath serv'd a dumb arrest upon his tongue;   1780
Who, mad that sorrow should his use control
Or keep him from heart-easing words so long,
Begins to talk; but through his lips do throng
   Weak words, so thick come in his poor heart's aid
     That no man could distinguish what he said.   1785

Yet sometime "Tarquin" was pronounced plain,
But through his teeth, as if the name he tore.
This windy tempest, till it blow up rain,
Held back his sorrow's tide, to make it more.
At last it rains, and busy winds give o'er;   1790
   Then son and father weep with equal strife
     Who should weep most, for daughter or for wife.

Then one doth call her his, the other his,
Yet neither may possess the claim they lay.

1768. *falt'ring*] foultring *Qq*.   1781. *mad*] *Q1*; made *Q2–9*.   1784. *come*]
Q1; comes *Q4–7*.   1787. *the*] *Q1*; his *Q4–9*.

1774. *key-cold*] cold as steel. Steevens
says: 'A key, on account of the coldness of the metal of which it is composed, was anciently employed to stop
any slight bleeding.' 'Key-cold' is a
common Elizabethan phrase, but
occurs elsewhere in Shakespeare only
in *R3*, I. ii. 5:

   Poor key-cold figure of a holy
     king.

1776.] And seems to die with her,
perhaps because he faints.

1780. *serv'd a dumb arrest*] forced a
dumbness, as if by warrant. Compare
Ham., v. ii. 329.

1784. *so thick come*] coming with such
hurry.

1788–90.] English weather-lore
holds that a high wind always brings
rain, and then drops.

The father says, "She's mine." "O mine she is," 1795
Replies her husband, "do not take away
My sorrow's interest; let no mourner say
    He weeps for her, for she was only mine,
    And only must be wail'd by Collatine."

"O," quoth Lucretius, "I did give that life 1800
  Which she too early and too late hath spill'd."
"Woe, woe," quoth Collatine, "she was my wife;
  I ow'd her, and 'tis mine that she hath kill'd."
"My daughter" and "my wife" with clamours fill'd
    The dispers'd air, who holding Lucrece' life 1805
    Answer'd their cries, "my daughter" and "my wife".

Brutus, who pluck'd the knife from Lucrece' side,
Seeing such emulation in their woe,
Began to clothe his wit in state and pride,
Burying in Lucrece' wound his folly's show. 1810
He with the Romans was esteemed so
    As silly jeering idiots are with kings,
    For sportive words and utt'ring foolish things.

But now he throws that shallow habit by,
Wherein deep policy did him disguise, 1815
And arm'd his long-hid wits advisedly,
To check the tears in Collatinus' eyes.
"Thou wronged lord of Rome," quoth he, "arise!
    Let my unsounded self, suppos'd a fool,
    Now set thy long-experienc'd wit to school. 1820

1815. deep] *Q1;* the *Q6–9.*

1797. *My sorrow's interest*] my right to sorrow.

1800–1.] Compare *3H6,* II. v. 92–3.
too late] because her death was too late to save her from Tarquin's crime.

spill'd] destroyed.

1803. *ow'd her*] was her rightful possessor. See *Ven.,* l. 411.

1805.] Brown says: '. . . the thought may be that the air having received the spirit of Lucrece now answers on her behalf'.

dispers'd] scattered, rent.

1807–20.] 'Livy's text gives sufficient authority for this description of Brutus' (Brown). Compare *H5,* II. iv. 37 f.:   the Roman Brutus,
  Covering discretion with a coat of
    folly.

1815. *policy*] calculation.

1816. *advisedly*] See l. 1527 and l. 180 n.

1819. *unsounded*] unplumbed, unexplored. Compare *2H6,* III. i. 57:
    Gloucester is a man
  Unsounded yet and full of deep
    deceit.

"Why Collatine, is woe the cure for woe?
Do wounds help wounds, or grief help grievous deeds?
Is it revenge to give thyself a blow
For his foul act by whom thy fair wife bleeds?
Such childish humour from weak minds proceeds;   1825
    Thy wretched wife mistook the matter so,
    To slay herself that should have slain her foe.

"Courageous Roman, do not steep thy heart
In such relenting dew of lamentations;
But kneel with me and help to bear thy part   1830
To rouse our Roman gods with invocations,
That they will suffer these abominations,—
    Since Rome herself in them doth stand disgraced,—
    By our strong arms from forth her fair streets chased.

"Now by that Capitol that we adore,   1835
    And by this chaste blood so unjustly stained,
    By heaven's fair sun that breeds the fat earth's store,
    By all our country rights in Rome maintained,
    And by chaste Lucrece' soul that late complained
        Her wrongs to us, and by this bloody knife,   1840
        We will revenge the death of this true wife."

This said, he strook his hand upon his breast,
And kiss'd the fatal knife to end his vow;

1829. relenting] *Q1;* lamenting *Q6.*   1831. invocations] *Q1;* innotations *Q5*
(*Huntington*).   1838. rights] *Q1;* rites *Q3–9.*

1821. *Why*] 'An exclamation of impatience, as in *Merchant of Venice*, II. v. 6' (Pooler).

1821–9.] Compare Livy, I. 59: 'Movet . . . tum Brutus castigator lacrimarum atque inertium querellarum auctorque quod viros, quod Romanos deceret, arma capiendi adversus hostilia ausos' (Ewig, *Anglia*, XXII. 23). Baldwin investigates further the sources of Shakespeare's treatment of Lucius Junius Brutus (*op. cit.*, pp. 149–52). Students should take note of the difference of identity between this Brutus and the Brutus of *Julius Cæsar*. See *Cæs.*, I. ii. 159–61 and II. i. 53–4.

1829. *relenting*] melting.

1834. *chased*] i.e. to be chased.

1836.] Ewig again compares Livy, I. 59: 'Per hunc . . . castissimum ante regiam iniuriam sanguinem iuro.'

1837. *store*] abundance. See l. 97.

1838. *country rights*] national or native rights.

1839.] Kittredge refers to *Fasti*, II. 842: 'Perque tuos manes' (see Appendix II, p. 198).

1842–8.] Ewig notes that these details are not in Ovid or Chaucer, but in Livy, I. 59: 'Cultrum deinde Collatino tradit, inde Lucretio ac Valerio, stupentibus miraculo rei, unde novum in Bruti pectore ingenium. Ut praeceptum erat iurant' (see Appendix II, p. 195).

And to his protestation urg'd the rest,
Who wond'ring at him, did his words allow.   1845
Then jointly to the ground their knees they bow,
    And that deep vow which Brutus made before,
    He doth again repeat, and that they swore.

When they had sworn to this advised doom,
They did conclude to bear dead Lucrece thence,   1850
To show her bleeding body thorough Rome,
And so to publish Tarquin's foul offence;
Which being done with speedy diligence,
    The Romans plausibly did give consent
    To Tarquin's everlasting banishment.   1855

1851. her] *Q1;* the *Q4–9.*   thorough] *Q1;* through out *Q6.*   Rome] Roome
Q1,2.   1854. plausibly] *Q1;* pausiblie *Q2,3.*

1844. *protestation*] vow. See l. 1700.
1845. *allow*] approve.
1849. *advised doom*] deliberate judgment.
1854. *plausibly*] with applause, i.e. with a general acclamation. See the

Argument, ll. 34 f. Pooler quotes from Greene, *Euphues his Censure to Philautus* (ed. Grosart, vi. 199): 'Ulysses having ended his tale with a plausible silence of both parties.'

THE PASSIONATE PILGRIM

THE PASSIONATE PILGRIM

I

When my love swears that she is made of truth,
I do believe her, though I know she lies,
That she might think me some untutor'd youth,
Unskilful in the world's false forgeries.
Thus vainly thinking that she thinks me young,   5
Although I know my years be past the best,
I smiling credit her false-speaking tongue,
Outfacing faults in love with love's ill rest.

1. 6. be] *Q1–3;* are *Folger MS. 2071.7.*

1.] Compare Sonnet cxxxviii:

When my love sweares that she is
    made of truth,
I do beleeve her though I know she
    lyes,
That she might thinke me some
    untuterd youth,
Unlearned in the worlds false
    subtilties.
Thus vainely thinking that she
    thinkes me young,
Although she knowes my dayes are
    past the best,
Simply I credit her false speaking
    tongue,
On both sides thus is simple truth
    supprest:
But wherefore sayes she not she is
    unjust?
And wherefore say not I that I am
    old?
O loves best habit is in seeming
    trust,
And age in love, loves not t'have
    yeares told.
    Therefore I lye with her, and she
        with me,
    And in our faults by lyes we
        flattered be.

As Pooler says, 'This is clearer and
more consistent than the form in the

text'. Other commentators agree,
though Sidney Lee deviates (see l. 9
n.). It is odd that most comments
assume that Sonnet cxxxviii is a
revision of the poem published ten
years earlier, when the earlier readings are just of the kind that might be
expected in an inaccurate report:
they confuse and weaken the poem as
a whole. A version of this poem,
together with iv, vi, vii, xi, and xviii,
is contained in a manuscript once
owned by J. P. Collier, and now in the
Folger Library. In the MS. the initials
'W.S.' have been added at the end of
i, iv, vi, vii, and xviii 'in a different
hand and different ink' (*Poems,* ed.
Rollins, p. 544).

4. *forgeries*] falsifications. See *Lucr.,*
l. 460. 'False' adds nothing to this, as it
does to 'subtilties'.

8. *Outfacing faults in love*] wilfully
ignoring the lover's faults. The lover
puts a bold or bland face upon the
matter.

with love's ill rest] A sense has been
forced out of this by some editors.
Dowden wrote: ' "Ill rest", I suppose,
means "uneasy sleep" '. Tucker explains: 'The remainder of the love,
which is (really) of inferior value';

But wherefore says my love that she is young?
And wherefore say not I that I am old?　　　　10
O, love's best habit's in a soothing tongue,
And age, in love, loves not to have years told.
　　Therefore I'll lie with love, and love with me,
　　Since that our faults in love thus smother'd be.

II

Two loves I have, of comfort and despair,
That like two spirits do suggest me still;

11. habit's in] *Q1;* habit is *Q2.*　　　soothing] *Q1–3;* smoothinge *Folger MS.*
14. smother'd] *Q1–3;* smothered *Folger MS.*

unlike most of Shakespeare's hard passages, the phrase does not suggest two or more strong meanings, but rather no meaning at all.

9. *she is young*] This is one of the worst variants, though Lee says: 'These lines,' (ll. 6–9) 'if less polished, are somewhat more pointed than the later version'. The logic of the situation and of the sonnet requires the reading we find in Sonnet cxxxviii. Dowden pointed this out, while holding that the superiority of the later version was due to revision: '[These lines] confuse the idea of the piece by bringing in a new motive. "My love" here not only asserts her truth when she is really false, but also asserts her youth (her youth being past): evidently the balance of the composition ... requires that there should be one lie on each side, and that the lady's lie should be an assertion of fidelity, the man's lie an implied assertion of his youth. And so it was worked out in the version of 1609.' It seems more likely that the vigour and consistency of the original idea are seen in Sonnet cxxxviii, and that they were marred in the reporting either because the reporter could not recall the somewhat unexpected 'unjust', for *unfaithful,* or because the notion of the lady also being past her youth seemed more obviously amusing.

11.] 'Love is best clothed in flattery'

(Pooler). It is doubtful whether Shakespeare's sense of metaphor would have let him write of anyone or anything being clothed in a tongue.

12. *told*] counted up. Compare *LLL.,* I. ii. 41, and *Ven.,* l. 277.

11.] Compare Sonnet cxliv:
Two loves I have of comfort and
　dispaire,
Which like two spirits do sugjest me
　still,
The better angell is a man right
　faire:
The worser spirit a woman
　collour'd il.
To win me soone to hell my femall
　evill,
Tempteth my better angel from my
　sight,
And would corrupt my saint to be
　a divel:
Wooing his purity with her fowle
　pride.
And whether that my angel be
　turn'd finde [*sic*],
Suspect I may, yet not directly tell,
But being both from me both to
　each friend,
I gesse one angel in an others hel.
　Yet this shal I nere know but live
　　in doubt,
　Till my bad angel fire my good
　　one out.

2. *suggest*] prompt or incite. See *Ven.,* l. 651 n. and *Lucr.,* l. 37 n.

My better angel is a man, right fair,
My worser spirit a woman, colour'd ill.
To win me soon to hell, my female evil 5
Tempteth my better angel from my side,
And would corrupt my saint to be a devil,
Wooing his purity with her fair pride.
And whether that my angel be turn'd fiend,
Suspect I may, yet not directly tell; 10
For being both to me, both to each, friend,
I guess one angel in another's hell:
   The truth I shall not know, but live in doubt,
   Till my bad angel fire my good one out.

8. *fair*] Pooler notes that the 'foul' of Sonnet cxliv 'gives a sense more in accordance with "colour'd ill", l. 4'. Dowden is perversely ingenious: 'the "faire pride" of the earlier text has a touch of happy audacity which is toned down in the tamer "foul pride" of the later version'. 'Foul' is decidedly the stronger word, and the fact that it evokes the woman's dark complexion does not make it less so.

10. *directly*] exactly. See *Mer. V.*, i. iii. 78:

No; not take interest; not, as you
  would say,
Directly interest: mark what Jacob
  did.

11. *to me*] 'Being both of them alike friends of mine and of each other' (Pooler). But while this reading seems at first sight smooth and obvious, it is inferior to the 'from me' of 1609; the latter conveys the reason for the lover's suspicion that his two friends may be deceiving him—and they have their opportunities when they are away from him, and may meet behind his back. Pooler compares *Lucr.*, l. 1144:

Some dark deep desert seated from
  the way.

12.] 'I suspect that she has him in her own place' (Pooler). Others have made the sexual allusion clearer by referring to Boccaccio (the 10th story of the 3rd day of the *Decameron*). The Elizabethans and later poets are fond of a similar joke about the game called 'barley-break', in which one of the players might be put 'in hell'. Compare Herrick, *Barly-Break: or, Last in Hell*.

14. *fire . . . out*] 'In its literal meaning of driving out by applying fire, "fire out" was freely used by men of letters down to the time of Swift. In the sixteenth and seventeenth centuries its cognate usage in the metaphorical sense of expelling violently . . . was only a little less common . . .' (Lee in *The Athenaeum*, 1901). Modern American 'fire' for 'dismiss' thus descends from 18th-cent. English. But here we have another obscene joke, which both Lee and Pooler illustrate by an epigram in Guilpin's *Skialetheia*, 1598. The phrase is discussed in *Notes and Queries*, 7 Dec. 1907, pp. 454 f. As so often in Elizabethan bawdy, there is also an allusion to some of the effects of venereal disease.

III

Did not the heavenly rhetoric of thine eye,
'Gainst whom the world could not hold argument,
Persuade my heart to this false perjury?
Vows for thee broke deserve not punishment.
A woman I forswore; but I will prove,   5
Thou being a goddess, I forswore not thee:
My vow was earthly, thou a heavenly love;
Thy grace being gain'd cures all disgrace in me.
My vow was breath, and breath a vapour is;
Then thou, fair sun that on this earth doth shine,   10
Exhal'st this vapour vow. In thee it is;
If broken then, it is no fault of mine.
    If by me broke, what fool is not so wise
    To break an oath, to win a paradise?

IV

Sweet Cytherea, sitting by a brook
With young Adonis, lovely, fresh and green,

III. 11. Exhal'st] *LLL, Malone;* Exhalt *Q1;* Exhale *Q2,3.*

v. 1. Sweet] *Q1–3;* ffaire *Folger MS. 1.8.*

III.] This, together with Nos. v and xvi, may have been taken from the 1598 Quarto of *Love's Labour's Lost,* though Lee thinks that the variations suggest that the publisher 'printed stray copies which were circulating "privately", and did not find the lines in the printed quarto of the play.' See *LLL.,* IV. iii. 56–69.

2. *whom*] for 'which'. Compare *Ven.,* l. 87.

11.] The sun draws up the vapour from the earth. Compare *Rom.,* III. v. 13:

    It is some meteor that the sun
        exhales.

12. *If broken then*] if it is broken now that it is exhaled and 'in' the sun, not in the earth.

13. *so*] For 'so' in this construction see Abbott, § 281 f.

14. *break*] *LLL.* has 'lose', which gives more point.

IV.] Not found elsewhere. Versions exist both in Folger MS. 2071.7 (see 1 n.) and Folger MS. 1.8, where it is accompanied by XI. This and Nos. VI, IX, and XI were thought by Malone to be 'Essays of the author when he first conceived the idea of writing a poem on the subject of Venus and Adonis, and before the scheme of his poem was adjusted.' Many 19th-cent. editors accepted this suggestion, or varied only slightly from it, in no case producing new arguments or evidence (Dyce, Collier, Bell, Hudson, Halliwell-Phillipps, and others). Some expressed doubt of Shakespeare's authorship (Boswell, Knight, Edmonds, Humphreys, Gollancz). Dowden in 1883 tried to take the matter further, writing: 'I think there can be little doubt that IV, VI, and ... IX come from the same hand. Nothing in any one of the three sonnets forbids the idea of

Did court the lad with many a lovely look,
Such looks as none could look but beauty's queen.
She told him stories to delight his ear; 5
She show'd him favours to allure his eye;
To win his heart, she touch'd him here and there;
Touches so soft still conquer chastity.
But whether unripe years did want conceit,
Or he refus'd to take her figur'd proffer, 10
The tender nibbler would not touch the bait,
But smile and jest at every gentle offer.
Then fell she on her back, fair queen, and toward:
He rose and ran away; ah fool too froward!

4. could] *Q1–3;* can *Folger MS. 1.8.* 5. ear] eare *Folger MS. 1.8;* eares *Q1–3.*
8. soft] *Q2;* soft, *Q1,3;* sought *Folger MS. 2071.7.* 10. refus'd] *Q1–3;* did
scorne *Folger MS. 1.8.* her] *Q2,3;* his *Q1.* figur'd] figurd *Folger MSS.;*
figured *Q1–3.* 11, 12. touch...smile...jest] *Q1–3;* take...blusht...smild
Folger MS. 1.8. 13. queen] *Q1–3; omitted Folger MS. 1.8.* 14. rose] *Q1–3;*
blusht *Folger MS. 1.8.* ah] *Q1–3;* ô *Folger MS. 1.8.*

Shakspere's authorship...At the same time there is nothing which decisively proves them to be by Shakspere'. He notes that the name 'Cytherea' for Venus (in IV and VI) does not occur in *Venus and Adonis.* 20th-cent. editors have given more weight to the fact that XI was previously printed as his own by Bartholomew Griffin (see p. 162 below), and that it cannot easily be dissociated from the other three pieces. Lee, Porter, Adams, and Chambers incline to look on the group as Griffin's work, while Feuillerat is actually able to produce a new argument on the matter: 'IV, VI, and IX are remarkable for their lack of imagery: they scarcely contain any simile and metaphor. The man who wrote them was singularly devoid of imagination, a thing which cannot be said of Shakespeare but which is certainly true of

Griffin, as XI and the whole of *Fidessa* demonstrates.' A later opinion is offered by Baldwin, *op. cit.,* pp. 43–5. See also Bullough, *op. cit.,* pp. 161–2.

2. *green*] new, young. See *Ven.,* l. 806.
3. *lovely*] amorous.
5.] 'Venus tells Adonis the story of Atalanta in Ovid, *Met.* x. 560–704' (Pooler).
9. *conceit*] understanding. See VIII. 7–8.
10. *take*] accept or understand. Compare XI. 12, and *MND.,* v. i. 90:
Our sport shall be to take what they
mistake.
figur'd] indicated by signs. Collier's suggested emendation to 'sugar'd' is unnecessary.
13. *toward*] ready, submissive.
14. *froward*] intractable. See *Ven.,* l. 570.

V

If love make me forsworn, how shall I swear to love?
O never faith could hold, if not to beauty vowed.
Though to myself forsworn, to thee I'll constant prove:
Those thoughts, to me like oaks, to thee like osiers bowed.
Study his bias leaves, and makes his book thine eyes,   5
Where all those pleasures live that art can comprehend.
If knowledge be the mark, to know thee shall suffice:
Well learned is that tongue that well can thee commend,
All ignorant that soul that sees thee without wonder;
Which is to me some praise, that I thy parts admire.   10
Thine eye love's lightning seems, thy voice his dreadful thunder,
Which, not to anger bent, is music and sweet fire.
    Celestial as thou art, O do not love that wrong,
    To sing heaven's praise with such an earthly tongue.

VI

Scarce had the sun dried up the dewy morn,
And scarce the herd gone to the hedge for shade,
When Cytherea, all in love forlorn,
A longing tarriance for Adonis made
Under an osier growing by a brook,   5
A brook where Adon us'd to cool his spleen;
Hot was the day, she hotter that did look

---

v. 11. Thine] *Q2,3;* Thin *Q1.*

v.] Compare *LLL.*, IV. ii. 100–13.

5. *Study his bias leaves*] 'The student abandons his inclination to learning' (Pooler). The 'bias' is the weight inserted in a bowl to give it a curving course; hence 'a special tendency or characteristic'. Compare *Lr.*, I. ii. 120.

makes his book thine eyes] Like the rest of the sonnet, this is a concentration of the theme of *LLL.*: see IV. iii. 350–3.

11–12.] Compare *Ant.*, v. ii. 83–6.

13–14.] These lines can only be a botched version of those in *LLL.*, which conclude:

    O! pardon love this wrong
    That sings heaven's praise with
      such an earthly tongue!

VI.] A version is given in Folger MS. 2071.7 (see I n.). Pooler observes: 'The subject is that of one of the pictures offered to Christopher Sly, *T.S.*, *Induction*, ii. 50:

    Dost thou love pictures? we will
      fetch thee straight
    Adonis painted by a running
      brook,
    And Cytherea all in sedges hid.'

This is suggested by Ovid's story of Salmacis and Hermaphroditus, which has also been absorbed into *Venus and Adonis* (see Baldwin, *op. cit.*, pp. 43–4).

4. *tarriance*] waiting. Compare *Gent.*, II. vii. 90:

    I am impatient of my tarriance.

5. *osier*] willow.

6. *spleen*] hot or proud temper. Compare *Rom.*, III. i. 163.

For his approach, that often there had been.
Anon he comes, and throws his mantle by,
And stood stark naked on the brook's green brim: 10
The sun look'd on the world with glorious eye,
Yet not so wistly as this queen on him.
   He spying her, bounc'd in; whereas he stood,
"O Jove," quoth she, "why was not I a flood?"

VII

Fair is my love, but not so fair as fickle,
Mild as a dove, but neither true nor trusty,
Brighter than glass, and yet, as glass is, brittle,
Softer than wax, and yet as iron, rusty:
   A lily pale, with damask dye to grace her,   5
   None fairer, nor none falser to deface her.

Her lips to mine how often hath she joined,
Between each kiss her oaths of true love swearing!
How many tales to please me hath she coined,
Dreading my love, the loss whereof still fearing!   10

vi. 8. there] *Q2,3;* heare *Folger MS.*   12. this] *Q2,3;* the *Folger MS.*   14. O] *Q2,3;* ah *Folger MS.*

vii. 7, 9. joined . . . coined] *Q2,3;* joynd . . . coynd *Folger MS.*   10. whereof] *Q2;* thereof *Q3.*

12. *wistly*] eagerly. Compare *Ven.,* l. 343, and *Lucr.,* l. 1355.
13. *whereas he stood*] and as he stood there.

vii.] In Folger MS. 2071.7 (see 1 n.). Not found elsewhere.
3. *brittle*] Editors point out that 'brickle' was a common form of 'brittle', and Pooler cites two passages from Spenser, *The Ruines of Time* and *F.Q.,*iv. x. 39:
    Yet glasse was not if one did
       rightly deeme;
    But being faire and brickle, likest
       glass did seeme.
5. *damask dye*] red. The Elizabethan use of 'damask' for rosy complexions derives from the mingled colour of the damask rose: 'The flowers . . . be

neither redde nor white but of a mixt colour betwixt red and white, almost carnation colour' (O.E.D.). Compare *AYL.,* iii. v. 120–3:
    There was a pretty redness in his lip,
    A little riper and more lusty red
    Than that mix'd in his cheek; 'twas
      just the difference
    Betwixt the constant red and
      mingled damask.
5–6.] Pooler suggests an improved punctuation: 'The antithesis between "grace" and "deface" seems to require a change: "A lily pale with damask dye: to grace her, None fairer, nor none falser, to deface her," i.e. To her honour it may be said that there is none fairer, and to her discredit that there is none more false.'

Yet in the midst of all her pure protestings,
Her faith, her oaths, her tears and all were jestings.

She burnt with love, as straw with fire flameth;
She burnt out love, as soon as straw out-burneth.
She fram'd the love, and yet she foil'd the framing;   15
She bade love last, and yet she fell a-turning.
    Was this a lover, or a lecher whether?
    Bad in the best, though excellent in neither.

VIII

If music and sweet poetry agree,
As they must needs, the sister and the brother,
Then must the love be great 'twixt thee and me,
Because thou lov'st the one and I the other.
Dowland to thee is dear, whose heavenly touch   5
Upon the lute, doth ravish human sense;
Spenser to me, whose deep conceit is such
As passing all conceit, needs no defence.
Thou lov'st to hear the sweet melodious sound
That Phoebus' lute, the queen of music, makes;   10
And I in deep delight am chiefly drown'd
Whenas himself to singing he betakes.
    One god is god of both, as poets feign;
    One knight loves both, and both in thee remain.

vii. 11. midst] *Q3, Folger MS.;* mids *Q2.*

13. *fire*] Pronounce as two syllables.
15. *foil'd*] frustrated.
17. *whether*] which of the two. See
xiv. 8, and *Ven.,* l. 304.

viii.] By Richard Barnfield. This
and No. xx appeared in Barnfield's
Poems: In diuers humors, added to *The
Encomion of Lady Pecunia* (1598). The
sonnet was addressed by Barnfield *To
his friend Maister R. L. In praise of
Musique and Poetrie.* R. L. has been
identified with Richard Linche, who
published *Diella: certaine Sonnets* in
1596. For the stages by which Barnfield was shown to be the author of this
poem, see Rollins, pp. 542 f.

5. *Dowland*] John Dowland (1563?–
1626?), one of the most famous com-
posers of the period.

7. *Spenser*] Barnfield produced in
Cynthia (1595) 'the first imitation of the
verse of that excellent Poet Maister
Spenser in his Fayrie Queene'
(Pooler).
    conceit] This and the next line show
both meanings: 'imagination', and
'understanding or conception'.

14. *One knight*] This was probably
Sir George Carey, K.G., to whom
Dowland dedicated his first book of
airs in 1597, and to whose wife (daugh-
ter of Sir John Spencer of Althorp)
Spenser dedicated *Muiopotmos* in 1590.

IX

Fair was the morn, when the fair queen of love,

.   .   .   .

Paler for sorrow than her milk-white dove,
For Adon's sake, a youngster proud and wild;
Her stand she takes upon a steep-up hill;   5
Anon Adonis comes with horn and hounds.
She silly queen, with more than love's good will,
Forbade the boy he should not pass those grounds.
"Once," quoth she, "did I see a fair sweet youth
Here in these brakes deep-wounded with a boar,   10
Deep in the thigh, a spectacle of ruth!
See in my thigh," quoth she, "here was the sore!"
    She showed hers, he saw more wounds than one,
    And blushing fled, and left her all alone.

X

Sweet rose, fair flower, untimely pluck'd, soon vaded,
Pluck'd in the bud and vaded in the spring!
Bright orient pearl, alack too timely shaded!
Fair creature kill'd too soon by death's sharp sting!
    Like a green plum that hangs upon a tree,   5
    And falls, through wind, before the fall should be.

I weep for thee, and yet no cause I have,
For why thou lefts me nothing in thy will;
And yet thou lefts me more than I did crave,
For why I craved nothing of thee still.   10
    O yes, dear friend, I pardon crave of thee:
    Thy discontent thou didst bequeath to me.

---

ix.] Not found elsewhere.

3.] Malone noted that a preceding line had been lost.

5. *steep-up*] Malone compared Sonnet vii, l. 5:

And having climb'd the steep-up heavenly hill.

8. *pass those grounds*] go through those valleys or low-lying places.

13. *one*] For the rhyme see *Ven.*, ll. 293–4.

x.] Not found elsewhere.

1. *vaded*] faded.

3. *orient*] oriental. Pearls from Indian seas were brighter than those found in Europe. See *Ven.*, l. 981 n.

timely] early.

5. *Like a green plum*] Compare *Ven.*, l. 527.

8. *For why*] because. See Abbott, § 75. Compare *Lucr.*, l. 1222.

9. *lefts*] For this form of the second person singular in verbs ending with -t, see Abbott, § 340. Compare xii. 12 below, and *Lucr.*, l. 878.

XI

Venus with Adonis sitting by her
Under a myrtle shade began to woo him;
She told the youngling how god Mars did try her,
And as he fell to her, she fell to him.
"Even thus," quoth she, "the warlike god embrac'd me,"   5
And then she clipp'd Adonis in her arms.
"Even thus," quoth she, "the warlike god unlac'd me,"
As if the boy should use like loving charms.
"Even thus," quoth she, "he seized on my lips,"
And with her lips on his did act the seizure;   10
And as she fetched breath, away he skips,
And would not take her meaning nor her pleasure.
Ah, that I had my lady at this bay,
To kiss and clip me till I run away!

xi. 1. with] *Q2,3;* and *Griffin, Folger MS. 1.8.*   3. god] *Q2,3;* great *Folger MS. 1.8.*   4. she fell] *Q2,3;* so fell she *Griffin, Folger MS. 1.8.*   5. warlike] *Q2,3;* wanton *Griffin.*   6. clipp'd] *Q2,3;* clasp'd *Griffin;* tooke *Folger MS. 1.8.* 7. Even] *Q2,3;* & *Folger MS. 2071.7.*   warlike] *Q2,3;* lusty *Folger MS. 1.8.* 9–12.] *Q2,3, Folger MSS.;* But he a wayward boy refusde her offer / And ran away, the beautious Queene neglecting: / Shewing both folly to abuse her proffer, / And all his sex of cowardise detecting. *Griffin.*   9. Even] *Q2,3;* Then *Folger MS. 2071.7.*   11. And] *Q2,3;* But *Folger MS. 1.8.*   fetched] *Q2,3;* tooke hir *Folger MS. 1.8.*   13. Ah, . . . this] *Q2,3;* Oh . . . that *Griffin, Folger MS. 1.8.* lady] *Q2,3;* mistris *Griffin, Folger MSS.*   14. kiss . . . me] *Q2,3;* clipp and kiss hir *Folger MS. 1.8.*   run] *Q2,3;* ranne *Griffin, Folger MS. 1.8.*

xi.] A version of this appeared as the third poem in Bartholomew Griffin's *Fidessa,* 1596 (see iv n.). Even this has not prevented some critics from attributing it to Shakespeare (see Rollins, pp. 644–6). The poem is also in Folger MSS. 2071.7 and 1.8 (see i n. and iv n.).

4.] The faulty rhythm and rhyme show that the reading from *Fidessa* is correct.

fell to] Pooler would interpret this metaphorically: 'To "fall to" is to begin or set about doing anything; and in modern provincial use means often to attack; thus "He fell to him like a day's work" means violently assaulted him'. He cites *Shr.,* i. i. 38, and *Ham.,* v. ii. 216, but adds: 'Prof. Case prefers the less idiomatic sense: "And as Mars

fell (or leant) towards her, so she fell towards Adonis." ' The literal sense is more in the spirit of these poems. See *Ven.,* ll. 592–6.

6. *clipp'd*] clasped. See *Ven.,* l. 600.

12. *take*] understand. See iv. 10.

13. *at this bay*] Pooler explains that 'the poet does not wish that he was hunting his lady, but that his lady was hunting him. He would like . . . to be in Adonis's shoes, i.e. to be the hunted not the hunter. And "to hold at a bay" could be said of the stag as well as of the hounds. See Cotgrave (*Dictionarie,* 1611): "Aux derniers abbois. . . A metaphor from hunting; wherein a Stag is said, Rendre les abbois when wearie of running he turns upon the hounds, and holds them at, or puts them to, a bay." ' See *Ven.,* l. 877.

XII

Crabbed age and youth cannot live together:
Youth is full of pleasance, age is full of care;
Youth like summer morn, age like winter weather;
Youth like summer brave, age like winter bare.
Youth is full of sport, age's breath is short;   5
    Youth is nimble, age is lame;
Youth is hot and bold, age is weak and cold;
    Youth is wild and age is tame.
Age, I do abhor thee; youth, I do adore thee:
    O my love, my love is young!   10
Age, I do defy thee. O sweet shepherd, hie thee,
    For methinks thou stays too long.

XIII

Beauty is but a vain and doubtful good,
A shining gloss that vadeth suddenly,
A flower that dies when first it 'gins to bud,
A brittle glass that's broken presently:

XII. 2. pleasance] *Q2,3;* pleasure *Deloney.*   3. summer . . . winter] *Q2,3;*
summers . . . winters *Deloney.*   4.] *Q2,3; omitted Deloney.*   12. stays] *Q2,3;*
stay'st *Deloney.*

XII.] This is the earliest known appearance of this song. It was published also, as *A Maidens choice twixt Age and Youth,* in Thomas Deloney's *Garland of Good Will,* the earliest surviving edition of which is that of 1631. But this ballad-anthology had probably first appeared in the early 1590's; it was certainly in existence by 1596, when it was mentioned by Thomas Nashe (*Works,* ed. McKerrow, 1958, III, p. 84). An edition of 1604 is mentioned by several editors, including Pooler, but it is unknown today. Since the contents of such collections as Deloney's varied from one edition to another, there is no means of telling whether the present poem was included in the *Garland of Good Will* before 1631. The song as given there is expanded by several stanzas of inferior quality, as popular songs were apt to be. Those who ascribe the present version to Shakespeare have no evidence but its undoubted charm; they generally say they 'like to think it his' (Furnivall, Quiller-Couch, Chambers, and others).

1. *Crabbed*] cross-tempered.
4. *brave*] finely dressed.
11. *defy*] reject. Compare *AYL.,* Epilogue 21.
hie thee] See *Ven.,* l. 3 n.

XIII.] Not found elsewhere. Several versions, purporting to come from MS. copies, appeared in 18th-cent. periodicals (*Gentlemen's Magazine,* Nov. 1750 and Jan. 1760; see Rollins, pp. 291–2). The variations they show are distinctly 18th-cent. in flavour and cast doubt on the authenticity of the MSS.

2. *vadeth*] See x. 1.
4. *presently*] instantly.

A doubtful good, a gloss, a glass, a flower,   5
Lost, vaded, broken, dead within an hour.

And as goods lost are seld or never found,
As vaded gloss no rubbing will refresh,
As flowers dead lie withered on the ground,
As broken glass no cement can redress: 10
    So beauty blemish'd once, for ever lost,
    In spite of physic, painting, pain and cost.

XIV

Good night, good rest: ah, neither be my share!
She bade good night that kept my rest away,
And daff'd me to a cabin hang'd with care,
To descant on the doubts of my decay.
    "Farewell," quoth she, "and come again tomorrow;"   5
    Fare well I could not, for I supp'd with sorrow.

Yet at my parting sweetly did she smile,
In scorn or friendship, nill I conster whether:
'T may be she joy'd to jest at my exile,
'T may be again to make me wander thither: 10
    "Wander," a word for shadows like myself,
    As take the pain, but cannot pluck the pelf.

Lord, how mine eyes throw gazes to the east!
My heart doth charge the watch; the morning rise

xiv. 3. care] *Q2;* eare *Q3.*

7. *seld*] seldom. See *Troil.,* iv. v. 150, and *Cor.,* ii. i. 229.

8.] The line suggests that 'gloss' is meant strictly as 'polish'.

10. *cement*] Stressed on the first syllable. See also *Ant.,* iii. ii. 29.

redress] repair.

xiv.] Not found elsewhere. The five stanzas form one poem, though divided after l. 12 by Malone and some later editors.

3. *daff'd*] dismissed, put off. Compare *Ado,* v. i. 78 and ii. ii. 76, and *1H4,* iv. i. 96:

And his comrades, that daff'd the
    world aside,
And bid it pass.

cabin] a small room or retreat. See *Ven.,* l. 637.

hang'd] hung as with tapestries.

4. *descant*] comment at length. Compare *R3,* i. i. 27.

doubts] fears.

decay] fall or grief.

8. *nill I conster whether*] I will not interpret which. See *Ven.,* l. 304.

12. *As*] who, such as.

pelf] booty or treasure.

14–16.] Pooler suggested the follow-

Doth cite each moving sense from idle rest. 15
Not daring trust the office of mine eyes,
   While Philomela sings, I sit and mark,
   And wish her lays were tuned like the lark.

For she doth welcome daylight with her ditty,
And drives away dark dreaming night. 20
The night so pack'd, I post unto my pretty;
Heart hath his hope and eyes their wished sight,
   Sorrow chang'd to solace, and solace mix'd with sorrow;
   For why, she sight, and bade me come to-morrow.

Were I with her, the night would post too soon, 25
But now are minutes added to the hours;
To spite me now, each minute seems a moon;
Yet not for me, shine sun to succour flowers!
   Pack night, peep day; good day, of night now borrow:
   Short night to night, and length thyself to-morrow. 30

XV

It was a lording's daughter, the fairest one of three,
That liked of her master as well as well might be,

ing amended version, though he did not adopt it:

> My heart doth charge them watch
> the morning rise,
> Doth cite each moving sense from
> idle rest,
> Not daring trust the office of mine
> eyes.

charge the watch] 'Perhaps the poet, wishing for the approach of morning, enjoins the watch to hasten through their nocturnal duties' (Malone).

15. *cite*] summon.

20.] 'Daylight' has probably been omitted before 'drives'.

21. *pack'd*] sent off or gone. Compare *R3*, I. i. 146:

> Till George be pack'd with post-
> horse up to heaven.

post] hasten. See *Lucr.*, l. 1.

22. *wished*] desired. See *Err.*, I. i. 91.

24. *For why*] because. See x. 8, 10.

27. *moon*] month. See *Ant.*, III. xii. 5, and *Oth.*, I. iii. 84:

Till now some nine moons wasted.

29. *Pack*] be off. See l. 21 n.

30.] 'To-morrow is addressed, the meaning being, "O Night, make thyself short, O To-morrow, make thyself long"' (Pooler).

xv.] Not found elsewhere.

1. *lording's*] lord's. There is some depreciation in the word, according to the *Arte of English Poesie*, where it is an example of *meiosis*: 'Also such terms are used to be given in derision and for a kind of contempt, as when we say Lording for Lord' (Pooler). See *2H6*, I. i. 145.

2. *liked of*] 'The *of* . . . is perhaps a result of the old impersonal use of the verb, "me liketh", "him liketh", which might seem to disqualify the verb from taking a direct object' (Abbott, § 177).

master] teacher. See *Shr.*, III. i. 54 and IV. ii. 7.

Till looking on an Englishman, the fairest that eye could see,
 Her fancy fell a-turning.
Long was the combat doubtful, that love with love did fight, 5
To leave the master loveless, or kill the gallant knight;
To put in practice either, alas, it was a spite
 Unto the silly damsel!
But one must be refused; more mickle was the pain,
That nothing could be used to turn them both to gain, 10
For of the two the trusty knight was wounded with disdain:
 Alas, she could not help it!
Thus art with arms contending was victor of the day,
Which by a gift of learning did bear the maid away:
Then lullaby, the learned man hath got the lady gay; 15
 For now my song is ended.

XVI

 On a day (alack the day)
 Love, whose month was ever May,
 Spied a blossom passing fair,
 Playing in the wanton air.
 Through the velvet leaves the wind 5
 All unseen 'gan passage find,
 That the lover, sick to death,
 Wish'd himself the heaven's breath:
"Air," quoth he, "thy cheeks may blow;
 Air, would I might triumph so! 10
 But, alas, my hand hath sworn
 Ne'er to pluck thee from thy throne:
 Vow, alack, for youth unmeet,
 Youth so apt to pluck a sweet!

---

xv. 3. that] *Q2; omitted Q3.*

xvi. *Entitled* The passionate Sheepheards Song *in Eng. Hel.* 2. was] *Q1–3; is LLL.* 6. 'gan] *Q1–3; can LLL.* 7. lover] *Q1–3; sheepheard Eng. Hel.*
8. Wish'd] *Q1–3; Wish LLL.* 11. alas . . . hath] *Q1–3; alacke . . . is LLL.*
12. throne] *Q1–3; thorne Eng. Hel.*

9. *more mickle*] greater.

xvi.] See *LLL.*, iv. iii. 101–20. The poem also appears in *England's Helicon*, 1600. The *LLL.* text gives two lines after l. 14, which are needed to complete the sense, but have been omitted presumably because they refer directly to the dramatic situation:
 Do not call it sinne in me,
 That I am forsworne for thee . . .
4. *wanton*] playful. See *Lucr.*, l. 401.
7. *That*] so that. See *Ven.*, l. 242.

Thou for whom Jove would swear   15
Juno but an Ethiope were,
And deny himself for Jove,
Turning mortal for thy love."

XVII

My flocks feed not, my ewes breed not,
My rams speed not, all is amiss:
Love is dying, faith's defying,
Heart's denying, causer of this.
All my merry jigs are quite forgot,   5
All my lady's love is lost, God wot:
Where her faith was firmly fix'd in love,
There a nay is plac'd without remove.
      One silly cross wrought all my loss:
      O frowning fortune, cursed fickle dame!   10
      For now I see inconstancy
      More in women than in men remain.

18. thy] *Q1–3;* my *Eng. Hel.*

xvii. *Entitled* The unknowne Sheepheards complaint *in Eng. Hel.*   1. flocks feed
. . . breed] *Q1–3;* flocke feedes . . . breeds *Harl. MS.*   2. speed . . . amiss]
Q1–3; speedes not in their blis *Harl. MS.*   3. dying] *Q1–3;* denying *Eng.
Hel.*   faith's defying] *Q1–3;* fayth defyinge *Harl. MS.;* Faith is defying *Eng.
Hel.*   4. Heart's denying] Harts denying *Q3;* harts denieng *Q1, Weelkes;* Harts
nenying *Q2;* her denyinge *Harl. MS.;* Harts renying *Eng. Hel.*   5. my] *Q1–3;*
our *Weelkes.*   quite] *Q1–3;* cleane *Harl. MS.*   6. lady's love is] *Q1–3;*
layes of Love are *Harl. MS.*   7. her] *Q1–3;* my *Harl. MS.;* our *Weelk*
faith was . . . fix'd in] *Q1–3;* joyes were . . . linkt by *Harl. MS.*   8. a nay is]
Q1–3; annoyes are *Harl. MS.;* annoy is *Weelkes.*   9. One silly] *Q1–3;* Our
seely *Weelkes.*   cross . . . my] *Q1–3;* poore cross hath wrought me this *Harl.
MS.*   10. frowning . . . cursed fickle] *Q1–3;* fickle . . . cruell cursed *Harl. MS.*
11. For . . . see] *Q1–3;* Now you may see that *Harl. MS.*   12.] *Q1–3;* In
women more then I my selfe have found *Harl. MS.*   men remain] *Q1–3;*
many men to be *Weelkes.*

16. *Ethiope*] negro. Compare *Gent.*,
ii. vi. 25–6:
      And Silvia—witness heaven that
            made her fair!—
      Shows Julia but a swarthy Ethiope.
17. *for Jove*] to be Jove.

xvii.] This first appeared in
Thomas Weelkes's *Madrigals To 3.4.5.*

and 6. *voyces,* 1597. It is printed also in
England's Helicon, and there is a version
in Harleian MS. 6910.
      3. *defying*] rejection. See xii. 11.
      8. *nay*] denial.
      9. *One silly cross*] Perhaps 'a single
small misfortune'; but grammar and
sense throughout are too weak to bear
much meaning.

In black mourn I, all fears scorn I,
Love hath forlorn me, living in thrall.
Heart is bleeding, all help needing,   15
O cruel speeding, fraughted with gall!
My shepherd's pipe can sound no deal.
My wether's bell rings doleful knell;
My curtal dog that wont to have play'd
Plays not at all, but seems afraid.   20
    With sighs so deep procures to weep,
    In howling wise, to see my doleful plight.
    How sighs resound through heartless ground,
    Like a thousand vanquish'd men in bloody fight!

Clear wells spring not, sweet birds sing not,   25
Green plants bring not forth their dye;
Herds stands weeping, flocks all sleeping,
Nymphs back peeping fearfully.
All our pleasure known to us poor swains,
All our merry meetings on the plains,   30
All our evening sport from us is fled;

---

13. fears] *Q1-3;* feare *Weelkes.*   14. Love . . . living] *Q1-3;* lo how forlorne I,
live *Harl. MS.*   15. help] *Q1-3;* helpes *Harl. MS.*   16. cruel] *Q1-3;*
cursed *Harl. MS.*   fraughted] *Q1-3;* fraught *Harl. MS., Weelkes.*   17. can]
Q1-3; will *Harl. MS., Weelkes.*   deal] *Q1-3;* omitted *Harl. MS.*   18. bell
rings] *Q1-3;* ringe a *Harl. MS.*   19. curtal dog] *Q1-3;* curtail'd dogge
Harl. MS.   that wont to] *Q1-3;* wch would *Harl. MS.*   20. at] *Q1,2;*
omitted Q3.   afraid] *Q1-3;* dismayd Harl. *MS.*   21. With . . . procures]
Q1-3; My sights so deepe, doth cause him *Harl. MS.;* My . . . procures *Weelkes.*
22. In howling wise] *Q1-3;* With howling noise *Harl. MS., Weelkes.*   see . . .
doleful] *Q1-3;* wayle . . . woefull *Harl. MS.*   23.] *Q1-3;* My shrikes resoundes,
through Arcadia groundes *Harl. MS.*   How] *Q1-3;* harke how *Weelkes.*
24. a] *Q1-3; omitted Harl. MS.*   thousand . . . bloody] *Q1-3;* thousandes . . .
deadly *Harl. MS.*   26.] *Q1-3;* Lowde bells ring not, cherefully, *Weelkes.*
plants] *Q1-3;* palmes *Harl. MS.*   forth their dye] *Q1-3;* foorth yor dye
Harl. MS.   27. stands] *Q1-3;* stand *Weelkes, Eng. Hel.*   flocks all] *Q1-3;*
ecchoes *Harl. MS.*   28. back peeping] *Eng. Hel.;* blacke peeping *Q1-3;*
looke peeping *Harl. MS.;* back creping *Weelkes.*   fearfully] *Q1-3;* pittyfully
Harl. MS.   29. our pleasure] *Q1-3;* the pleasures *Harl. MS.;* our pleasures
Weelkes.   30. meetings] *Q1-3;* meeting *Eng. Hel.*   31. sport . . . is] *Q1-3;*
sportes . . . are *Harl. MS., Weelkes., Eng. Hel.*   us] *Q1-3;* greenes *Harl. MS.*

---

16. *speeding*] lot.
fraughted] charged.
17. *no deal*] not at all (Onions).
19. *curtal*] with docked tail.
21. *procures*] causes.
23. *heartless ground*] Steevens says
that the ground is 'heartless' because
exhausted by over-cultivation: 'To
plough soil out of *heart* is still a common
phrase'. Malone suggests that the
meaning is 'uncultivated, desolated
ground, corresponding in appearance
with the unhappy state of its owner'.

All our love is lost, for love is dead.
Farewell, sweet love, thy like ne'er was
For a sweet content, the cause of all my woe!
Poor Corydon must live alone: 35
Other help for him I see that there is none.

XVIII

Whenas thine eye hath chose the dame,
And stall'd the deer that thou shouldst strike,
Let reason rule things worthy blame,
As well as fancy, partial might;
    Take counsel of some wiser head,   5
    Neither too young nor yet unwed.

32. our love is] *Q1-3; alas is Harl. MS.; our loves are Weelkes.* for love] *Q1-3;*
now Dolus *Harl. MS.* 33-6.] *Q1-3; omitted Harl. MS.* 33. love] *Q1-3;*
lasse *Weelkes.* thy] *Q1-3; the Weelkes.* 34. a] *Q1-3; omitted Eng. Hel.*
woe] *Q1-3; moane Eng. Hel.* 36. see . . . is] *Q1-3; know ther's Weelkes.*

xviii. 1. Whenas] *Q1-3; When yᵗ Folger MS.* 2. shouldst] *Q1-3; wouldest*
Folger MS. 1.112; wouldst Folger MS. 2071.7. 4. fancy, partial might;] fancy
(partyall might) *Q1,2;* fancy (party all might) *Q3;* fancye parcyall like *Folger*
MS. 1.112; parciall fancie like *Folger MS. 2071.7;* fancy, partial wight *conj.*
Malone. 5. Take] *Q1-3;* Aske *Folger MS. 2071.7.* wiser] *Q1-3;* other
Folger MSS. 6. too young] *Q1-3;* unwise *Folger MSS.* unwed] *Q1-3;*
unwayde *Folger MS. 1.112.*

xviii.] Not printed elsewhere. 'In
Halliwell-Phillipps's folio edition of
Shakespeare there is a facsimile of a
MS. copy of the poem supposed to be
the same as that formerly in the possession of Samuel Lysons, from which
Malone took some readings' (Pooler).
The Lysons MS. is now in the Folger
Library (see Rollins, p. 311). Another
version is in Folger MS. 2071.7 (see
1 n.). If the piece is to be attributed to
Shakespeare, it can only be on some
external evidence; the verses themselves provide none. The poem has
been connected with *Willobie his Avisa*
(1594), on the ground that it is written
in the same stanza-form. For some un-
rewarding opinions on authorship and
significance see Rollins, pp. 553-4.

1-2.] Pooler compares Ovid, *Ars*
Amatoria, i. 45-50:
    Scit bene venator, cervis ubi retia
        tendat,
    Scit bene, qua frendens valle
        moretur aper: . . .
    Tu quoque, materiam longo qui
        quaeris amori,
    Ante frequens quo sit disce puella
        loco.
    2. *stall'd*] According to Craig 'en-
closed; got within range of. A term
of venery'. Case suggested 'stalk'd'.
Compare *Ven.*, l. 39.
    4. *partial might*] Pooler inclines to-
wards Furnivall's conjecture, 'fancy's
partial might'; but no emendation has
yet made sense of the line.
    fancy] love.

And when thou com'st thy tale to tell,
Smooth not thy tongue with filed talk,
Lest she some subtle practice smell,—
A cripple soon can find a halt,—   10
    But plainly say thou lov'st her well,
    And set her person forth to sale.

And to her will frame all thy ways;
Spare not to spend, and chiefly there
Where thy desert may merit praise,   15
By ringing in thy lady's ear:
    The strongest castle, tower and town,
    The golden bullet beats it down.

Serve always with assured trust,
And in thy suit be humble true;   20
Unless thy lady prove unjust,
Press never thou to choose a new:
    When time shall serve, be thou not slack,
    To proffer, though she put thee back.

---

7. com'st] *Q1–3;* commest *Folger MSS.*   8. Smooth] *Q1–3;* Whett *Folger MSS.*
10. find] *Q1–3;* spie *Folger MS. 2071.7.*   a halt] *Q1–3;* one haulte *Folger MS.*
1.112.   11. say] *Q1–3; omitted Folger MS. 2071.7.*   12. her . . . sale] *Q1–3;*
thy . . . sell *Folger MSS.*   person] *Q1–3;* body *Folger MS. 2071.7.*   13–24
precede 25–36 in Q1, follow 25–36 in Q2,3.   13. And to] *Q1–3;* Unto *Folger*
MS. 2071.7.   15. desert . . . merit] *Q1–3;* expences . . . sounde thy *Folger MS.*
1.112; expence . . . sound thy *Folger MS. 2071.7.*   16. By] *Q1–3;* & still be
Folger MS. 2071.7.   in thy lady's] *Q1–3;* allwayes in her *Folger MS. 1.112;*
in in her *Folger MS. 2071.7.*   17. castle, tower] *Q1–3;* towres fort *Folger MS.*
2071.7.   and] *Q1–3;* or *Folger MSS.*   18. beats it] *Q1–3;* hathe beat
Folger MS. 1.112; beateth *Folger MS. 2071.7.*   20. humble] *Q1–3;* ever
Folger MS. 2071.7.   21. Unless] *Q1–3;* untill *Folger MS. 2071.7.*   22. Press]
Q1–3; seeke *Folger MS. 1.112.*   choose] *Q1–3;* change *Folger MSS.*   a new]
Q1–3; anew *Folger MS. 1.112;* for newe *Folger MS. 2071.7.*   23. shall . . . be
thou] *Q1–3;* dothe . . . then be *Folger MS. 1.112;* doth . . . thee be *Folger MS.*
2071.7.   24. thee] *Q1,2;* it *Q3, Folger MSS.*

---

8. *filed talk*] polished phrases.
9. *practice*] plot, deception.
10.] There are various forms of this
proverb. See *Troilus and Criseyde,* iv.
ccix. 1, and O.D.E.P., p. 234.
12. *And set her person forth to sale*]
Steevens proposed 'sell' for 'sale'.
' "To set forth to sell" is "to set off to

advantage, as a salesman by praising
his goods" ' (Pooler).

13–24.] The order of stanzas in Q1
and the Lysons and Folger MSS. is
clearly correct.
21. *unjust*] Perhaps 'unfaithful', as in
Sonnet cxxxviii, l. 19. See i. 1 n. and
i. 9 n. above.

What though her frowning brows be bent?   25
Her cloudy looks will calm ere night,
And then too late she will repent,
That thus dissembled her delight;
    And twice desire, ere it be day,
    That which with scorn she put away.   30

What though she strive to try her strength,
And ban and brawl, and say thee nay?
Her feeble force will yield at length,
When craft hath taught her thus to say:
    "Had women been so strong as men,   35
    In faith, you had not had it then."

The wiles and guiles that women work,
Dissembled with an outward show,
The tricks and toys that in them lurk,
The cock that treads them shall not know.   40
    Have you not heard it said full oft,
    A woman's nay doth stand for nought?

---

25. though . . . frowning] *Q1–3;* if shee frowne w^th *Folger MS. 2071.7.*   26. calm ere] calme yer *Q1–3;* cleare ere *Folger MS. 1.112;* calme at *Folger MS. 2071.7.*   27. And . . . will] *Q1–3;* And she perhappes will sone *Folger MS. 1.112;* When y^t perhaps shee will *Folger MS. 2071.7.*   28. thus] *Q1–3;* she *Folger MS. 1.112;* so *Folger MS. 2071.7.*   29. ere it] *Folger MS. 1.112;* yer it *Q1–3;* it ere *Folger MS. 2071.7.*   30. which with] *Q1–3;* wth suche *Folger MSS.* 31. though . . . her] *Q1–3;* if . . . thy *Folger MS. 2071.7.*   32. ban] *Q1–3;* chide *Folger MS. 1.112.*   say] *Q1–3;* sweare *Folger MS. 2071.7.*   34. When] *Q1–3;* & *Folger MSS.*   hath taught] *Q1–3;* will cause *Folger MSS.*   35. so] *Q1–3;* as *Folger MSS.*   36. In faith] *Q1–3;* by cock *Folger MS. 2071.7.*   had it] *Q1–3;* got it *Folger MS. 1.112.*   37–42 *precede 48 in Q1–3, follow 48 in Folger MSS.*   37.] *Q1–3;* A thousand wiles in wantons lurkes *Folger MS. 2071.7.*   women work] *Q1–3;* in them lurkes *Folger MS. 1.112.*   39. that . . . lurk] *Q1–3;* & meanes to woorke *Folger MS. 1.112;* he meanes to worke *Folger MS. 2071.7.*   40. shall] *Q1–3;* doth *Folger MS. 2071.7.*   41. Have you] *Q1–3;* Hast y^u *Folger MS. 2071.7.*   it] *Q1–3;* that *Folger MS. 1.112.*

---

32. *ban*] curse. See *Ven.*, l. 326.

42.] According to the proverb, 'Maids say nay, and take it'. Compare *R2,* III. vii. 51:

    Play the maid's part, still answer
        nay and take it.

43–6.] Malone read, following the

Lysons MS. (Folger MS. 1.112):

    Think, women love to match with
        men,
    And not to live so like a saint:
    Here is no heaven; they holy then
    Begin, when age doth them attaint.

'This seems impossibly bad, but the

Think women still to strive with men,
To sin and never for to saint:
There is no heaven, by holy then,   45
When time with age shall them attaint.
    Were kisses all the joys in bed,
    One woman would another wed.

But soft, enough,—too much,—I fear
Lest that my mistress hear my song: 50
She will not stick to round me on th'ear,
To teach my tongue to be so long.
    Yet will she blush, here be it said,
    To hear her secrets so bewray'd.

43. still to strive] *Q1–3;* love to matche *Folger MS. 1.112;* seeke to matche *Folger MS. 2071.7.*   44.] *Q1–3;* and not to live soe like a sainte *Folger MS. 1.112;* to live in sinne & not to saint *Folger MS. 2071.7.*   45. There] *Q1–3;* Here *Folger MSS.*   by holy then] *Q1–3;* they holye then *Folger MS. 1.112;* be holy then *Folger MS. 2071.7.*   46. When . . . them] *Q1–3;* Beginne when age dothe them *Folger MS. 1.112;* Till time shall thee wth age *Folger MS. 2071.7.*   47. kisses] *Q1–3;* kyssinge *Folger MSS.*   49. But] *Q1–3;* Nowe *Folger MS. 1.112;* Ho *Folger MS. 2071.7.*   soft, enough,] soft enough, *Q1–3;* hoe inoughe *Folger MS. 1.112;* now enough *Folger MS. 2071.7.*   too . . . fear] too much I feare *Q1–3;* & more I feare *Folger MS. 2071.7.*   50. Lest . . . mistress] *Q1–3;* For if my ladye *Folger MS. 1.112;* For if my Mrs *Folger MS. 2071.7.*   hear my] *Q1–3;* heare this *Folger MS. 1.112;* hard this *Folger MS. 2071.7.*   51. will] *Q1–3;* would *Folger MS. 2071.7.*   round me on th'ear] round me on th'are *Q1,2;* round me on th'ere *Q3;* ringe my eare *Folger MS. 1.112;* warme my eare *Folger MS. 2071.7.*   53. will] *Q1–3;* would *Folger MSS.*   blush] *Q1–3;* smile *Folger MS. 2071.7.*   54. so bewray'd] *Q1–3;* thus bewrayede *Folger MS. 1.112;* thus bewrayde *Folger MS. 2071.7.*

text is inexplicable', comments Pooler.

    51. *stick*] hesitate. Compare *H8,* ii. ii. 127.

    round] The usual meaning of 'whisper' (A.S. runian) is seen in *John,* ii. i. 566: rounded in the ear With that same purpose-changer, that sly devil. From this sense, 'round in the ear' came to mean also 'to take (one) privately to task', which is the meaning here, despite the substitution of 'on' for 'in'.

XIX

Live with me and be my love,
And we will all the pleasures prove
That hills and valleys, dales and fields,
And all the craggy mountains yield.

There will we sit upon the rocks,   5
And see the shepherds feed their flocks,
By shallow rivers, by whose falls
Melodious birds sing madrigals.

There will I make thee a bed of roses,
With a thousand fragrant posies,   10
A cap of flowers, and a kirtle
Embroidered all with leaves of myrtle;

A belt of straw and ivy buds,
With coral clasps and amber studs:
And if these pleasures may thee move,   15
Then live with me and be my love.

LOVE'S ANSWER

If that the world and love were young,
And truth in every shepherd's tongue,
These pretty pleasures might me move   20
To live with thee and be thy love.

XIX. *Entitled* The passionate Sheepheard to his love *in Eng. Hel.*   I. Live]
Q2,3; Come live *Eng. Hel.*   3.] *Q2,3;* That vallies, groves, hills and fieldes,
Eng. Hel.   4. And ... craggy] *Q2,3;* Woods, or steepie *Eng. Hel.*   mountains]
Q2,3; mountaine *Eng. Hel.*   yield] *Q2,3;* yeeldes *Eng. Hel.*   5. There will
we] *Q2,3;* And wee will *Eng. Hel.*   6. And see] *Q2,3;* seeing *Eng. Hel.*
7. by] *Q2,3;* to *Eng. Hel.*   7, 8. falls ... madrigals] *Q2;* tales ... madrigales *Q3.*
8. sing] *Q2,3;* sings *Eng. Hel.*   9. There will I] *Q2,3;* And I will *Eng. Hel.*
a bed] *Q2,3;* beds *Eng. Hel.*   10. With ... posies] With ... poses *Q2,3;*
And ... poesies *Eng. Hel.*   16. Then] *Q2,3;* Come *Eng. Hel.*   17. Love's
Answer] *Q2,3;* The Nimphs reply to the Sheepheard *Eng. Hel.*   18. that]
Q2,3; all *Eng. Hel.*   21. thy] *Q2;* my *Q3.*

XIX.] By Christopher Marlowe. It
appeared also in *England's Helicon*, and,
in another version, in Izaak Walton's
Complete Angler, 1655.

7–10.] Sung by Sir Hugh Evans in
Wiv., III. i. 17 ff.

8. *madrigals*] Here simply 'songs'.
Compare *Comus*, l. 495.

XX

As it fell upon a day
In the merry month of May,
Sitting in a pleasant shade
Which a grove of myrtles made,
Beasts did leap and birds did sing,   5
Trees did grow and plants did spring;
Everything did banish moan,
Save the nightingale alone:
She, poor bird, as all forlorn,
Lean'd her breast up-till a thorn,   10
And there sung the dolefull'st ditty,
That to hear it was great pity.
"Fie, fie, fie," now would she cry,
"Tereu, Tereu," by and by;
That to hear her so complain,   15
Scarce I could from tears refrain,
For her griefs so lively shown
Made me think upon mine own.
Ah, thought I, thou mourn'st in vain!
None takes pity on thy pain.   20
Senseless trees they cannot hear thee,
Ruthless bears they will not cheer thee;
King Pandion he is dead,
All thy friends are lapp'd in lead,
All thy fellow birds do sing,   25
Careless of thy sorrowing.
Whilst as fickle fortune smiled,
Thou and I were both beguiled.

---

xx. *Entitled* An Ode *in Barnfield*, Another of the same Sheepheards *in Eng. Hel.*
10. up-till] *Q2,3;* against *Eng. Hel.*   22. bears] *Q2,3;* beasts *Eng. Hel.*   27–
56.] *Q2,3; omitted Eng. Hel. which adds after l. 26* Even so poore bird like thee, /
None a-live will pitty me.

xx.] By Richard Barnfield. It appeared first in his *Poems: In diuers humors*, 1598. The first twenty-six lines appeared also in *England's Helicon*, followed by a concluding couplet not found elsewhere.

10. *up-till*] up against.

14. *by and by*] at once. Compare *Lucr.*, l. 1292.

The story of Philomela is told in Ovid, *Metam.*, vi. 424–676: 'Tereus, king of Thrace, married Progne, daughter of Pandion, king of Athens, and had a son, Itys. Tereus violated his wife's sister, Philomela, cut out her tongue, and imprisoned her. Progne released Philomela and killed and cooked Itys as a cannibal feast for his father. She was changed into a swallow, Philomela to a nightingale, Tereus to a hoopoe' (Pooler).

24. *lapp'd*] wrapped.

Every one that flatters thee
Is no friend in misery. 30
Words are easy, like the wind;
Faithful friends are hard to find.
Every man will be thy friend
Whilst thou hast wherewith to spend;
But if store of crowns be scant, 35
No man will supply thy want.
If that one be prodigal,
Bountiful they will him call,
And with such-like flattering:
"Pity but he were a king." 40
If he be addict to vice,
Quickly him they will entice;
If to women he be bent,
They have at commandement.
But if fortune once do frown, 45
Then farewell his great renown:
They that fawn'd on him before,
Use his company no more.
He that is thy friend indeed,
He will help thee in thy need: 50
If thou sorrow, he will weep;
If thou wake, he cannot sleep:
Thus of every grief in heart
He with thee doth bear a part.
These are certain signs to know 55
Faithful friend from flatt'ring foe.

41. *addict*] addicted. See Abbott, § 342.
44. *They have*] they have women.
at commandement] at their disposal.

Compare *2H4*, III. ii. 26: 'we knew where the *bona-robas* were, and had the best of them all at commandment.'

THE PHOENIX AND TURTLE

THE PHOENIX AND TURTLE

Let the bird of loudest lay
On the sole Arabian tree
Herald sad and trumpet be,
To whose sound chaste wings obey.

But thou shrieking harbinger,　　　　　　　　　　5
Foul precurrer of the fiend,
Augur of the fever's end,
To this troop come thou not near.

1. *the bird of loudest lay*] Most commentators agree that this bird's identity is left uncertain (Grosart suggested it might be the nightingale). Wilson Knight argues that it is the Phoenix itself, re-born from its ashes, which celebrates its own and the Turtle's obsequies (*op. cit.*, pp. 202–4), although we are told in l. 59 that the two birds left 'no posterity'. This interpretation goes with Knight's idea that the Phoenix is a symbol of the whole of Shakespeare's poetry; he half-admits that it 'weakens the point and pathos' here (*op. cit.*, p. 204). It seems unlikely that Shakespeare would have left the bird's identity so vague if it were one of the two chief characters in the poem. The meaning is probably that whatever bird proves able to sing loudest should act as herald.

2. *the sole Arabian tree*] Florio's Italian Dictionary, 1598, defines '*Rasin*, a tree in Arabia, whereof there is but one found, and upon it the Phenix sits'. Compare *Tp.*, III. iii. 23:

　　　　　　that in Arabia
There is one tree, the phoenix'
　　throne; one phoenix
　At this hour reigning there.

Grosart declares: 'The Palm is meant.

In Greek *phoinix*, and meaning both phoenix and palm-tree'.

3. *trumpet*] trumpeter. Compare *John*, I. i. 27 f.:

　　Be thou the trumpet of our wrath
　　And sullen presage of your own
　　　decay.

See also *Troil.*, IV. v. 6 f.

4. *To*] *Obey* was often used with *to* in Elizabethan English. See *F.Q.*, III. xi. 35:

　Lo! now the hevens obey to me
　　alone.

chaste wings] the wings of the good birds summoned.

5. *shrieking harbinger*] the screech-owl. Compare *MND.*, V. i. 383–5:

　　the screech-owl, screeching loud,
　　Puts the wretch that lies in woe
　　In remembrance of a shroud.

See also *Ham.*, I. i. 121 f.:

　　　the like precurse of fierce events,
　As harbingers preceding still the
　　fates.

6. *precurrer*] precursor. This is the only example quoted in O.E.D. Note collocation of 'precurse' and 'harbinger' in the lines just quoted from *Hamlet*.

7. *Augur*] prophet or soothsayer: 'a religious official among the Romans,

From this session interdict
Every fowl of tyrant wing,   10
Save the eagle, feather'd king;
Keep the obsequy so strict.

Let the priest in surplice white,
That defunctive music can,
Be the death-divining swan,   15
Lest the requiem lack his right.

And thou treble-dated crow,
That thy sable gender mak'st
With the breath thou giv'st and tak'st,
'Mongst our mourners shalt thou go.   20

---

whose duty it was to predict future events and advise upon the course of public business, in accordance with omens derived from . . . birds . . . and other portents' (O.E.D.). See Sonnet cvii, l. 6:

>   And the sad augurs mock their own
>   presage.

10. *Every fowl of tyrant wing*] every bird of prey.

14.] that is skilled in funeral music.

15. *the death-divining swan*] The swan singing before its own death was one of the most used emblems in Elizabethan poetry. See *Lucr.*, l. 1611 n.

16. *his right*] It is characteristic of this poem that many phrases have ambiguous, or double or triple, meanings. Thus it is impossible to decide whether 'right' here means 'due' or 'rite', or whether 'his' refers to swan or requiem. The general sense is clear: without the swan and its song the requiem would lack something essential. But the alternative meanings remain suspended in the words, and all add something to their tone and weight.

17. *treble-dated crow*] In classical and medieval natural history and in later popular belief, the crow was supposed to live for a hundred or even four hundred years. Steevens quoted Lucretius, v. 1084; this gives no estimate of the

bird's longevity. Pooler cites Holland's *Pliny*, VII. xlviii, p. 180: 'Hesiodus . . . saith forsooth, That the crow liveth 9 times as long as we; and the harts or stags 4 times as long as the crow; but the ravens thrice as long as they'. He adds: 'Possibly "crow" is for raven, and "treble-dated" means living as long as three stags'. But no stags are even hinted at by Shakespeare, who simply evokes popular belief in a deliberately vague and ponderous epithet. See Baldwin, *op. cit.*, p. 372, in connection with this and the next two lines. See *Lucr.*, l. 949.

18–19.] This has been referred to a popular belief that 'the crow can change its sex at will' (*Shakespeare's England*, I. 520): but the exploration of Elizabethan natural history shows that 'the reference is to the belief that the crow (or rather the raven) engendered by the mouth; a belief mentioned . . . by Martial and discredited by Aristotle and Pliny . . .' (Grosart). Halliwell-Phillipps quoted from Swan's *Speculum Mundi*, 1635, p. 397: 'Neither (as is thought) doth the raven conceive by conjunction of male and female, but rather by a kinde of billing at the mouth, which *Plinie* mentioneth as an opinion of the common people'. Pooler gives a passage concerning ravens from *Hortus Sanitatis*, bk III,

Here the anthem doth commence:
Love and constancy is dead;
Phoenix and the Turtle fled
In a mutual flame from hence.

So they lov'd, as love in twain   25
Had the essence but in one:
Two distincts, division none;
Number there in love was slain.

Hearts remote, yet not asunder;
Distance and no space was seen   30
'Twixt this Turtle and his queen:
But in them it were a wonder.

So between them love did shine
That the Turtle saw his right
Flaming in the Phoenix' sight;   35
Either was the other's mine.

para. 34 (to be found in Seager, *Natural History in Shakespeare's Time*): 'They are said to conceive and lay their eggs at the bill. The young become black on the seventh day.' 'Sable gender' would thus mean 'black offspring'.

25. *as*] that. See *Lucr*., ll. 1372 and 1420.

27. *distincts*] separate, distinct things or persons (no other instance of this use is known). According to M. R. Ridley, 'In the language of the schools "distinction" implies a verbal, "division" a real, difference.' Shakespeare certainly wishes to give an impression of scholastic subtlety, and does so; but, since his theme is a paradox, and his method is to work on our *imagination*, his use of analytic terms cannot be judged by strictly philosophical standards.

28.] Adams says that the line 'refers to the mathematical dictum "one is no number". That is, by the "two" being "one" they "slay" number' (Rollins).

32.] 'But' means 'except', and 'were' is conditional. Malone para-phrases: 'So extraordinary a phenomenon as *hearts remote, yet not asunder*, etc., would have excited admiration, had it been found anywhere else except in these two birds. In them it was not wonderful.'

34. *his right*] what was due to him; Pooler explains by adding 'love in return, and this he sees shining in her eyes.' Steevens in proposing 'light' seeks only to smooth and flatten the sense.

36.] The line surely means that the lovers were so identified with each other that each was the other's self, or held the other's self in his own being. Certainly the use of 'mine' as referring to an unspoken 'I', or *ego*, is unparalleled, and would be unintelligible in another context. But the paradox of love has already been fully stated twice, and the line is only a variation on what we already understand. To explain 'mine' as 'a rich source of wealth' (Schmidt), or 'the source of inexhaustible treasure' (Feuillerat), is to introduce a new and strange image which Shakespeare

Property was thus appalled
That the self was not the same:
Single nature's double name
Neither two nor one was called.　　　　40

Reason, in itself confounded,
Saw division grow together,
To themselves yet either neither,
Simple were so well compounded:

That it cried, How true a twain　　　　45
Seemeth this concordant one!
Love hath reason, reason none,
If what parts, can so remain.

very uncharacteristically fails to make vivid or to develop further. It may be noted that this explanation was first put forward by two scholars whose native tongue was not English, though Rollins gives it his approval and Baldwin accepts it (*op. cit.*, pp. 374–5. See also A. Alvarez in *Interpretations*, p. 12). There are only two passages in which Shakespeare certainly uses 'mine' in the sense proposed, and he makes the context support that meaning emphatically in each case:

The bawdy wind that kisses all it meets
Is hush'd within the hollow mine of earth
                    (*Oth.*, IV. ii. 77–8).
Today the French
All clinquant, all in gold, like heathen gods,
Shone down the English; and to-morrow they
Make Britain India: every man that stood
Show'd like a mine
                    (*H8*, I. i. 18–22).

37–8.] 'Property is a Latinism, "proprietas", peculiar or essential property. . . "Property" was appalled to find out that personality had been destroyed, since each lover's identity was merged into the other's, and was no longer itself' (Feuillerat).

39–40.] 'They could not be called one because their persons were distinct . . . or two, because their nature or essence was the same' (Pooler).

41–4.] The syntax is beyond repair, but Fairchild's paraphrase is adequate (*Englische Studien*, 1904, XXXIII. 371): 'Pure reason had seen those unlike and, according to its insight, quite incompatible, unite together. In the union neither had a separate identity, simple, that is, simples or elementary elements, were so perfectly compounded or united.' Another version was suggested by R. H. Case (quoted by Pooler): 'Reason . . . saw division grow together, yet saw neither grow to or become absorbed in the other, so well were simple compounded; So that it cried,' etc.

45–6.] Reason cries: 'How true this pair is, that seems to agree as one together!'

47–8.] Reason continues its comment and then abdicates in favour of love. Feuillerat paraphrases: 'So that Love is right while Reason, which ought to be right, is wrong—since there remains a union where there should be a division.'

Whereupon it made this Threne
To the Phoenix and the Dove,   50
Co-supremes and stars of love,
As Chorus to their tragic scene.

THRENOS

Beauty, truth and rarity,
Grace in all simplicity,
Here enclos'd, in cinders lie.   55

Death is now the Phoenix' nest,
And the Turtle's loyal breast
To eternity doth rest.

Leaving no posterity,
'Twas not their infirmity,   60
It was married chastity.

Truth may seem, but cannot be;
Beauty brag, but 'tis not she;
Truth and beauty buried be.

To this urn let those repair   65
That are either true or fair:
For these dead birds sigh a prayer.

---

49. *Threne*] funeral song; from Greek *threnos*. The word appears as *trenes* and *trenys* in the 15th cent., and as *threnes* in the 16th.

51. *Co-supremes*] joint rulers. For 'supreme' in this sense see *Lucr.*, l. 780 n.

55.] The comma after 'enclos'd' is omitted in many editions, with a consequent distortion of the sense. 'Beauty, truth', etc., now *are* cinders, lying enclosed in 'this urn' (l. 65); they are not enclosed *in* cinders. Compare Cleanth Brooks, *The Well-Wrought Urn*, 1949, p. 20.

APPENDIX I

The Stories of Venus and Adonis and of Hermaphroditus and Salmacis from The XV Bookes of P. Ovidius Naso, entytuled Metamorphosis, translated oute of Latin into English meeter, by Arthur Golding Gentleman. . . 1567.

(*a*)   Shee [Venus] lovd *Adonis* more
  Than heaven. To him shee clinged ay, and bare him companye.
And in the shadowe woont she was too rest continually,
And for too set her beawtye out most seemely too the eye
By trimly decking of her self. Through bushy grounds and groves,
And over Hills and Dales, and Lawnds and stony rocks shee roves,
Bare kneed with garment tucked up according too the woont
Of *Phebe*, and shee cheerd the hounds with hallowing like a hunt,
Pursewing game of hurtless sort, as Hares made lowe before,
Or stagges with lofty heades, or bucks. But with the sturdy Boare
And ravening woolf, and Bearewhelpes armd with ugly pawes, and eeke
The cruell Lyons which delyght in blood, and slaughter seeke,
Shee meddled not. And of theis same shee warned also thee
Adonis for too shoonne them, if thou wooldst have warned bee.
Bee bold on cowards (*Venus* sayd) for whoso dooth advaunce
Himselfe against the bold, may hap too meete with sum mischaunce.
Wherfore I pray thee my sweet boy forbeare too bold too bee,
For feare thy rashnesse hurt thy self and woork the wo of mee.
Encounter not the kynd of beastes whom nature armed hath,
For dowt thou buy thy prayse too deere procuring thee sum scath.
Thy tender youth, thy beawty bryght, thy countnance fayre and brave
Although they had the force too win the hart of *Venus*, have
No powre ageinst the Lyons, nor ageinst the bristled swyne.
The eyes and harts of savage beasts doo nought too theis inclyne.
The cruell Boares beare thunder in theyr hooked tushes, and
Exceeding force and feercenesse is in Lyons too withstand.
And sure I hate them at my hart. Too him demaunding why?
A monstrous chaunce (quoth *Venus*) I will tell thee by and by,
That hapned for a fault. But now unwoonted toyle hath made
Mee weerye: and beholde, in tyme this Poplar with his shade
Allureth, and the ground for cowch dooth serve too rest uppon.
I prey thee let us rest us heere. They sate them downe anon.
And lying upward with her head uppon his lappe along,

Shee thus began: and in her tale shee bussed him among.
[Venus tells the story of Atalanta, and then points the moral:]
>   Shonne
Theis beastes [lions], deere hart; and not from theis alonely see
>   thou ronne,
But also from eche other beast that turnes not backe too flight
But offreth with his boystows brest too try the chaunce of fyght:
Anemis least thy valeantnesse bee hurtfull to us both.
>   This warning given, with yoked swannes away through aire she
>   goth.
>   But manhod by admonishment restreyned could not bee.
By chaunce his hounds in following of the tracke, a Boare did see,
And rowsed him. And as the swyne was comming from the wood,
Adonis hit him with a dart askew, and drew the blood.
The Boare streyght with his hooked groyne the huntingstaffe out drew
Bestayned with his blood, and on *Adonis* did pursew
Who trembling and retyring back, too place of refuge drew
And hyding in his codds his tuskes as farre as he could thrust
He layd him all along for dead uppon the yellow dust.
Dame *Venus* in her chariot drawen with swannes was scarce arrived
At *Cyprus*, when shee knew a farre the sygh of him depryved
Of lyfe. Shee turned her Cygnets backe, and when shee from the skye
Beehilld him dead, and in his blood beweltred for to lye:
Shee leaped downe, and tare at once hir garments from hir brist,
And rent her heare, and beate uppon her stomack with her fist,
And blaming sore the destnyes, sayd. Yit shall they not obteine
Their will in all things. Of my greefe remembrance shall remayne
(*Adonis*) whyle the world doth last. From yeere too yeere shall growe
A thing that of my heaviness and of thy death shall showe
The lively likeness. In a flowre thy blood I will bestowe.
Hadst thou the powre *Persephonee* rank sented Mints to make
Of womens limbes? and may not I lyke powre upon mee take
Without disdeine and spyght, too turne *Adonis* too a flowre?
This sed, shee sprinckled Nectar on the blood, which through the
>   powre
Therof did swell like bubbles sheere that ryse in weather cleere
On water. And before that full an howre expyred weere,
Of all one colour with the blood a flowre she there did fynd
Even like the flowre of that same tree whose frute in tender rynde
Have pleasant graynes inclosde. Howbeet the use of them is short,
For why the leaves doo hang so looce through lightnesse in such sort,
As that the windes that all things perce, with every little blast
Doo shake them of and shed them so as that they cannot last.

>   (*Metamorphoses*, x. 614–47 and 826–63)

(b) And (as it chaunst) the selfe same time she [Salmacis] was a sorting
      gayes
To make a poisie, when she first the yongman did espie,
And in beholding him desirde to have his companie.
But though she thought she stoode on thornes untill she went to him:
Yet went she not before she had bedect hir neat and trim,
And pride and peerd upon hir clothes that nothing sat awrie,
And framde hir countnance as might seeme most amrous to the eie.
   Which done she thus begon: O childe most worthie for to bee
   Estemde and taken for a God, if (as thou seemste to mee)
   Thou be a God, to *Cupids* name thy beautie doth agree.
Or if thou be a mortall wight, right happie folke are they,
By whome thou camste into this worlde, right happy is (I say)
Thy mother and thy sister too (if any bee:) good hap
That woman had that was thy nurce and gave thy mouth hir pap.
But farre above all other, far more blist than these is shee
Whome thou vouchsafest for thy wife and bedfellow for to bee.
Now if thou have alredy one, let me by stelth obtaine
That which shall pleasure both of us. Or if thou doe remaine
A Maiden free from wedlocke bonde, let me then be thy spouse,
And let us in the bridelie bed our selves togither rouse.
   This sed, the Nymph did hold hir peace, and therewithall the boy
   Waxt red: he wist not what love was: and sure it was a joy
To see it how exceeding well his blushing him became.
For in his face the colour fresh appeared like the same
That is in Apples which doe hang upon the Sunnie side:
Or Ivorie shadowed with a red; or such as is espide
Of white and scarlet colours mixt appearing in the Moone
When folke in vaine with sounding brasse would ease unto hir done.
When at the last the Nymph desirde most instantly but this,
As to his sister brotherly to give hir there a kisse,
And therewithall was clasping him about the Ivorie necke:
Leave of (quoth he) or I am gone and leave thee at a becke
With all thy trickes. Then *Salmacis* began to be afraide,
And to your pleasure leave I free this place my friend she sayde.
Wyth that she turnes hir backe as though she would have gone
      hir way:
But evermore she looketh backe, and (closely as she may)
She hides her in a bushie queach, where kneeling on hir knee
She alwayes hath hir eye on him. He as a childe and free,
And thinking not that any wight had watched what he did
Romes up and downe the pleasant Mede: and by and by amid
The flattring waves he dippes his feete, no more but first the sole
And to the ancles afterward both feete he plungeth whole.
And for to make the matter short, he tooke so great delight
In coolenesse of the pleasant spring, that streight he stripped quight
His garments from his tender skin. When *Salmacis* behilde
His naked beautie, such strong pangs so ardently hir hilde,

That utterly she was astraught. And even as *Phebus* beames
Against a myrrour pure and clere rebound with broken gleames:
Even so hir eys did sparcle fire. Scarce could she tarience make:
Scarce could she any time delay hir pleasure for to take:
She wolde have run, and in hir armes embraced him streight way:
She was so far beside hir selfe, that scarsly could she stay.
He clapping with his hollow hands against his naked sides,
Into the water lithe and baine with armes displayde glydes,
And rowing with his hands and legges swimmes in the water cleare:
Through which his bodie faire and white doth glistringly appeare,
As if a man an Ivorie Image or a Lillie white
Should overlay or close with glasse that were most pure and bright.
    The price is won (cride *Salmacis* aloud) he is mine owne.
    And therewithall in all post hast she having lightly throwne
Hir garments off, flew to the Poole and cast hir thereinto
And caught him fast betweene hir armes, for ought that he could doe:
Yea maugre all his wrestling and his struggling to and fro,
She held him still, and kissed him a hundred times and mo.
And willde he nillde he with hir handes she toucht his naked brest:
And now on this side now on that (for all he did resist
And strive to wrest him from hir gripes) she clung unto him fast:
And wound about him like a Snake which snatched up in hast,
And being by the Prince of Birdes borne lightly up aloft,
Doth writhe hir selfe about his necke and griping talants oft:
And cast hir taile about his wings displayed in the winde:
Or like as Ivie runnes on trees about the utter rinde:
Or as the Crabfish having caught his enmy in the Seas,
Doth claspe him in on every side with all his crooked cleas.
    But *Atlas* Nephew still persistes, and utterly denies
    The Nymph to have hir hoped sport: she urges him likewise,
And pressing him with all hir weight, fast cleaving to him still,
Strive, struggle, wrest and writhe (she said) thou froward boy thy fill:
Doe what thou canst thou shalt not scape. Ye Goddes of Heaven agree
That this same wilful boy and I may never parted bee.
The Gods were pliant to hir boone. The bodies of them twaine
Were mixt and joyned both in one.

                                    (*Metamorphoses*, IV. 382–462)

APPENDIX II

(*a*) Chaucer, *The Legende of Good Women*, ll. 1680–1885

Incipit Legenda Lucrecie, Rome, Martiris.

Now mote I seyn the exilynge of kynges   1680
Of Rome, for here horrible doinges,
And of the laste kyng Tarquinius,
As seyth Ovyde and Titus Lyvius.
But for that cause telle I nat this storye,
But for to preyse and drawe to memorye   1685
The verray wif, the verray trewe Lucresse,
That, for hyre wif hod and hire stedefastnesse,
Nat only that these payens hire comende,
But he that cleped is in oure legende
The grete Austyn, hath gret compassioun   1690
Of this Lucresse, that starf at Rome toun;
And in what wise, I wol but shortly trete,
And of this thyng I touche but the grete.
    Whan Ardea beseged was aboute
With Romeyns, that ful sterne were and stoute,   1695
Ful longe lay the sege, and lytel wroughten,
So that they were half idel, as hem thoughten;
And in his pley Tarquinius the yonge
Gan for to jape, for he was lyght of tonge,
And seyde that it was an ydel lyf;   1700
No man dide there no more than his wif.
"And lat us speke of wyves, that is best;
Preyse every man his owene, as hym lest,
And with oure speche lat us ese oure herte."
    A knyght, that highte Colatyn, up sterte,   1705
And seyde thus: "Nay, sire, it is no nede
To trowen on the word, but on the dede.
I have a wif," quod he, "that, as I trowe,
Is holden good of alle that evere hire knowe.
Go we to-nyght to Rome, and we shal se."   1710
    Tarquinius answerde, "That liketh me."
To Rome be they come, and faste hem dyghte
To Colatynes hous and doun they lyghte,
Tarquinius, and ek this Colatyn.
The husbonde knew the estris wel and fyn,   1715
And prively into the hous they gon,
Nor at the yate porter nas there non,
And at the chambre-dore they abyde.
This noble wif sat by hire beddes side
Dischevele, for no malyce she ne thoughte;   1720

And softe wolle oure bok seyth that she wroughte
To kepen hire from slouthe and idelnesse;
And bad hire servaunts don hire besynesse,
And axeth hem, "What tydyngs heren ye?
How seyth men of the sege, how shal it be?   1725
God wolde the walles were falle adoun!
Myn husbonde is to longe out of this toun,
For which the drede doth me so to smerte
That with a swerd it stingeth to myn herte
Whan I thynke on the sege or on that place.   1730
God save my lord, I preye hym for his grace!"
And therwithal ful tenderly she wep,
And of hire werk she tok no more kep,
And mekely she let hyre eyen falle;
And thilke semblaunt sat hire wel withalle.   1735
And eek hire teres, ful of honeste,
Embelished hire wifly chastite,
Hyre contenaunce is to hire herte dygne,
For they acorde bothe in dede and sygne.
And with that word hire husbonde Colatyn,   1740
Or she of him was war, com stertynge in
And seyde, "Drede the nat, for I am here!"
And she anon up ros, with blysful chere,
And kiste hym, as of wives is the wone.
    Tarquinius, this proude kynges sone,   1745
Conceyved hath hire beaute and hyre cheere,
Hire yelwe her, hire shap, and hire manere,
Hire hew, hire wordes, that she hath compleyned
(And by no craft hire beaute nas nat feyned),
And caughte to this lady swich desyr   1750
That in his herte brende as any fyr
So wodly that his wit was al forgeten.
For wel thoghte he she wolde nat ben geten;
And ay the more that he was in dispayr,
The more he coveytyth and thoughte hire fayr.   1755
His blynde lust was al his coveytynge.
    A-morwe, whan the brid began to synge,
Unto the sege he cometh ful privily,
And by hymself he walketh soberly,
Th'ymage of hire recordynge alwey newe: 1760
"Thus lay hire her, and thus fresh was hyre hewe;
Thus sat, thus spak, thus span; this was hire chere;
Thus fayr she was, and this was hire manere."
Al this conseit hys herte hath newe ytake.
And as the se, with tempest al toshake,   1765
That after, whan the storm is al ago,
Yit wol the water quappe a day or two,
Ryght so, thogh that hire forme were absent,

The plesaunce of hire forme was present;
But natheles, nat plesaunce but delit,   1770
Or an unrigh[t]ful talent, with dispit—
"For, maugre hyre, she shal my leman be!
Hap helpeth hardy man alday," quod he,
"What ende that I make, it shal be so."
And girte hym with his swerd, and gan to go,   1775
And forth he rit til he to Rome is come,
And al alone his wey than hath he nome
Unto the hous of Colatyn ful ryght.
Doun was the sonne, and day hath lost his lyght;
And in he cometh into a prive halke,   1780
And in the nyght ful thefly gan he stalke,
Whan every wight was to his reste brought,
Ne no wight hadde of tresoun swich a thought.
Were it by wyndow or by other gyn,
With swerd ydrawe, shortly he com in   1785
There as she lay, this noble wif Lucresse.
And as she wok, hire bed she felte presse.
"What beste is that," quod she, "that weyeth thus?"
"I am the kynges sone, Tarquinius,"
Quod he, "but, and thow crye or noyse make,   1790
Or if there any creature awake,
By thilke God that formed man alyve,
This swerd thurghout thyn herte shal I ryve."
And therwithal unto hire throte he sterte,
And sette the poynt al sharp upon hire herte.   1795
No word she spak, she hath no myght therto.
What shal she seyn? hire wit is al ago.
Ryght as a wolf that fynt a lomb alone,
To whom shal she compleyne, or make mone?
What! shal she fyghte with an hardy knyght?   1800
Wel wot men that a woman hath no myght.
What! shal she crye, or how shal she asterte
That hath hire by the throte, with swerd at herte?
She axeth grace, and seyth al that she can.
"Ne wilt thow nat," quod he, this crewel man,   1805
"As wisly Jupiter my soule save,
As I shal in the stable slen thy knave,
And ley hym in thy bed, and loude crye
That I the fynde in swich avouterye.
And thus thow shalt be ded, and also lese   1810
Thy name, for thow shalt non other chese."
    These Romeyn wyves lovede so here name
At thilke tyme, and dredde so the shame
That, what for fer of sclaunder and drede of deth,
She loste bothe at ones wit and breth,   1815
And in a swogh she lay, and wex so ded,

Men myghte smyten of hire arm or hed;
She feleth no thyng, neyther foul nor fayr.
 Tarquinius, that art a kynges eyr,
And sholdest, as by lynage and by ryght,   1820
Don as a lord and as a verray knyght,
Whi hastow don dispit to chivalrye?
Whi hastow don this lady vilanye?
Allas! of the this was a vileyns dede!
 But now to purpos; in the story I rede,   1825
Whan he was gon, and this myschaunce is falle,
This lady sente after hire frendes alle,
Fader, moder, husbonde, alle yfeere;
And al dischevele, with hire heres cleere,
In habit swich as women used tho   1830
Unto the buryinge of hire frendes go,
She sit in halle with a sorweful sighte.
Hyre frendes axen what hire eylen myghte,
And who was ded; and she sit ay wepynge;
A word, for shame, forth ne myght she brynge,   1835
Ne upon hem she durste nat beholde.
But atte last of Tarquyny she hem tolde
This rewful cas and al thys thing horryble.
The woo to tellen were an impossible,
That she and al hir frendes made attones.   1840
Al hadde folkes hertes ben of stones,
Hyt myght have maked hem upon hir rewe,
Hir herte was so wyfly and so trewe.
She sayde that, for hir gylt ne for hir blame,
Hir husbonde shulde nat have the foule name,   1845
That wolde she nat suffre, by no wey.
And they answerden alle, upon hir fey,
That they forgave yt hyr, for yt was ryght;
It was no gilt, it lay not in hir myght;
And seyden hir ensamples many oon.   1850
But al for noght; for thus she sayde anoon:
"Be as be may," quod she, "of forgyvying,
I wol not have noo forgyft for nothing."
But pryvely she kaughte forth a knyf,
And therwithal she rafte hirself hir lyf;   1855
And as she fel adoun, she kaste hir lok,
And of hir clothes yet she hede tok.
For in hir fallynge yet she had a care,
Lest that hir fet or suche thyng lay bare;
So wel she loved clennesse and eke trouthe.   1860
Of hir had al the toun of Rome routhe,
And Brutus by hir chaste blood hath swore
That Tarquyn shulde ybanysshed be therfore,
And al hys kyn; and let the people calle,

idelnes, but late in the night occupied and busie amonges her maydes in the middes of her house spinning of wool. The victory and prayse wherof was given to Lucretia, who when she saw her husband, gentlie and loving-lie intertained him, and curteously badde the Tarquinians welcome. Immediately Sextus Tarquinius the sonne of Tarquinius Superbus (that time the Romaine king) was incensed wyth a libidinous desire, to constru-pate and defloure Lucrece. When the yonge gentlemen had bestowed that night pleasantly with their wives, they retourned to the Campe. Not long after, Sextus Tarquinius with one man retourned to Collatia unknowen to Collatinus, and ignorant to Lucrece and the rest of her houshold, for what purpose he came. Who being well intertayned, after supper was con-veighed to his chamber. Tarquinius burninge with the love of Lucrece, after he perceived the housholde to be at reste, and all thinges in quiet, with his naked sworde in his hande, wente to Lucrece being a sleepe, and keeping her downe with his lefte hande, saide: "Holde thy peace Lucrece, I am Sextus Tarquinius, my sworde is in my hande, if thou crie, I will kill thee." The gentlewoman sore afrayed, being newely awaked oute of her sleepe, and seeing imminent death, could not tell what to do. Then Tarquinius confessed his love, and began to intreate her, and therewithall used sundry menacing wordes, by all meanes attempting to make her quiet: when he saw her obstinate, and that she would not yelde to his request, notwithstanding his cruell threates, he added shameful and villanous speach, saying: That he would kill her, and when she was slaine, he woulde also kill his slave, and place him by her, that it might be reported howe she was slaine, being taken in adulterie. She vanquished with his terrible and infamous threate, his fleshlye and licentious enterprice overcame the puritie of her chaste and honest hart, which done he depart-ed. Then Lucrece sent a post to Rome to her father, and an other to Ardea to her husbande, requiringe them that they would make speede to come unto her, with certaine of their trustie frendes, for that a cruell facte was chaunced. Then Sp. Lucretius with P. Valerius the sonne of Volesius, and Collatinus with L. Junius Brutus, made hast to Lucrece: where they founde her sitting, very pensive and sadde, in her chamber. So sone as she sawe them she began pitiously to weepe. Then her husband asked her, whether all thinges were well: unto whome she sayde these wordes:

"No, deare husbande, for what can be wel or safe unto a woman, when she hath lost her chastitie? Alas Collatine, the steppes of an other man be now fixed in thy bed. But it is my bodye onely that is violated, my minde God knoweth is guiltles, whereof my death shalbe witnesse. But if you be men give me your handes and trouth, that the adulterer may not escape unrevenged. It is Sextus Tarquinius whoe being an enemie, in steede of a frende, the other night came unto mee, armed with his sword in his hand, and by violence caried away from me (the Goddes know) a woful joy."

Then every one of them gave her their faith, and comforted the pensive and languishing lady, imputing the offence to the authour and doer of the same, affirming that her bodye was polluted, and not her minde, and where consent was not, there the crime was absente. Whereunto shee added: "I praye you consider with your selves, what punishmente is due for the malefactour. As for my part, though I cleare my selfe of the offence, my body shall feele the punishment: for no unchast or ill woman, shall hereafter impute no dishonest act to Lucrece."

Then she drewe out a knife, which she had hidden secretely, under her kirtle, and stabbed her selfe to the harte. Which done, she fell downe grouelinge uppon her wound and died. Whereupon her father and husband made great lamentation, and as they were bewayling the death of Lucrece, Brutus plucked the knife oute of the wound, which gushed out with aboundance of bloude, and holding it up said: "I sweare by the chast bloud of this body here dead, and I take you the immortall Gods to witnes, that I will drive and extirpate oute of this Citie, both L. Tarquinius Superbus, and his wicked wife, with all the race of his children and progenie, so that none of them, ne yet any others shall raigne anye longer in Rome." Then hee delivered the knife to Collatinus, Lucretius and Valerius, who marveyled at the strangenesse of his words; and from whence he should conceive that determination. They all swore that othe. And followed Brutus, as their captaine, in his conceived purpose. The body of Lucrece was brought into the market place, where the people wondred at the vilenesse of that facte, every man complayning uppon the mischiefe of that facinorous rape, committed by Tarquinius. Whereupon Brutus perswaded the Romaynes, that they should cease from teares and other childishe lamentacions, and to take weapons in their handes, to shew themselves like men.

Then the lustiest and most desperate persons within the citie, made themselves prest and readie, to attempte any enterprise: and after a garrison was placed and bestowed at Collatia, diligent watche and ward was kept at the gates of the Citie, to the intent that the kinge should have no advertisement of that sturre. The rest of the souldiours followed Brutus to Rome. When he was come thither, the armed multitude did beate a marveilous feare thorughout the whole Citie: but yet because they sawe the chiefeste personages goe before, they thought that the same enterprise was [not] taken in vaine. Wherefore the people out of all places of the citie, ranne into the market place. Where Brutus complained of the abhominable Rape of Lucrece, committed by Sextus Tarquinius. And thereunto he added the pride and insolent behaviour of the king, the miserie and drudgerie of the people, and howe they, which in time past were victours and conquerours, were made of men of warre, Artificers, and Labourers. He remembred also the infamous murder of Servius Tullius their late kinge. These and such like he called to the people's remembraunce, whereby they abrogated and deposed Tarquinius, banishing him, his wife, and children. Then he levied an army of chosen and piked men, and marched to the Campe at Ardea, committing the governemente of the Citie to Lucretius, who before was by the king appointed Lieutenant. Tullia in the time of this hurlie burlie, fledde from her house, all the people cursing and crying vengeaunce upon her. Newes brought into the campe of these eventes, the king with great feare retourned to Rome, to represse those tumultes, and Brutus hearinge of his approche, marched another waye, because hee woulde not meete him. When Tarquinius was come to Rome, the gates were shutte against him, and he himselfe commaunded to avoide into exile. The campe received Brutus with great joye and triumphe, for that he had delivered the citie of such a tyraunte. Then Tarquinius with his children fledde to Caere, a Citie of the Hetrurians. And as Sextus Tarquinius was going, he was slaine by those that premeditated revengemente, of old murder and injuries by him done to their predecessours. This L. Tarquinius Superbus raigned XXV yeares. The raigne of the kinges from the first foundation of the Citie continued CCXLIV yeares. After which governmente two Consuls were appointed, for the order and administration of the Citie. And for that yeare L. Junius Brutus, and L. Tarquinius Collatinus.

(c) Ovid, *Fasti*, II. 721–852

Text as in *P. Ovidii Nasonis fastorum libri diligenti emendatione . . . commentatoribus Antonio Constantio fanensi: Paulo Marso piscinate.* Venetiis. Joh. Tacuinus de Tridino, 1520.[1]

Liber II

Cingitur interea Romanis Ardea signis   721
   Et patitur longas obsidione moras.
Dum vacat, & metuunt hostes committere pugnam
   Luditur in castris ocia miles agit:
Tarquinius juvenes socios dapibusque meroque
   Accipit ex illis rege creatus ait:
Dum nos solicitos pigro tenet Ardea bello
   Nec sinit ad patrios arma referre deos:
Ecquid in officio thorus est socialis & ecquid
   Conjugibus nostris mutua cura sumus: 730
Quisque suam laudant. studiis certamina crescunt
   Et fervent multo linguaque corque mero:
Surgit cui dederat clarum Collatia nomen;
   Non opus est verbis credite rebus ait:
Nox superest: tollamur equis, urbemque petamus:
   Dicta placent: frenis impediuntur equi:
Pertulerant dominos regalia, protinus ipsi
   Tecta petunt custos in fore nullus erat
Ecce nurum regis fusis per colla coronis
   Inveniunt posito pervigilare mero: 740
Inde cito passu petitur Lucretia: cujus
   Ante thorum calathi lanaque mollis erant:
Lumen ad exiguum famulae data pensa trahebant
   Inter quas tenui sic ait illa sono:
Mittenda est domino (nunc, nuncuperate) puellae
   Quamprimum nostra facta lacerna manu:
Quid tamen audistis (nam plura audire potestis)

[1] See Bullough, *op. cit.*, p. 179.

Quantum de bello dicitur esse super:
Postmodo victa cades melioribus Ardea restas
   Improba: quae nostros cogis abesse viros: 750
Sint tantum reduces. sed enim atmerarius ille
   Est meus & stricto qualibet ense ruit:
Mens abit & morior quotiens pugnantis imago
   Me subit & gelidum pectora frigus habet:
Desinit in lachrymas inceptaque fila remisit
   In gremio vultum deposuitque suo.
Hoc ipsam decuit: lachrymae decuere pudicam,
   Et facies animo dignaque parque fuit.
Pone metum venio conjux ait: illa revixit
   Deque viri collo dulce pependit onus 760
Interea juvenis furiales regius ignes
   Concipit & caeco raptus amore fuit:
Forma placet, niveusque color flavique capilli
   Quique aderat nulla factus ab arte decor:
Verba placent, & vox & quod corrumpere none st:
   Quoque minor spes est: hoc magis ille cupit
Jam dederat cantum lucis praenuntius ales
   Cum referunt juvenes in sua castra pedem:
Carpitur attonitos absentis imagine sensus
   Ille: recordanti plura magisque placent: 770
Sic sedit; sic culta fuit sic stamina nevit
   Neglectae collo sic jacuere comae:
Hos habuit vultus haec illi verba fuerunt
   Hic color haec facies hic decor oris erat:
Ut solet a magno fluctus languescere flatu:
   Sed tamen a vento, qui fuit, unda tumet:
Sic, quamvis aberat placitae praesentia formae:
   Quem dederat praesens forma: manebat amor.
Ardet: & injusti stimulis agitatus amoris
   Comparat indigno vimque metumque toro. 780
Exitus in dubio est: audebimus ultima dixit.
   Viderit: audentes forsque Venusque juvant.
Cepimus audendo Gabios quoque talia fatus
   Ense latus cinxit: tergaque pressit equi.
Accipit aerata juvenem Collatia porta,
   Condere jam vultus Sole parante suos.
Hostis ut hospes init penetralia Collatini:
   Comiter excipitur: sanguine junctus erat.
Quantum animis erroris inest. parat inscia rerum
   Infelix epulas hostibus illa suis. 790
Functus erat dapibus: poscunt sua tempora somnum:
   Nox erat: & tota lumina nulla domo.
Surgit: & auratum vagina liberat ensem:
   Et venit in thalamos nupta pudica tuos,
Utque torum pressit ferrum, Lucretia mecum est,

Natus ait regis, Tarquiniusque vocor.
Illa nihil: neque enim vocem viresque loquendi
Aut aliquid toto pectore mentis habet
Sed tremit, ut quondam stabulis deprensa relictis,
Parva sub infesto cum jacet agna lupo.   800
Quid faciat? pugnet? vincetur foemina pugnans.
Clamet? at in dextra, qui vetet, ensis erat:
Effugiat? positis urgentur pectora palmis:
Tunc primum externa pectora tacta manu.
Instat amans hostis, pretio, precibusque minisque:
Nec prece, nec pretio, nec movet ille minis.
Nil agis, eripiam dixit per crimina vitam:
Falsus adulterii testis adulter ero.
Interimam famulum: cum quo deprensa fereris.
Succubuit famae victa puella metu.   810
Quid victor gaudes? haec te victoria perdet.
Heu quantum regnis nox stetit una tuis.
Jamque erat orta dies: sparsis sedet illa capillis,
Ut solet ad nati mater itura rogum
Grandaevumque patrem fido cum conjuge castris
Evocat: & posita venit uterque mora.
Utque vident habitum: quae luctus causa requirunt:
Cui paret exsequias, quove sit icta malo.
Illa diu reticet, pudibundaque caelat amictu
Ora: fluunt lachrymae more perennis aquae.   820
Hinc pater, hinc conjux lachrymas solantur: & orant,
Indicet: & caeco flentque paventque metu.
Ter conata loqui: ter destitit: ausaque quarto:
Non oculos ideo sustulit illa suos.
Hoc quoque Tarquinio debebimus: eloquar, inquit,
Eloquar infelix dedecus ipsa meum.
Quodque potest narrat: restabant ultima: flevit:
Et matronales erubuere genae.
Dant veniam genitor facto conjuxque coacto,
Quam dixit veniam vos datis, ipsa nego.   830
Nec mora, caelato fixit sua pectora ferro:
Et cadit in patrios sanguinolenta pedes.
Tunc quoque jam moriens, ne non procumbat honeste:
Respicit: haec etiam cura cadentis erat.
Ecce super corpus communia damna gementes
Obliti decoris virque paterque jacent.
Brutus adest: tandemque animo sua nomina fallit:
Fixaque semianimi corpore tela rapit.
Stillantemque tenens generoso sanguine cultrum,
Edidit impavidos ore minante sonos: 840
Per tibi ego hunc juro fortem, castumque cruorem:
Perque tuos manes, qui mihi numen erunt:
Tarquinium profuga poenas cum stirpe daturum:

Jam satis est virtus dissimulata diu.
Illa jacens ad verba oculos sine lumine movit:
Visaque concussa dicta probare coma.
Fertur in exequias animi matrona virilis:
Et secum lachrymas, invidiamque trahit.
Vulnus inane patet: Brutus clamore Quirites
Convocat, & regis facta nefanda refert.   850
Tarquinius cum prole fugit: capit annua Consul
Jura: dies regnis illa suprema fuit.   852

(d) Translation of Ovid, *Fasti*, ii. 721–852 (ed. J. G. Frazer (London, 1929), Vol. i, pp. 101–9)

Meantime the Roman legions had compassed Ardea, and the city suffered a long and lingering siege. While there was naught to do, and the foe feared to join battle, they made merry in the camp; the soldiers took their ease. Young Tarquin entertained his comrades with feast and wine: among them the king's son spake: "While Ardea keeps us here on tenterhooks with sluggish war, and suffers us not to carry back our arms to the gods of our fathers, what of the loyalty of the marriage-bed? and are we as dear to our wives as they to us?" Each praised his wife: in their eagerness dispute ran high, and every tongue and heart grew hot with the deep draughts of wine. Then up and spake the man who from Collatia took his famous name: "No need of words! Trust deeds! There's night enough. To horse! and ride we to the city." The saying pleased them; the steeds are bridled and bear their masters to the journey's end. The royal palace first they seek: no sentinel was at the door. Lo, they find the king's daughters-in-law, their necks draped with garlands, keeping their vigils over the wine. Thence they galloped to Lucretia; she was spinning: before her bed were baskets of soft wool. By a dim light the handmaids were spinning their allotted stints of yarn. Amongst them the lady spoke in accents soft: "Haste ye now, haste, my girls! The cloak our hands have wrought must to your master be instantly dispatched. But what news have ye? For more news comes your way. How much do they say of the war is yet to come? Hereafter thou shalt be vanquished and fall: Ardea, thou dost resist thy betters, thou jade, that keepest perforce our husbands far away! If only they came back! But mine is rash, and with drawn sword he rushes anywhere. I faint, I die, as oft as the image of my soldier spouse steals on my mind and strikes a chill into my breast." She ended weeping, dropped the stretched yarn, and buried her face in her lap. The gesture was becoming; becoming, too, her modest tears; her face was worthy of its peer, her soul. "Fear not, I've come," her husband said. She revived and on her spouse's neck she hung, a burden sweet.

Meantime the royal youth caught fire and fury, and transported by blind love he raved. Her figure pleased him, and that snowy hue, that yellow hair, and artless grace; pleasing, too, her voice and words and virtue incorruptible; and the less hope he had, the hotter his desire. Now had the bird, the herald of the dawn, uttered his chant, when the young men retraced their steps to camp. Meantime the image of his absent love preyed on his senses crazed. In memory's light more fair and fair she grew. " 'Twas thus she sat, 'twas thus she dressed, 'twas thus she spun the yarn, 'twas thus her tresses careless lay upon her neck; that was her look, these were her words, that was her colour, that her form, and that her lovely face." As after a great gale the surge subsides, and yet the billow heaves, lashed by the wind now fallen, so, though absent now that winsome form and far away, the love which by its presence it had struck into his heart remained. He burned, and, goaded by the pricks of an unrighteous love, he plotted violence and guile against an innocent bed. "The issue is in doubt. We'll dare the utmost," said he. "Let her look to it! God and fortune help the daring. By daring we captured Gabii too."

So saying he girt his sword at his side and bestrode his horse's back. The bronze-bound gate of Collatia opened for him just as the sun was making ready to hide his face. In the guise of a guest the foe found his way into the home of Collatinus. He was welcomed kindly, for he came of kindred blood. How was her heart deceived! All unaware she, hapless dame, prepared a meal for her own foes. His repast over, the hour of slumber came. 'Twas night, and not a taper shone in the whole house. He rose, and from the gilded scabbard he drew his sword, and came into thy chamber, virtuous spouse. And when he touched the bed, "The steel is in my hand, Lucretia," said he, "I that speak am the king's son and Tarquin." She answered never a word. Voice and power of speech and thought itself fled from her breast. But she trembled, as trembles a little lamb that, caught straying from the fold, lies low under a ravening wolf. What could she do? Should she struggle? In a struggle a woman will always be worsted. Should she cry out? But in his clutch was a sword to silence her. Should she fly? His hands pressed heavy on her breast, the breast that till then had never known the touch of stranger hand. Her lover foe is urgent with prayers, with bribes, with threats; but still he cannot move her by prayers, by bribes, by threats. "Resistance is vain," said he, "I'll rob thee of honour and of life. I, the adulterer, will bear false witness to thy adultery. I'll kill a slave, and rumour will have it that thou wert caught with him." Overcome by fear of infamy, the dame gave way. Why, victor, dost thou joy? This victory will ruin thee. Alack, how dear a single night did cost thy kingdom! And now the day had dawned. She sat with hair dishevelled, like a mother who must attend the funeral pyre of her son. Her aged sire and faithful spouse she summoned from the camp, and both came without delay. When they saw her plight, they asked why she mourned, whose obsequies she was preparing, or what ill had befallen her. She was long silent, and for shame hid her face in her robe: her tears flowed like a running stream. On this side and on that her father and her spouse did soothe her grief and pray her to tell, and in blind fear they wept and quaked. Thrice she essayed to speak, and thrice gave o'er, and when the fourth time she summoned up courage she did not for that lift up her eyes. "Must I owe this too to Tarquin? Must I utter," quoth she, "must I utter, woe's me, with my own lips my own disgrace?" And what she can she tells. The end she left unsaid, but wept and a blush o'erspread her matron cheeks. Her husband and her sire pardoned the deed enforced. She said, "The pardon that you give, I do refuse myself." Without delay, she stabbed her breast with the steel she had hidden, and weltering in her blood fell at her father's feet. Even in dying she took care to sink down decently: that was her thought even as she fell. Lo, heedless of appearances, the husband and father fling themselves on her body, moaning their common loss. Brutus came, and then at last belied his name; for from the half-dead body he snatched the weapon stuck in it, and holding the knife, that dripped with noble blood, he fearless spake these words of menace: "By this brave blood and chaste, and by thy ghost, who shall be god to me, I swear to be avenged on Tarquin and on his banished brood. Too long have I dissembled my manly worth." At these words, even as she lay, she moved her lightless eyes and seemed by the stirring of her hair to ratify the speech. They bore her to burial, that matron of manly courage; and tears and indignation followed in her train. The gaping wound was exposed for all to see. With a cry Brutus assembled the Quirites and rehearsed the king's foul deeds. Tarquin and his brood were banished. A consul undertook the government for a year. That day was the last of kingly rule.